Sinfree Makoni

Languages and Language Planning in Zimbabwe

Selected papers
Volume 4
Including papers written in collaboration with
Janina Brutt-Griffler, Busi Makoni, Pedzisai Mashiri,
Nicholus Nyika and Charles Pfukwa

Edited by David Bade

International Association for the Integrational Study of
Language and Communication

This collection ©2020 by Sinfree Makoni.
Acknowledgements:
A critical analysis of the historical and contemporary status of minority languages in Zimbabwe, ©2011 originally published in *Current Issues in Language Planning*, 12, 437-455
The use of "indigenous" and urban vernaculars in Zimbabwe, ©2007 Sinfree Makoni, Janina Brutt-Griffler, Pedzisai Mashiri. Originally published in *Language in Society*, 36(1), 25-49.
In the beginning was the missionaries' word: The European invention of an African language: The case of Shona in Zimbabwe, ©1998 originally published in Kwesi Prah (Ed.), *Between Distinction and Extinction: the Harmonisation and Standardisation of African Languages*, Johannesburg: Witwatersrand University Press, 157–164.
The pragmatic import of pronoun usage in chiShona discourse, ©2003 Sinfree Makoni & Pedzisai Mashiri. Originally published in *Per Linguam*, 19(1), 13-38.
Is Zimbabwean English a type of new English?, ©1992 originally published in *African Study Monographs* 14 (2), 97-107.
Naming practices and language planning in Zimbabwe ©2007 by Sinfree Makoni, Busi Makoni and Pedzisai Mashiri. Originally published *Current Issues in Language Planning* 8(3):437-467
Language planning, language ideology and entextualization: war naming practices, ©2010 by Busi Makoni, Sinfree Makoni, Charles Pfukwa. Originally published in *Names*, 58(4), 197-208.
Language planning from below: the case of the Tonga in Zimbabwe, ©2008 by Sinfree Makoni, Busi Makoni and Nicholus Nyika. Originally published in *Current Issues in Language Planning,* 9(4), 413-439.
Zimbabwe colonial and post colonial language policy and planning practices, ©2006 by Sinfree Makoni, Busi Makoni and Pedzisai Mashiri. Originally published in *Current Issues in Language Planning,* 7(4), 377-414.

Contents

Preface..7

I. *A critical analysis of the historical and contemporary status of minority languages in Zimbabwe*..................................9

II. *The use of "Indigenous" and urban vernaculars in Zimbabwe*
(with Janina Brutt-Griffler and Pedzisai Mashiri)..................47

III. *In the beginning was the missionaries' word: The European invention of an African language: The case of Shona in Zimbabwe*..87

IV. *The pragmatic import of pronoun usage in chiShona discourse* (with Pedzisai Mashiri)..99

V. *Is Zimbabwean English a type of new English?*..............145

VI. *Naming practices and language planning in Zimbabwe*
(with Busi Makoni and Pedzisai Mashiri)............................163

VII. *Language planning, language ideology and entextualization: War naming practices*
(with Busi Makoni and Charles Pfukwa)............................217

VIII. *Language planning from below: The case of the Tonga in Zimbabwe* (with Busi Makoni and Nicholus Nyika)..........237

IX. *Zimbabwe colonial and post colonial language policy and planning practices*
(with Busi Makoni and Pedzisai Mashiri)............................283

Preface

This fourth and final volume of Sinfree Makoni's selected papers contains papers on the linguistic situation in his homeland Zimbabwe. While numerous papers in the previous volumes dealt in part or even primarily with the linguistic situation in Zimbabwe, all of the papers in this volume are devoted solely to language in Zimbabwe. Of the nine papers reprinted here, four were written in collaboration with Busi Makoni and four with another Zimbabwean linguist, Pedzisai Mashiri; the three other co-authors are Janina Brutt-Griffler, Nicholus Nyika and Charles Pfukwa. The papers range in date from 1992 to 2011 and cover a few topics not otherwise treated in the previous volumes: the status of English in Zimbabwe, Shona pragmatics, minority languages in education, Tonga language planning, and naming practices.

    Although this volume concludes his selected papers series of volumes, there is in fact more to come: a volume of papers by Cristine Severo on the sociolinguistics of Lusophone Africa is in preparation and will include several papers written in collaboration with Sinfree Makoni. We also expect that Sinfree will continue writing (and he is indeed currently working with Vicky Khasandi and the editor on a monograph devoted tothe use of proverbs in political speech in Africa) and thus at some future date we may wish to compile yet another volume. I at least, am hoping for more.

David Bade
Rachel's Farm
20 September 2020

I

A critical analysis of the historical and contemporary status of minority languages in Zimbabwe

Abstract
Although a voluminous amount of literature addresses language-in-education policy in Africa, one area in which the literature remains sparse is the role of minority languages in education. This article presents an overview of complex issues regarding the hegemony claims of different minority language groups in Zimbabwe. Given the relatively small research base dealing explicitly with controversies in the promotion of minority languages as the media of instruction, this article uses archival and historical literature to trace intricate controversies about language in education within minority African languages groups. This article argues that the interrelationships between the dynamics of the state, ethnic composition, and history vary considerably and impact the success of minority language policies.

Introduction
Discussions about minority[1] languages have achieved little prominence in Zimbabwean academic discourses because Zimbabwe has been imagined largely as a Shona and Ndebele state, with the former as the dominant ethnic group. Thus, the main thrust in Zimbabwean sociolinguistics has been the dynamics of English and its relationship with Shona and Ndebele or the languages of the 'super tribes' (Werbner, 2003). The historical and contemporary constructions of the super tribes inversely created and marginalized ethnic minorities. The search for a new status by these minorities, therefore, runs counter to this ideological and sociological trend. The constitutional debates of the 1990s created space for minority language groups to demand linguistic recognition.

In this article, the nature of language planning and policies of ethnic minorities in Zimbabwe are analyzed. In particular, the focus is on the multiple dimensions of language planning: (a) top-down and bottom-up planning; (b) national policies and transnational language practices; (c) external support and community autonomy; and (d) use of partially non-standardized varieties of language in education. The main thrust of this article is a critical analysis of the promotion of ethnic minority languages, such as Kalanga, Sotho, Shangani, and Tonga. We also argue that promotion of these languages to indigenous status has, ironically, further marginalized other minority languages, such as Yao, Barwe, Hwesa, and languages of European and Asian minorities, which are spoken by groups that do not actively campaign for recognition.

Language promotion, especially of minority languages, is inherently discriminatory. Sizeable Asian and European communities in Zimbabwe live in specific residential areas, with their children attending specific schools and universities in

---

[1] In Zimbabwe, the term *minority* is racialized and refers to the White minority. However, we use the term differently from its conceptualization in Zimbabwean political discourse.

South Africa, and have a considerable impact on the Zimbabwean economy. Yet, their languages have not been included in the minority language debate in Zimbabwe, rendering Asian and Europeans as 'invisible minorities'. While this article does not delve deeper into the reasons for other minorities being rendered 'invisible', it does point out the need for studies into language planning that explore the impact, if any, of these communities on local language practices at a grassroots level.

When discussing European languages, language policy studies in Zimbabwe have often been restricted to English and its effects on indigenous African languages. Such an approach to language policy is too narrow because between 1960 and the late 1970s, there were more European non-native speakers of English who were natives of Greece and Italy and who were Jews from the former Soviet Union and Afrikaans speakers in southwestern Zimbabwe (Ranger, 2010). The wide variety of non-standard varieties of English in Zimbabwe might, in part, be due to the extensive contact between European non-native speakers of English who were also second language speakers of African languages. The effects of Afrikaans, for instance, are apparent in most indigenous Zimbabwean languages, especially at the level of lexical borrowing. In Shona, for instance, words such as *fasitera* (window) seem to have their origins in the Afrikaans *venster* (window), *kereke* (church) seems to originate from *kerk* (in Afrikaans), and *sawuti* (salt) seems to be derived from *sout* (Afrikaans for salt). Even though Afrikaans is widely spread and African languages have borrowed extensively from it, no language policy study in Zimbabwe has ever explored the colonial and post-colonial status and impact of Afrikaans on African languages since more emphasis is placed on English.

It is, therefore, not surprising that the well-documented argument with regard to language in education in most African contexts is that African parents prefer their children to be taught in English rather than in indigenous African languages. One of the reasons for the preference for English, it is argued, is that

English will provide children with a global future. In this article, we contend that while this argument may be correct, another debate on language in education is often sidelined. This particular debate relates to the controversy within indigenous African languages themselves about which of the multiple varieties of minority languages are to be used as languages of instruction. In this article, we argue that, while little attention has been paid to the debate among different minority language groups, the call for mother tongue education has revived the debate regarding which of the varieties of minority languages are to be used as languages of instruction. This tension is not new but has been evident in the 'major' indigenous African languages that were developed through missionary education and later accorded official status after independence. The most common practice during the colonial period was to make use of European language orthography; hence, 'for a number of African languages, there was often no fully uniform practice of representation across dialects or agreement on which of the many competing forms should be recognized as the standard form of a language' (Simpson, 2008, p. 5). Harmonization efforts have been unsuccessful because these competing forms have become solidified and associated with "ethnic identities that were previously less clearly defined" (Simpson, 2008, p. 3).

In order to explore this tension, it has been situated in different minority language groups to see how it manifests itself both historically and in contemporary Zimbabwe. The choice of certain languages as the subject for analysis is strategic. Shangani is situated in the southern part of Zimbabwe, sharing borders with South Africa. In both Zimbabwe and South Africa, Shangani is an officially recognized minority language. However, in Zimbabwe, Shangani attained official minority status after extensive lobbying by community organizations. On the other hand, Kalanga is also a recognized minority language in Zimbabwe and Botswana. Like Shangani, Kalanga attained official minority status after a protracted period of lobbying by community organizations in Zimbabwe and Botswana (Chebanne, 2002; Nyati-Ramahobo, 2000). Ndau, as it will become evident, has a rather ambivalent status, depending on whether it is viewed as a language different from or as a variety of Shangani.

The fact that these minority languages have, in some instances, significant status in other states creates opportunities for transnational language policies and possibly provision of teaching materials from other states. Yet, as will be evident in this article, any attempts at transnational language planning have been fraught with varying problems, depending on the aspirations of the ethnic group in question.

Lastly, the sociolinguistic landscape of contemporary Zimbabwe has, in recent years, been complicated by the emerging role of China's political and economic engagement in Africa and its potential effects on language policy. This article, therefore, analyzes whether the introduction of Chinese language teaching in Zimbabwe is significantly different from the introduction of English in colonial Zimbabwe and whether the current interest in Chinese suggests that Mandarin Chinese will, at some point in the future, be Zimbabwe's new lingua franca. Thus, this article explores the extent to which the modus operandi of the Chinese is significantly different from that of the former colonial powers that introduced European languages in Africa.

This article is divided into three sections. In the first section, we provide a background in order to contextualize the issues related to minority language planning. In this section, we describe the activities of the Zimbabwean Indigenous Languages Promotion Association (ZILPA) as well as provide a brief overview of the two Education Acts in an attempt to establish the degree and extent to which minority languages have attained meaningful status in education. The rationale in this overview is to show how language policies reflect "power, politics and status differentials" (Lo Bianco, 2009, p. 113). Different languages are accorded different statuses, thereby perpetuating systems of inequality in that some languages acquire dominant status while others are marginalized (Wickert, 2001). The question for this article is whether the 2006 Education Act accords minority languages the same status as the languages of the super tribes.

The second section focuses on the sociolinguistic contexts of a number of minority languages in Zimbabwe that are rarely written about – (a) Shangani; (b) Ndau; (c) Kalanga; (d) Fengu; (e) Nambya; and (f) CiNyanja – and the different contestations in which the different groups are engaged. In this section, we comment on the status of each language, the nature of minority language promotion activities, and their role and status in the Zimbabwean educational system.

In the third section, we briefly comment on the theoretical relevance of minority language research in Zimbabwe and the challenges it poses for language planning, including: (a) standardization (orthography creation and reform); (b) the development of language teaching materials; (c) implications for top-down status planning; and (d) the opportunities and constraints of transnational language policies. Lastly, this article analyzes the gaps and silences in Zimbabwean language planning literature and proposes areas for future research.

Historical and political context
Zimbabwe's history has to be traced back to its predecessor state, Rhodesia. Rhodesia was a British colony characterized by seizure of land, marginalization, and exploitation of Africans. In 1965, during the period when most African countries were attaining their independence from Britain, the White community tried to preempt African independence by declaring their own Unilateral Declaration of Independence (UDI) from Britain under the leadership of Ian Smith. The establishment of UDI prompted intense nationalistic wars led by Robert Mugabe and Joshua Nkomo's liberation armies, Zimbabwe African National Union and Zimbabwe People's Union, respectively. Zimbabwe

attained its independence in 1980 as a result of the impact of the liberation and nationalist armies and withdrawal of South African armies from Zimbabwe.

In the 1990s, Zimbabwe's successful mineral and agriculture-based economy collapsed due to a combination of factors ranging from mismanagement of the agricultural sector and the general decline of the mineral sectors. Frequent and sustained unrest led to the formation of the Movement for Democratic Change, led by a trade unionist, Morgan Tsvangirai. The seizure of land by Robert Mugabe from the White commercial farmers and violation of human rights led to its ostracization from Western countries, which resulted in Zimbabwe becoming increasingly dependent on Chinese assistance. It is against this political background that the developments outlined in this article should be read.

In Africa, the choice of languages in education has been based mainly on the historical experience of colonialism. That each colonial power imposed its own language on the countries it colonized is a well-known fact. Colonial language-in-education policies often determined the level of entrenchment of the colonial language and the extent to which indigenous African languages were consciously promoted within the educational system. British colonies encouraged the teaching of African languages up to the end of secondary education, and Christian missionaries provided instruction in indigenous African languages to the early grades. A prominent feature of the teaching of indigenous African languages during the colonial period was the constant use of English as a reference point. Thus, the grammatical categories of English (which were derived from Latin) were applied to African languages. Grammatical categories used are important because languages are, to a large extent, abstractions, metaphors, an artifact of the analytical postulates used, and do not necessarily exist independently of the analytical templates used as entries into communicative practices (Harris, 2009; Hutton, 2010). The meta-language for African languages was an extension of the meta-language used in descriptions of English and/or Latin. Whether the categories described using this Anglicized meta-language actually existed in these languages was considered irrelevant. Similarly, translation of African languages into English was particularly widespread. In essence, the meta-language used in any instruction was English. Hence, mother tongue education was, for all intents and purposes, an extension of learning English.

The irony is that the promotion of indigenous African languages in post-colonial Africa is, inadvertently, a continuation of a colonial project. It is, therefore, not surprising that the continuation of the colonial project is often met with resistance, especially when African languages are introduced as languages of instruction in mother tongue instruction programs. Although in contemporary Zimbabwe the argument against the use of indigenous African languages appears, *prima facie*, to be one of a preference for English, the fundamental issue is, as it was in the early 1930s, that the standardized varieties that are used in classrooms are not mother tongues to anyone but, rather, foreign languages or, as Rusike (1936) neatly described them, 'whiteman's language' (*The Bantu Mirror,* Rhodesia 18 April 1936).

It is also not surprising that standardization in both colonial and post-colonial Africa has been a source of controversy because it was, and still is, perceived as radically changing indigenous languages to suit a particular worldview. The controversy surrounding the standardization of African languages is not unique to Zimbabwe. For instance, Peterson (2004), referring to Gikuyu in Kenya, argued convincingly that grammar was fixed in central Kenya because everyone reworked vernacular languages for different objectives. This statement echoes framework on the lack of regularity or absence of fixed structure in grammar, which reflects that it cannot be taken for granted that there is a natural fixed structure to language (Bybee & Hopper, 2001). Rather, speakers borrow heavily from their previous experiences of communication in similar circumstances, on comparable subjects, and with a similar audience (Peterson, 2004). From this perspective, linguistic structure is not 'a set of independent pre-given laws but rather a response to discourse needs' (Bybee & Hopper, 2001, p. 2). The structural fixity arose as a result of standardization, a reification that led to the description of African languages as subject–verb–object languages, and all the other permutations that were used in syntax became a source of consternation.

Another controversy sparked by the standardization of African languages seems to have been in-group and related to the question of which variety of the same language is to be used as a medium of instruction for the same ethnic group. In the Zimbabwean context, the most well known of these debates relates to whether Zulu or the variety of Ndebele spoken by all should be used as a medium of instruction in Matebeleland. This controversy draws heavily on the historical nature of the Ndebele society. The Ndebele society is heterogeneous and, therefore, divided along caste lines into *abezansi*, *abenhla*, and *amahole*. The aristocracy, *abezansi*, often identified itself with the Nguni clan and the Zulu language, while the commoners were a heterogeneous group that had been drawn from the Sotho and the Tswana and were often referred to as *amahole* (commoners). This act of naming other group members using derogatory names reflects the tension between Zulu aristocrats and the Ndebele commoners; the latter preferred the use of Ndebele to subvert aristocratic powers of the *abezansi*. The *abenhla* or *amahole* who had been integrated into the Ndebele advocated for the use of Ndebele to promote a much broader Ndebele identity than that predicated on Zulu as a prestige variety. From the standpoint of the Ndebele aristocrats, 'pure' Ndebele was associated with the use of the Zulu language. Learning and speaking Ndebele were then associated with the political and social history of the Ndebele. The debates between the different groups reflected different 'moral and social stand points' (Msindo, 2005, p. 79) about what it meant to be Ndebele. The conventional view in African studies attributes the invention of African ethnicities to colonialists, missionaries, and African elites (Ranger, 1989), yet the case of the Ndebele demonstrates the active role of 'commoners' in shaping the nature of their identities.

Introductory overview: role of ZILPA and the two Education Acts

The Education Acts were facilitated by a series of events, including extensive lobbying by ZILPA and Silveira House. Although Zimbabwe's minorities came together in ZILPA to claim their rights to more inclusive policies regarding language in schools and national broadcasting and to share concerns over stigmatizing stereotypes, poverty, and access to resources, sharp differences and tensions exist between them. For example, Zimbabwe minorities differ in their relationships with the ruling party. Within Matabeleland, minority groups differ in their historical relations with 'the Ndebele' and 'the Shona' and with each other. Promoting ethnic minorities and boundaries between 'self' and 'other', including demands for cultural rights, has generated conflict with the majority ethnicities and among the minority groups themselves, thus engendering tensions between essentialized identities and dynamic constructions of ethnic identity.

The socio-cultural contexts for the production of the two Education Acts were shaped by the prevailing political contexts, such as efforts toward a wider inclusion of minori-ties into Zimbabwe in the 1980s and the space created by the 1990s' constitutional forum. The space for minority languages was narrowed by the President of Zimbabwe, who referred to a 1987 agreement of the super tribes as "a charter which would bind once and for all, the two major tribes of Zimbabwe, namely the Shona and Ndebele, into one … The Unity Accord thus forms the bedrock upon which peace, democracy, social justice and prosperity should be built" (Mugabe). Minority language groups were clearly excluded from a political and linguistic standpoint, which is evident in both Education Acts.

ZILPA's main objective (see Appendix 1) was to challenge the provisions of Section 62 of the Education Act of 1987 and propose changes to the act (see Appendix 2). Notably, the names of these languages are written using an orthography that ZILPA preferred and not the orthography commonly used in Zimbabwe. By choosing a different orthography, it seems that ZILPA was resisting what it perceived as the hegemony of the languages of the super tribes since the orthography used in postcolonial Zimbabwe is based either in Shona or in Ndebele.

In response to ZILPA's demands, the government of Zimbabwe amended the Education Act in 2006. Specifically, the category of indigenous languages was broadened to include what, in the 1987 Act, were described as minority languages. The 'new' indigenous languages were Shangani, Tonga, Venda, and Nambya, but Fengu (Xhosa) and Ci-Nyanja were excluded from this category, indicating the ranking order of languages that often reflects a 'hierarchy of power' (Pelinka, 2007, p. 141). Both CiNyanja and Fengu speakers are treated as immigrants, even though some have been in Zimbabwe since the mid-twentieth century. Fengu speakers have been treated as non-Zimbabwean. In fact, the Fengu regard themselves as a nation outside the Zimbabwean state, prefer to be part of South Africa, and provide social justification for being part of a bigger Xhosa nation. The CiNyanja, speakers of Mozambican languages, and their descendants (even if born in Zimbabwe) have also been excluded by the ways in which the categories of indigenous are used. Even though CiNyanja speakers are dominant in some areas of Zimbabwe, such as northwestern Zimbabwe, they fall into a third space in which they are neither foreign nor indigenous.

In both the Education Act of 1987 and that of 2006 (see Appendix 3), the status of Shona, Ndebele, and English as the three main languages remains unchanged; if anything, their status has been enhanced. The expression 'main languages' is, in fact, a depoliticized manner of referring to dominant languages described in a quasi-neutral form as official languages (Williams, 1992). What is implied in this euphemism is that these three languages are the common and possibly nationally unifying languages of Zimbabwe. As a result, the other minority or indigenous languages are rendered negligible and of secondary importance. In fact, in both acts, it is mandatory for schools to teach English, Shona, and Ndebele, as captured in the use of the deontic modal 'shall', which, in a legal sense, is equivalent to 'must'. There is no room for either the school or minister to exercise any discretion, unlike in the teaching of other languages in which the minister 'may authorize [author emphasis]' their use as the media of instruction. The use of the modal auxiliary may indicates possibility but leaves room for the minister to propose the use of one of the main languages instead, thus underscoring the secondary importance of these languages.

Even though English, Shona, and Ndebele are the dominant languages in the two acts, there are subtle differences between the two acts in relation to the educational status of the languages. The 1987 Act states that the three 'main' languages 'shall be taught' but not necessarily on an 'equal-time-allocation basis'. However, the 2006 Act contains an attempt to close the gap in the time allocated to teaching the three main languages by explicitly stating that the languages shall be taught on an 'equal basis', which seems to be a rhetorical strategy for achieving parity of esteem. Despite the inherent status differential in the 'main languages', the notion of an 'equal-time-allocation basis' suggests peaceful coexistence in a shared physical space, despite their status differentials. The idea that the main languages may be taught on an equal basis is indicative of the government's attempt pedagogically to establish some form of linguistic equality between the languages. Yet, the notion of an 'equal basis' creates a 'fiction of language equality' by disguising a 'hierarchy of power' (Pelinka, 2007, p. 141) between

English, on the one hand, and Shona and Ndebele, on the other hand. It disguises the power hierarchy between the main languages and other indigenous languages and also between minority languages and excluded languages such as Yao, Chikunda, Barwe, and Asian languages. There is no explicit directive that, when the minister exercises discretion, the 'indigenous' or, for that matter, the minority languages may be taught on an 'equal-time-allocation basis' with the three main languages. This silence in the act suggests that these other languages are viewed, as has already been pointed out, as of secondary importance.

The status of English is also different between the two acts. The 2006 Act states that English is to be taught from the first grade, whereas the 1987 Act states that English is to be deferred until the fourth grade. The 1987 Act states that English is to be taught in both areas in which Shona and Ndebele are spoken, suggesting that the bilingualism expected was one between English and either Shona or Ndebele but not a multilingualism in which the pupils are proficient in Shona, Ndebele, *and* English, as is implied in the 2006 Act.

In a sense, the 2006 Act is more inclusive. For example, sign languages are mentioned as the media of instruction for the 'deaf and hard hearing'. Unlike in the teaching of either the main languages or indigenous languages, the medium of instruction for sign language is calibrated by introducing a notion of 'priority medium of instruction', which leaves room for other languages to be used as the media of instruction. Although the 2006 Act is more inclusive, it excludes other minority languages such as Barwe, Yao, Chikunda, and CiNyanja. Ironically, CiNyanja was used as a medium of instruction prior to Zimbabwe's attainment of independence in 1980. This practice was discontinued after 1980, suggesting that, as far as CiNyanja is concerned, colonial language policy was more inclusive than contemporary Zimbabwean language policy. Arguably, speakers of CiNyanja may be discriminated against more in post-independent Zimbabwe than during the colonial era. Furthermore, they do not fall under either the indigenous or 'foreign' language category. Thus, while the 1987 Act discriminated against most African languages, the 2006 Act discriminates against what are considered to be 'small' minority languages or the so-called immigrant languages such as CiNyanja and Fengu.

By and large, the formation of ZILPA as a grassroots movement that lobbied the government for the promotion and development of minority languages has been somewhat successful. The success of ZILPA is, however, ambivalent. First, by rejecting the use of the term *minority language*, the group managed, at least on an ideological level, to equate these languages with those of the super tribes. Secondly, the inclusion of languages of instruction suggests some legal gains. Yet, the promotion of indigenous languages in both Zimbabwean Education Acts has only created a rank order of languages. The 'main languages' are not functionally equal to the indigenous languages, just as the indigenous languages are not functionally equal to the 'invisible' minority languages. The mere fact that languages such as Kalanga and Shangani are elevated from minority to indigenous language status but are not examinable subjects like the indigenous languages of the super tribes indicates that the new language-in-education act has concealed certain power relations. Since the Zimbabwean educational system is examination driven, the fact that these languages, although taught and used as the media of instruction, are not examined means that, from the government's perspective and possibly from the students' viewpoint, these languages are not that important after all. In fact, this echoes an argument by McGroarty, Beck, and Butler (1995), who, with reference to Navajo communities, stated that:

> For indigenous languages, often disparaged or at least neglected by the dominant society, tests can be powerful pieces of evidence that a hitherto 'invisible' language does indeed exist in terms that an educational bureau-

cracy can understand and, consequently, must acknowledge. (p. 324)

In light of this comment, it is indeed possible that the Zimbabwean state is not as committed to minority languages as their inclusion in the new language-in-education act might suggest.

CiNyanja: Neither a foreign nor a minority language

Northwestern Zimbabwe is a fascinating linguistic landscape because of the number of different languages that are widely used there. These languages include: (a) CiNyanja; (b) Nambya; (c) Tonga; (d) Ndebele; (e) Shona; and (f) English, in part because of tourist ventures as well as the area's status as a mining location. Hwange, for instance, is a coal-mining town with a majority of Nambya and CiNyanja speakers, whereas the official languages in the schools have been Ndebele and English; however, in recent years, there has been an attempt to use Nambya and CiNyanja as languages of instruction in grades 1–4. Even though Nambya is the language spoken by the original inhabitants of Hwange, previously the most widely used language for official business was Ndebele, while CiNyanja was used largely for communication. It appears that CiNyanja became a dominant language because of a relatively large number of Zambians and Malawians in the mining areas. While Malawians may define themselves as Nyanja when in Zimbabwe, they may view themselves as belonging to different ethnicities, such as Ngoni or Kunda, while in Malawi. Consequently, CiNyanja is a broad linguistic category that includes a wide range of languages and ethnicities. Even though Nambya and, to some extent, CiNyanja are dominant languages in specific locales, they are not officially used in education or recognized as minority languages in Zimbabwe. Speakers of these languages are not considered citizens of Zimbabwe, despite the fact that they were born in Zimbabwe and know no other place as home.

Shangani and Ndau: an overview
Borders have variable effects on ethnicities. For example, the label Shangani is much more complicated than one might initially assume because its referents and symbolic meanings vary depending on the situational context and the person using the term. The referent Shangani is not a stable one, rendering it difficult to determine the number of speakers, even if the problematic nature of what constitutes 'speakerhood' is resolved (Makoni, Makoni, & Nyika, 2008; Moore, Pietkainen, & Blommaert, 2010). For example, a Zimbabwean ethnic group referred to as Ndau may be referred to as Shangani in South Africa because when the Ndau migrate to South Africa, they appropriate the term Shangani and use it to refer to themselves. They do so because of the perceived preferential treatment accorded to Shangani speakers in South African manual jobs. Because most Ndau eventually return home, a new category of migrant Ndau speakers leads to yet another distinction between ex-migrants and those who never left Zimbabwe.

The South African/Zimbabwean border on the Shangani produces different Ndau 'ethnic' groups, whereas the Zimbabwean/Mozambican border does not have the same effect. Thus, Ndau in Mozambique, which has been strongly influenced by Portuguese, has not produced distinct Ndau groups on either side of the border. Similarly, the Kalanga in Botswana and Zimbabwe retain a strong sense of ethnic identity despite being separated by the Zimbabwe/Botswana border. In certain cases, the converse also takes place: individuals who might have been regarded as belonging to different ethnicities in one country redefine themselves as members of the same group in a third place.

Changes in the ways people define themselves may also be the result of historical factors. For example, while contemporary Ndau speakers may refer to themselves as Ndau, their ancestors would have defined themselves as both Ndau and Zulu as they had Zulu surnames (McGonagle, 2002). Self- and group identities are, therefore, not permanently fixed in time and geographical space. The same language may evoke different associations and engender multiple and, at times, conflicting associations that are in a constant state of flux.

Shangani language in education
Shangani speakers are found in Zimbabwe, Mozambique, and South Africa. Bearing in mind that Shangani speakers found in Mozambique and in South Africa refer to themselves as Tsonga, the presence of the Zimbabwe/South Africa border has led to a fractured Shangani identity in South Africa and among their Mozambican counterparts, thereby working against efforts to synchronize language planning strategies in Mozambique, South Africa, and Zimbabwe. Even though materials for teaching Shangani in Zimbabwe are lacking, unlike in South Africa, if Shangani speakers in Zimbabwe do not subscribe to the same identity as their South African counterparts, they may not readily accept language teaching materials produced in South Africa because using such materials may make them feel inferior to their South African counterparts.

Although Shangani was a minority language in the 1987 Zimbabwe Education Act, it is categorized in the 2006 Act as an indigenous language. Even though Shangani is referred to as 'indigenous', the Shangani still find this term objectionable and prefer their language to be referred to as a 'community language'. The construct of a 'community' arguably captures the multi-layered and interconnected nature of their individual and collective histories as speakers of Shangani. However, the discourse implied by the use of the term may undermine their efforts because community languages rarely have status as formal languages that can be used in educational contexts.

Currently, Shangani is taught up to the fourth year of elementary education. Students have to switch to either Shona or Ndebele as second African languages. Pedagogically, Shangani students are heavily disadvantaged because they are treated as if Ndebele and Shona were their primary languages. Plans are underway to extend the teaching of Shangani to the end of primary education; however, the use of common Zimbabwean Shangani teaching materials is complicated by the diversity of views on what constitutes Shangani. If Shangani is viewed from the bottom up, it can be more appropriately defined as a continuum characterized by Shona, on the one end, and Ndebele, on the other end. With the prevalence of migrant labor in Mozambique and South Africa, cross-national varieties of Shangani are found in Zimbabwe. Thus, the promotion of Shangani has to resolve a tension or take advantage of a creative tension between the state's perceptions of the development of Shangani as a discrete entity, on the one hand, and as an amalgam, on the other hand.

The use of Shangani in education, therefore, raises questions about standardization. Because Shangani is in the early stages of standardization, a wide range of competing orthographies are in use, including the following:

1) An orthography based on one or more of the earlier versions of Ndebele or Shona (e.g. Shangane versus Shangani).
2) An orthography based on Tsonga (e.g. XiTshangana).
3) An orthography dependent upon different denominations and religious affiliations of the congregation (e.g. Cha-angan by the Dutch Reformed Church or Changana by the Anglican Church).

Efforts have been made to harmonize the diverse orthographies because orthographical variation is considered a problem in literacy acquisition. The desire to unify the orthographies is driven by a standard language ideology (Milroy, 2001) that sees variation as problematic and uniformity as a solution. Because orthographies are both linguistic and social, it is critically important to determine which orthography to use. The challenge is to find an orthography that baances technical acumen with sociological insight. As Schiefflin and Doucet (1992) pointed out, orthographies are seen as "sites of contested identities rather than as neutral academic or linguistic arguments without political, social or educational consequences" (p. 427).

Possibilities and constraints of transnational language policies: the case of Kalanga

Kalanga speakers can be found in southwestern parts of Zimbabwe and northern parts of Botswana. Historically, the Kalanga were separated from the main Shona communities by the Ndebele, which has strongly influenced the Kalanga. The Kalanga, both in Zimbabwe and in Botswana, are multilingual. Those found in Zimbabwe speak Ndebele and Shona and, if formally educated, they speak English as well. Similarly, the Kalanga in Botswana speak Tswana and English. The Kalanga in both Botswana and Zimbabwe actively collaborate in the production of teaching materials and participate in common cultural festivals. However, because of the collapse of the Zimbabwean economy, the Kalanga in Zimbabwe are more aggressively reasserting their shared origins with the Kalanga in Botswana by claiming their membership in a larger Kalanga ethnicity that predated the formation of Botswana. In doing so, the Kalanga are, by default and possibly for purposes of economic expediency, claiming to be citizens of Botswana. Yet, when the Zimbabwean economy was still viable, the Kalanga in Botswana were emphatic that their 'roots' lie in Zimbabwe.

Demands for the recognition of Kalanga, more so than of other ethnic groups, are likely to be perceived by the Zimbabwean government as political demands because of the long historical activism of the Kalanga. They have, at times, entered into astute political alliances with the Ndebele even though they have long objected to being taught through Ndebele, which was sanctioned in 1930 by Doke (the South African University of Witwatersrand Linguist), who recommended that Kalanga should not be the medium of instruction (Msindo, 2005).

Promotion of Kalanga has always been justified on grounds of political secession. Hence, campaigns to promote Kalanga initially resulted from a deep desire to resist Ndebele political and linguistic hegemony (Msindo, 2005). Historically, the Kalanga revolted against the colonial government because they were resisting colonial encounters, and in post-colonial Zimbabwe, the Kalanga have continued their defiance, although this time it was against the Zimbabwean government. The issue revolves around the classification of Kalanga as a minority language, in which case Kalanga-speaking children are to be taught either in Ndebele or in Shona. It seems that changes in language policy in Zimbabwe have been partially influenced by a relatively long and sustained history of dissent at the grassroots level by both parents and teachers.

The discourses used in the promotion of Kalanga as well as Shangani are based on an assumption that the boundaries between these languages and their attendant ethnicities are tightly drawn. At times, the promotion of minority languages created and enhanced the boundaries, some of which did not necessarily exist in the form which they later took as a direct consequence of language promotion. The discourses of language promotion founded on notions of ethnicity and language as tightly knit together created the impression that the groups were homogeneous.

Fengu: an ethnic group with 'static' heritage demanding alternative citizenship

The Fengu are, historically, Xhosa-speaking communities that originated from the Eastern Cape (South Africa) and were brought to Zimbabwe by Cecil John Rhodes as domestic workers and wagon drivers (Ndhlovu, 2009). The Fengu are a close-knit community living in areas such as Mbembezi, Fort Rixon, Gwatemba, and some parts of Mashonaland and Midlands (Hachipola, 1998; Ndhlovu, 2009).

There are indications that the term Fengu was originally used broadly to include anyone who was destitute or a refugee, including Europeans during the colonial period. However, the meaning of the term was subsequently racialized to refer to a specific ethnic group, the Xhosa who had fled Shaka during the Mfecane in the mid-nineteenth century and those who came with Cecile John Rhodes. The Fengu, like other minority groups, are increasingly vocal in promoting their interests, although they have never argued for the promotion of their language as a language of instruction, notwithstanding that their language has never been used as a language of instruction in Zimbabwe. The government has always argued that the number of speakers is not sufficiently significant to warrant the language any status in education (Ndhlovu, 2009). Unlike other minorities, the Fengu have been motivated by a powerful sense of ethnic identity and strong allegiance to the Xhosa in South Africa and, thus, view their language-in-education needs as met by the South African national language policy since it recognizes Xhosa as 1 of the 11 official languages.

Hence, the Fengu in sharp contrast with the Kalanga adamantly argue to be relocated to their 'mythical' home in the Eastern Cape in South Africa. While the Kalanga recognize their Zimbabwean citizenship (while quietly aspiring to be citizens of Botswana), the Fengu feel that they are foreigners in Zimbabwe but part of a bigger Xhosa ethnicity in South Africa. They still maintain some of Xhosa cultural practices, although these appear to have been influenced by Ndebele. Despite the fact that the Fengu have lived in Zimbabwe since the late nineteenth century, they strongly believe that they speak Xhosa and are part of the South African Xhosa-speaking community. However, what the Fengu do not realize is that the language they speak is, in all probability, significantly different from the variety of Xhosa spoken in South Africa because "all groups that come into contact with others, over time, develop their own unique 'codes', 'dialects' or 'languages' that emerge through these interactions and shared knowledge, leading to the development of unique and collective identities" (Shohamy, 2006, p. 8).

For the Fengu, it seems, ethnicity is not fluid, boundaries are not permeable, and geography and physical space define each other. Yet, as Shohamy (2006) and Mignolo (2000) pointed out, geographical location and language are disarticulated because languages are not permanently situated or located in any space. The presence of the Fengu in Zimbabwe and their strong yet 'imagined' association with the Xhosa in South Africa raise interesting issues about language, citizenship, and transnational language policies. The Fengu sense of group identity and demands to be relocated to South Africa suggest that transnational language policies are irrelevant because they do not address their sense of not being citizens. Other ethnic groups argue that being born in Zimbabwe guarantees their citizenship as Zimbabweans, although some have been deprived of citizenship (e.g. Ci-Nyanja speakers and all children of Malawian and Zambian immigrants born in Zimbabwe have been denied Zimbabwean citizenship). The Fengu, although born in Zimbabwe, argue that Zimbabwean citizenship is being imposed on them. As the Fengu wait to be relocated to South Africa, they consider themselves a people without national citizenship. Because of their sense of not being Zimbabwean citizens, they have not taken part in the language minority movement or in organizations addressing the problems of language minorities.

Clearly, cross-border language planning among the Xhosa in South Africa is likely to be rejected by the Fengu in Zimbabwe because they have different objectives. In addition, there may be intergenerational differences regarding language planning policies. Young Fengu speakers may not necessarily identify with the variety of Xhosa spoken in South Africa but may entertain the idea of being in South Africa for economic reasons, such as job opportunities they may not have in Zimbabwe. Similarly, young Ndau speakers who recast their identities as Shangani in South Africa may welcome language policies that provide opportunities for learning minority languages other than their own. Elderly Ndau speakers may be indifferent to the promotion of other Zimbabwean minority languages but welcome transnational cooperation that may provide them opportunities to be exposed to Zulu texts since they define themselves as both Ndau and Zulu.

One of the recurring assumptions in the promotion of minority languages in Zimbabwe is that language users are able to identify the linguistic community to which they belong. The distinction between 'hard' and 'soft' boundaries is relevant to a key construct in minority language planning: heritage. Yet, heritage means different things to communities with hard boundaries as opposed to those with soft boundaries. Because the Fengu identity is firmly situated in the past, heritage is fixed and retained regardless of differences in time and geographical location. For groups with soft boundaries, such as the Shangani, Kalanga, and Ndau, heritage is dynamic and 'reinvented' by each generation.

The dynamic nature of heritage has challenging implications for designing language teaching materials and language planning. Contemporary youth may be unable to relate to language teaching materials that overly emphasize the past, as their lives are heavily influenced by technology and popular culture. On the other hand, teaching materials that frame heritage as constantly evolving and are relevant to the youth may be regarded by the elderly as frivolous and not sufficiently educational (Pennycook, 2008).

Language planning and teaching materials: challenges for minority languages

Efforts to enhance the status and widen the spread of the teaching of minority/indigenous languages have been constrained by the reluctance of commercial publishers to develop learning materials for use in minority language classes. Publishers view such projects as not economically viable because the market is limited due to two factors:

1) Minority language speakers tend to identify themselves with one of the super tribes and, therefore, will learn either Shona or Ndebele.
2) Most teachers are not from these minority language groups and, therefore, are not proficient enough to use minority languages for instruction.

In such contexts, social ideology is confronted with commercial realities.

These publishing constraints could be alleviated by collaborating with other minority speakers in neighboring countries on textbook production. However, collaboration between minority language groups in Zimbabwe and other countries is faced with ideological constraints due to potential tension between speakers of the same minority languages across boundaries. In Zimbabwe, most of the teaching materials for minority languages are produced in the Curriculum Development Unit at the University of Zimbabwe in Harare and translated from English into minority languages. From the state's perspective and top-down language planning, translation is a useful strategy for creating uniformity. Translation is also a strategy for improving the availability of materials in minority languages. After all, materials in other languages already exist, and there is no need to undertake research (as would be the case for the newly introduced minority languages) to develop materials in all the minority languages.

While the move to make teaching materials in minority languages readily available is welcome, it may unintentionally undermine efforts toward minority language planning. Translation of materials from 'major' languages in order to 'improve availability of materials may inadvertently contribute to the view that "real" knowledge is knowledge' not codified in minority languages but in either the languages of the super tribes or in former colonial languages (Stroud 2001, p. 342). In this regard, translation may give the impression that minority language cultures and ways of knowing are insignificant in education. Thus, using teaching materials translated from English or from any of the major indigenous African languages may inadvertently reinforce the marginalization of minority languages, undermining the very goals the minority language activists are seeking to accomplish.

Uniform materials may still need to be adapted to local contexts in which minority languages are used. However, the fluidity of political boundaries and their transnational nature means that appropriate language teaching materials in relatively homogeneous cities may not be directly relevant to the complex heterogeneity of communities at political boundaries. Arguably, what might be required in such contexts is not so much the promotion of specific languages, which tend to be construed as formal objects, but the development of strategies for facilitating students' ability to communicate and move with relative ease 'into and out of' diverse communities (Canagarajah, 2007). This means creating language teaching materials founded on constructs such as crossing and accommodation (Rampton, 2003). Yet, materials based on such constructs may radically differ from those produced at the national level, which focus on a single national identity rather than on multiple group identities.

In addition, producing materials for languages in the early stages of standardization raises questions about which variety to use or what constitutes the correct form of spelling (Sebba, 2007). When language varieties and orthographies are distinct, they project a differentiated identity. Language varieties are then associated with "specific and pure identities" (Simpson, 2008, p. 10). Choosing one form of spelling over another may create undue tensions as much as will choosing one variety of the same language over another (Bird, 2001; Sebba, 2007).

In order to make the materials more suitable to local contexts of minority language speakers, it may be necessary to involve local communities in the design of the teaching materials. Although sacrificing uniformity of materials across the state, the involvement of local communities makes for locally relevant materials that might be considered 'authentic' (Stroud, 2001). Although enhancing ecological validity, this involvement may be regarded as time-consuming and difficult because of potential conflicts regarding what communities might consider desirable.

Top-down language planning and local initiatives
It is considered axiomatic that initiatives for the promotion and development of teaching materials, compilation of dictionaries, and writing of grammars should be left to the local communities, as involvement by external agencies may be interpreted as undermining their sense of agency. For this reason, Hale (1969) called for the professionalization of native speakers and informants so that they can take the lead in the design and development of their languages. His argument is based on both "scientific and moral grounds" (Dobrin, 2008, p. 201). If local community members are trained in the necessary disciplines, engaging them is a productive way of proceeding because they would have both the expertise and the inside knowledge about how the communities function. In the case of Zimbabwe, the professionalization and extensive utilization of local expertise are feasible because of the presence of a small but active group of locally trained linguists from different ethnic minorities.

As part of these local initiatives, the Zimbabwean government has also committed itself to introducing minority languages through the end of elementary education, and universities are beginning to offer degrees in minority languages. For example, the University of Great Zimbabwe offers degrees in Shangani, whereas the University of Zimbabwe has an institute dedicated to research and development of standardized orthography for minority languages. The participation of local universities in the promotion of minority languages is critically important, but it is also a double-edged sword. On the one hand, it contributes toward the overall 'intellectualization' of African languages (Finlayson & Madiba, 2002); on the other hand, the minority languages are discursively constructed as parochial. By offering degrees in minority languages in geographical areas in which these languages are most widely spoken, universities provide credibility to the programs. The involvement of the local communities also contributes to establishing rapport between academic institutions and local initiatives. In spite of these advantages, the localization of these languages leads to assumptions that they do not have wider relevance, undercutting the success of local initiatives.

Nonetheless, in some cases, local communities may value sustained engagement by external agencies. Dobrin (2008) pointed out that:

> So while the idea that outsiders should limit their involvement in local communities in an effort to respect their autonomy might seem commonsensical, it is at odds with the perspectives of... most villagers for whom foreign sponsored projects of all kinds (economic, religious, health-centered, etc.) are valued precisely because of the exchange relationships they bring with the outsiders who promote them. This applies to language projects no less, whether their aim is vernacular schooling, community literacy, Bible translation, language documentation, etc. (p. 309)

In such situations, more involvement is a sign of commitment to partnership with communities, rather than a compromise of their sense of agency. The degree to which the active involvement of local communities is warranted for the success of minority language development can only be determined on a case-by-case basis, taking into account the tensions and conflicts within the communities that may be exacerbated by the presence of outsiders. Reception to engagement with outsider agencies might also be strongly shaped by the communities' own history of relationships with outside agencies. If such relationships have been negative, communities are not likely to respond positively.

Chinese language in Zimbabwe
More recently, the introduction of Mandarin Chinese as a foreign language in schools and universities has raised another important issue in Zimbabwean language planning. Chinese seems to be playing a prominent role in the Zimbabwean sociolinguistic landscape, one that used to be played by former colonial languages such as English. The introduction of Chinese in Zimbabwe has to be understood in the context of China's increasing economic role in Africa, as China relies heavily on the importation of oil and minerals from the continent.

Mandarin Chinese has been introduced in all political regions, cutting across Francophone, Lusophone, and Anglophone regions. Confucius Institutes have been established in a number of different countries, including Zimbabwe. These institutes are a powerful instrument in the promotion of Chinese interests and the development of its international language policy. In a standard Memorandum of Agreement with African countries through Confucius Institutes, the Chinese Language Council International commits itself to four key obligations that are attractive to Africa:

(1) the provision of start-up funds for setting up new Confucius Institutes;
(2) training and deployment of Chinese teachers and/or volunteers for Confucius Institutes;
(3) payment of teachers' salaries and allowances; and
(4) provision of language teaching materials.

Language teaching materials are developed in China and used in different African countries, with very little adaptation to local contexts. Yet, Chinese is proving to be very popular in Zimbabwe. The Confucius Institute at the University of Zimbabwe has enrolled a large number of students for non-degree short-term courses in Foundational Chinese and Chinese for Business Purposes; the latter is in great demand in the business community. Chinese has also been introduced as a foreign language in secondary schools for students who may have English as a mother tongue with restricted proficiency in an African language.

The popularity of Chinese might also be related to the fact that, similar to the employment guarantee provided by knowledge of English in the past, knowledge of Mandarin Chinese currently guarantees employment in those areas of business controlled by the Chinese as well as in some locally owned businesses. For example, some hotels in Zimbabwe require their employees to have knowledge or basic proficiency in Chinese as they serve a large number of visitors from China. In addition, Air Zimbabwe flight attendants and some National Baggage Handling Services staff are required to communicate with Chinese speakers, read Chinese documents, and provide interpreting and translation services at the airport. With the collapse of the Zimbabwean health system, use of Chinese traditional medicine has also increased, and those who sell these medicines need to be proficient in Chinese in order to read the instructions on the packaging.

However, it is not only Zimbabweans who have been interested in learning Chinese. Members of some of the Chinese communities in Zimbabwe that have been in the country since the early twentieth century are also taking advantage of the Chinese international language policy. Young children from local Chinese communities are also attending language courses in Chinese in order to negotiate their identities.

Conclusion: silences and gaps in the literature
This article has demonstrated the various ways in which ethnic groups interact with the dominant group and the impact of these interactions on language planning. Minority grievances have been used to both enhance the status of ethnic minorities and construct patronage networks by the ruling party (McGregor, 2009). In addition, although languages such as Kalanga, Shangani, and Nambya have been elevated to indigenous language status in the new language-in-education policy, there are significant differences between the functions of these languages and those of the super tribes, indicating some power differential.

This opens up a possible avenue for a comparative textual analysis of the two Education Acts in order to establish whether any status differentials are embedded in their texts. Such an analysis could utilize critical discourse analysis (CDA) as an analytic and interpretive framework. Since language policy texts are a form of social practice reflecting power differences and social and political inequalities (Tollefson, 2006), CDA renders it possible to interpret the power dynamics concealed in the language used in policy documents, illustrating how texts are connected to each other and informed by their socio-cultural contexts (Abdelhay, Makoni, & Makoni, 2010).

The Zimbabwean diaspora and technology raise new challenges for most countries including Zimbabwean language planning. The issue of diaspora language planning is urgent because one-third of the Zimbabwean population lives outside the country, with the largest numbers in South Africa and the UK. Diaspora language planning raises new challenges because of the tendency of Zimbabweans like other people from other countries to congregate in specific geographical areas. It is possible that much more intense interaction occurs among Zimbabweans in a relatively small area who use their 'home' languages because these, to a large extent, create a community away from home. Yet, the conundrum for diaspora language planning is that migration to another country/continent by its very nature engenders a certain degree of loss of linguistic identity; for migrants, there is "a compelling need for new languages of communication" (Falola, Afolabi, & Adesanya, 2008, p. 13). The implications and consequences of such intense interaction in home country languages and the linguistic needs of the 'receiving' country require attention for sociolinguistic studies of language planning. Because of the connection between those in the diaspora and Zimbabwe through electronic communication (e-mail, Facebook, Twitter, etc.), the nature of diaspora language practices may have an impact on 'local' Zimbabweans who never migrated. There is, therefore, a gap in the current language planning literature as it has focused exclusively on traditional forms of language planning and maintenance.

Acknowledgement
I would like to thank Mai Tino for her kindness.

References
Abdelhay, A., Makoni, B., & Makoni, S. (2010). "The Naivasha language policy: A study of the language of politics and the politics of language in the Sudan" *Journal of Language Policy*, 10, 1–8.
Bird, S. (2001). "Orthography and identity in Cameroon" *Written Language and Literacy*, 4(2), 131–162.
Bybee, J., & Hopper, P (2001). *Frequency and the Emergence of Linguistic Structure*. Amsterdam: Benjamins.
Canagarajah, S. (2007). "After disinvention: possibilities for communication, community and competence" In S. Makoni & A. Pennycook (Eds.), *Disinventing and Reconstituting Languages* (pp. 233–249). Clevedon: Multilingual Matters.
Chebanne, A. (2002). "Shifting identities in eastern Khoe: ethnic and language endangerment" *Pula: Botswana Journal of African Studies*, 16(2), 147–157.
Dobrin, L. (2008). "From linguistic elicitation to eliciting

the linguist: Lessons in community empowerment from Melanesia" *Language*, 84(2), 300–324.

Falola, T., Afolabi, N., & Adesanya, A. (2008). "Introduction: Migrating souls, resistant spirits" In T. Falola, N. Afolabi, & A. Adesanya (Eds.), *Migrations and Creative Expressions in Africa and Africa Diaspora* (pp. 3–28). Durham, NC: Carolina Academic Press.

Finlayson, R., & Madiba, M. (2002). "The intellectualization of the indigenous languages of South Africa: challenges and prospects" *Current Issues in Language Planning*, 3(1), 40–61.

Hachipola, H. (1998). *A Survey of the Minority Languages of Zimbabwe*. Harare: University of Zimbabwe Press.

Hale, K. (1969). "Some questions about anthropological linguistics: The role of native knowledge" In D. Hymes (Ed.), *Reinventing Anthropology* (pp. 382–397). New York, NY: Random House.

Harris, R. (2009). *After Epistemology*. Gamlingay: Bright Pen.

Hutton, C. (2010). "Who owns language? Mother tongues as intellectual property and the conceptualization of human linguistic diversity" *Language Sciences*, 32(6), 638–647.

Lo Bianco, J. (2009). "Critical discourse analysis and language policy and planning (LPP): Constraints and applications of the critical in language planning" In T. Le, M. Short, & W. Le (Eds.), *Critical Discourse Analysis: An Interdisciplinary Perspective* (pp. 101–119). New York, NY: Nova Science.

Makoni, S., Makoni, B., & Nyika, N. (2008). "Language planning from below: The case of the Tonga" *Current Issues in Language Planning*, 9(4), 413–439.

McGonagle, E. (2002). *A Mixed Pot: History and Identity in the Ndau Region of Mozambique*. (Unpublished doctoral dissertation). Michigan State University, East Lansing.

McGregor, J. (2009). *Crossing the Zambezi: The Politics of*

Landscape on a Central African Frontier. Harare: Weaver.

McGroarty, M., Beck, A., & Butler, F. (1995). "Policy issues in assessing indigenous languages: A Navajo case" *Applied Linguistics,* 16(2), 323–343.

Mignolo, W.D. (2000). *Local Histories/Global Designs.* Princeton, NJ: Princeton University Press.

Milroy, L. (2001). "Language ideologies and the consequences of standardization" *Journal of Sociolinguistics,* 5(1), 530–555.

Moore, R., Pietkainen, S., & Blommaert, J. (2010). "Counting the losses: Numbers as the language of endangerment" *Sociolinguistic Studies,* 4(1), 1–26.

Msindo, E. (2005). "Language and ethnicity in Matabeleland: Ndebele–Kalanga relations in Southern Zimbabwe, 1930–1960. *International Journal of African Historical Studies,* 38(1), 79–103.

Ndhlovu, F. (2009). *The Politics of Language and Nation Building in Zimbabwe.* Oxford: Peter Lang.

Nyati-Ramahobo, L. (2000). "Linguistic and cultural domination: The case of theWayeyi of Botswana" In H. Batibo & B. Smieja (Eds.), *Botswana: The Future of Minority Languages* (pp. 217–234). Duisberg: Peter Lang.

Pelinka, A. (2007). "Language as a political category: The viewpoint of political science" *Journal of Language and Politics,* 61(1), 129–143.

Pennycook, A. (2008). *Global Englishes and Transcultural Flows.* New York, NY: Routledge.

Peterson, D. (2004). "Casting characters: Autobiography and political imagination in central Kenya" *Research in African Literatures,* 37(3), 176–192.

Rampton, B. (2003). "Ethnicity and the crossing of boundaries" In R. Mesthrie (Ed.), *Concise Encyclopedia of Sociolinguistics* (pp. 321–323). Oxford: Elsevier.

Ranger, T. (1989). *Democracy and Traditional Political Struc-*

    tures in Zimbabwe, 1890–1999. Harare: University of Zimbabwe Press.
Ranger, T. (2010). *Bulawayo Burning: The Social History of a Southern African City*. Harare: Weaver.
Rusike, M. (1936). *Bantu Mirror*. Salisbury: Rhodesia.
Schiefflin, B.B., & Doucet, R. (1992). "The 'real' Haitian Creole: metalinguistics and orthographic choice" *Pragmatics*, 2–3, 427–445.
Sebba, M. (2007). *Spelling and Society: The Culture and the Politics of Orthography Around the World*. Cambridge: Cambridge University Press.
Shohamy, E. (2006). *Language Policy: Hidden Agendas and New Approaches*. New York, NY: Routledge.
Simpson, A. (2008). "Introduction" In A. Simpson (Ed.), *Language and Identity in Africa* (pp. 1–25). Oxford: Oxford University Press.
Stroud, C. (2001). "African mother-tongue programmes and the politics of language: Linguistic citizenship versus linguistic human rights" *Journal of Multilingual and Multicultural Development*, 22(4), 339–355.
Tollefson, J.W. (2006). "Critical theory in language policy" In T. Ricento (Ed.), *An Introduction to Language Policy: Theory and Method* (pp. 42–60). Oxford: Blackwell.
Werbner, R. (2003). "Challenging minorities: difference and tribal citizenship in Botswana" *Journal of Southern African Studies*, 28(4), 671–684.
Wickert, R. (2001). "Politics, activism and processes of policy production: Adult literacy in Australia" In J. Lo Bianco & R. Wickert (Eds.), *Australian Policy Activism in Language and Literacy* (pp. 67–84). Melbourne: Language Australia.
Williams, G. (1992). *Sociolinguistics: A Sociological Critique*. London: Routledge.

Appendix 1: The two Education Acts
1. Zimbabwe Education Act (Chapter 25:04 part XII, 62)
62 Languages to be taught in schools:
- (1) Subject to this section, the three main languages of Zimbabwe, namely, Shona, Ndebele, and English, shall be taught in all primary schools from the first grade as follows:
    - (a) Shona and English in all areas where the mother tongue of the majority of the residents is Shona; or
    - (b) Ndebele and English in all areas where the mother tongue of the majority of the residents is Ndebele.
- (2) Prior to the fourth grade, either of the languages referred to in paragraph (a) or (b) of subsection (1) may be used as the medium of instruction, depending upon which language is more commonly spoken and better understood by the pupils.
- (3) From the fourth grade, English shall be the medium of instruction: Provided that Shona or Ndebele shall be taught as subjects on an equal-time allocation basis as the English language.
- (4) In areas where minority languages exist, the Minister may authorize the teaching of such languages in primary schools in addition to those specified in subsections (1), (2), and (3).

2. Zimbabwe Education Act of 2006 (Chapter 25: 04)

PART XII
GENERAL
62 Languages to be taught in schools:

- (1) Subject to this section, all three main languages of Zimbabwe, namely, Shona, Ndebele and English, shall

be taught on an equal-time allocation basis in all schools up to form one level.
(2) In areas where the indigenous languages other those mentioned in subsection (1) are spoken, the Minister may authorize the teaching of such languages in addition to those specified in subsection (1).
(3) The Minister may authorize the teaching of foreign languages in schools.
(4) Prior to Form One, any of the languages referred to in subsection (1) and (2) may be used as medium of instruction depending upon which language is more commonly spoken and better understood by the pupils.
(5) Sign languages shall be the priority medium of instruction for the deaf and hard hearing.

Appendix 2: ZILPA proposed changes to the Zimbabwean Education Act (1987)

Zimbabwe proposed amendment to Section 62 of the Educa-tion Act of Zimbabwe 1987
Interpretation of terms
In this section:

i) **Indigenous languages** means the following languages: Ndebele, Shona, Tonga, Sotho, Venda, Shangani and Nambya.
ii) **Area(s)** means district(s)

1. Subject to this Section, the indigenous languages of Zimbabwe including English and the Sign language shall be treated equally, taught and examined from first grade to university provided that, in each area or part of the area, the predominant indigenous language and English shall be taught.
2. The medium of instruction in any area or part of the area, shall depend upon which indigenous language is

more commonly spoken and understood by the majority of the peoples and shall be used in addition to the English language.
3. All indigenous languages shall be taught as subjects on equal time allocation basis as the English language.
4. Subjection four of the Education Act is to be deleted.

Appendix 3: Objectives of ZILPA

4. The objectives of the Association are to operate on a non-profit basis and to:

    4.1 Promote the teaching of TjiKalanga, ChiTonga, ChiNambya, Chichangana and SeSotho in schools, colleges and universities.

    4.2. Lobby the government of Zimbabwe to recognize and permit the use of TjiKalanga, ChiTonga, and TshiVenda, ChiNambya, ChiChangana, and SeSotho as official languages.

    4.3 Assist and encourage the writing and production of literature in TjiKalanga, ChiTonga, TshiVenda, ChiNambya, ChiChangana and SeSetho languages for use in schools, colleges, and universities.

    4.4 Promote the use of TjiKalanga, ChiTonga, TshiVenda, ChiNambya, ChiChangana, and SeSotho languages on national radio and television.

    4.5 Network with organizations with similar objectives in Africa and beyond the six languages.

    4.6 Solicit for and receive donations.

    4.7 Organise literacy exhibitions and competitions in order to generate interest in creative writing in these languages.

    4.8 Do all things necessary to further these objectives and for the general and cultural well being of the association's beneficiary.

II

The use of "indigenous" and urban vernaculars in Zimbabwe
(with Janina Brutt-Griffler and Pedzisai Mashiri)

Abstract
This article analyzes the reasons for and the effects of the language shift in Zimbabwe represented by the increasing use of pan-ethnic lingua francas, or urban vernaculars, of local origin. It is suggested that essentialist/primordialist assumptions about "indigenous" languages that feature prominently in current accounts of language endangerment should be made more complex by understanding their historical and social origins. In Zimbabwe, this means understanding the origins of Shona and Ndebele during the colonial period as the product of a two-stage process: codification of dialects by missionaries, and creation of a unified standard by the colonial regime. In the postcolonial context, these languages and the ethnic identities they created/ reified are giving way to language use that indexes not ethnic affiliation but urbanization. The article adduces data showing that as Zimbabweans move with relative ease across language boundaries, urban vernaculars express their shared social experience of living in postcolonial urban environments.

Introduction

The continuing interest on research into language endangerment / language death has served to refocus our attention on issues of language shift (Bradley & Bradley 2002, Crystal 2000, Skutnabb-Kangas 2000, Nettle & Romaine 2002, Phillipson 2003). Although most of the literature on language endangerment has centered on the Americas, Australasia, and the Pacific, the African context has frequently been invoked (e.g., Nettle & Romaine 2000, Mufwene 2002). Most directly, Nettle & Romaine note that English spread "is leading to the top-down displacement of numerous other tongues" (2000: 144). Similarly, Phillipson (1999:6) writes about the threat posed by English, including in southern Africa, "to other languages and cultures," perhaps even portending language attrition and "a loss of cultural vitality" (1999:176). Implicating the learning of English in "postethnicity," he contrasts to it the use of African languages, which, he implies, carry the "wellsprings of ethnic identification" (1999:104). In common with the mainstream of the literature on language rights and language endangerment, he assumes that English currently represents the greatest threat to "indigenous" languages in Africa. There is now, in addition, a growing literature explicitly directed to Africa that draws its inspiration from research into language endangerment from other geographical regions (see Batibo 1992, 1998, 2001, 2005; Trail 1995).

Much of the literature is analytically rooted in the binary notion of "indigenous" and "dominant" languages—one that is often put forward as though it usefully describes and explains the contexts of all of the world's speakers of allegedly threatened "indigenous" languages. Such a conception tends toward the primordialization of languages and other artifacts, such as customary law, which are thus conceived as if they were authentic, timeless, "stable depositor[ies] of culture" (Fabian 1986:5). That approach reductively treats language shift from the standpoint of its purported effects on allegedly authentic, "traditional" African culture, to the exclusion of considering its signaling the emergence of new and creative adaptive strategies (Batibo 2005).

Despite powerful critiques by such scholars as Mudimbe 1988, Ranger 1989, and Mamdani 1996, which highlight the socially and historically constructed nature of ideas about Africa, ethnicity, and other social processes, much work on African languages remains rooted in an essentialist/primordial paradigm. In this article, we analyze the reasons for and the effects of the language shift in Zimbabwe represented by the increasing use and spread of pan-ethnic lingua francas of local origin. When essentialist/primordial assumptions about the nation's "indigenous" languages are replaced by a more complex understanding of their historical and social constructions and their current linguistic makeup, ongoing processes of language shift and change require greater analytical depth than the paradigm of language endangerment provides. Our argument is thus that, whatever the merits of such paradigms for specific contexts, they are far from having universal validity, and they are particularly inapt when applied to postcolonial Zimbabwe.

In particular, notions that the peoples of Zimbabwe are uniformly, or even primarily, concerned with preserving ethnic affiliations through the use and promotion of language boundaries that mark ethnicity fail to capture the sociolinguistic dynamic. Rather, the Zimbabwean context features:

> * closely related—generally partially or even fully mutually intelligible—languages that make up a southern African regional language continuum, rather than an ecology of independent systems;
> * a situation in which precolonial identities have been reconstructed to the point that their reconstitution is impossible, while neither the colonial-constructed ethnicities (Ranger 1989) nor the postcolonial Zimbabwean unified identity exert a particularly strong hold;

* a sociopolitical crisis of government and a concomitant (or perhaps precipitating) economic collapse that has pushed basic survival strategies to the forefront of everyday experience. Further aggravating the endemic problems is the perception, or reality—as in much of the global South—that urban location provides a privileged socioeconomic status, which the recent urban removals undertaken by the Mugabe regime have made even more precarious.

In these specific conditions, a considerable portion of language use among many Zimbabweans aims at asserting neither ethnic nor national affiliation, but at an urban identity conveyed through what are known as URBAN VERNACULARS. Because these conditions, though currently unusually acute in Zimbabwe, more or less prevail throughout much of sub-Saharan Africa, the Zimbabwean experience can illuminate processes seen on a larger regional and continental level, as witnessed by the rise of such languages as Wolof in Senegal, Lingala in Congo, Town Bemba in Zambia, and isiCamtho in South Africa.

"Indigenous" languages and cultural authenticity
The premise that "indigenous" languages are in need of special protection (Nettle & Romaine 2000, Skutnabb-Kangas 2000) has relied in large part on the assumption that they constitute the authentic products of indigenous cultures. Recent work has shown that such seemingly common-sense assumptions require substantial modification in light of the complex legacy of colonialism. In southern Africa, historical examination of languages like Tswana, Zulu, Xhosa, and chiShona reveals a much more complicated picture. Current national boundaries in southern Africa were purely colonial impositions, for the most part without precolonial precursors. Linguistically, much of the entire region was dominated by a language ecology consisting of widespread language continua over large areas, bordering on

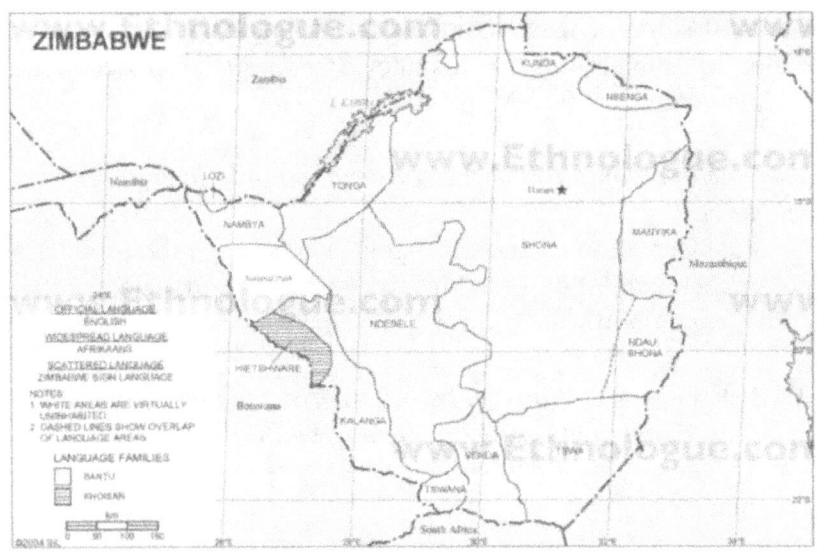

MAP 1: The languages of Zimbabwe (Ethnologue.com; reproduced with permission).

other language continua that belonged to closely related linguistic systems. belonged to closely related linguistic systems. This situation was true, for example, of the geographical whole of present-day Zimbabwe. Though we cannot with precision re-create the precolonial language ecology, all available evidence agrees on the absence of both a unified language encompassing entire presently recognized identities (like chiShona or isiNdebele) as well as of the subidentities, or dialects, into which these are divided (e.g. in the case of chiShona, the varieties chiZezuru, chiKoreKore, chiManyika, chiKaranga, and chiNdau [Ranger 1989]). In Zimbabwe, the current language ecology—as represented, for example, in the *Ethnologue*, whose classification of the world's languages figures so prominently in the language endangerment literature—is represented as consisting of two main indigenous ethnic languages, chiShona and isiNdebele. ChiShona divides into a number of major dialects, with some other languages/dialects more or less proximate to each, and the status of some of these as independent languages or dependent dialects is subject to some dispute (*Ethnologue*); isiNdebele has no known dialects (see Map 1).

The role of colonialism in the construction of indigenous languages
The representation of such a linguistic ecology is the product of colonialism, and it unfolded in two stages. The first stage entailed the creation of standard ver sions of what came to be labeled

TABLE 1. *The relationship between African dialects and religious denominations (Chimhundu 1992:80).*

Language variety	Missionaries working in the region
Korekore	None
Zezuru	Roman Catholic Church and Wesleyan Methodist
Manyika	Anglican Church, United Methodist
Ndau	American Board Mission (American Methodist)
Kalanga	London Missionary Society
Karanga	Dutch Reformed Church

"dialects" by European Christian missionaries. Their concerns were twofold: (i) to learn the languages for the purpose of proselytizing among the people living there; and (ii) to create written versions of these languages for the primary purpose of translating the Bible (and other religious tracts) into them. A missionary put it this way in 1905: "We never forget that the primary object of our work is to give the native the Bible and enable him to read it" (quoted in Ranger 1989: 127). Faced with complex linguistic ecologies featuring continua that defied easy categorization, European missionaries differentiated or grouped together what they saw as "dialects," often based on rudimentary understanding and superficial investigation of local language practices (see Makoni 2003; Brutt-Griffler 2002; MacGonagle2001). As such, the principal dialects recognized today correspond not to precolonial indigenous linguistic, ethnic, or even regional divisions, but to the location and SPHERES OF INFLUENCE of the major missionary denominations—their ability to exert religious hegemony by creating, reifying, and spreading the dialects and the concomitant "ethnic affiliations" those dialects came to represent, or allegedly to represent (since they had no precolonial antecedents).

Decades later, after colonial boundaries had arbitrarily carved up African societies and regimes had been established on the usual basis of force, the British colonial regimes of southern Africa conceived that the pragmatic demands of administration required what Brutt-Griffler calls the "manufacture [of] national languages to correspond with colonial boundaries" (2002: 82). That project was the synthetic product of two constituent components: the contest for control by the missionary bodies, and the imposition of a particular linguistic model by a leading South African linguist of the 1930s, Clement Doke. The Southern Rhodesia administration in 1929 appointed a colonial commission of missionaries, colonial officers and Doke, which decreed that the "four or five languages" spoken in the part of the colony they named Mashonaland were really "four or five dialects of one language." The imprint of the missionaries in the process was unmistakable, as they vied for advantage by asserting the respective claims of the dialect in which their literature was translated, their schools conducted and their followers trained.

Doke, though he lacked substantive proficiency in the language he was called upon to codify, served as arbiter, overseeing the creation of a vocabulary by choosing representative words from each of the different languages and working out a standard grammar (Brutt-Griffler 2002: 81-82). The resulting language was standardized on the basis of two dialects, chiZezuru and chiKaranga, with the former serving as the primary basis of Shona syntax and orthography. He justified this political choice on the dubious grounds that Zezuru had less phonetic variation than the other dialects. Elements of Korekore and Ndau were omitted because he judged them to be "Zuluisms." Because of these judgments and subsequent revisions of Shona orthography in 1955 and 1967, phonemes such as /l/ and /x/ used in Ndau, Karanga, and Korekore were omitted, meaning that for speakers of these dialects, the written language became quite distinct from their spoken variety.

In this standardization and codification process, native speakers of southern African languages were displaced and rendered irrelevant to the process of codifying their "own" languages, the alleged repositories of their cultural authenticity. One of the missionaries who took part in the work (on chiShona), for example, relied on an English-speaking Mozambican teacher who knew isiZulu, who in turn relied on a few children as informants. The direct sources of the constructed language were, therefore, at best second-language speakers of the language they were recording (Makoni & Mashiri 2006).

The colonial commission created to aid the Southern Rhodesian administration opted to call the language it had created "Shona," although even that body could find no reasonable basis for its choice:

> It has been widely felt that the name 'Shona' is inaccurate and unworthy, that it is not the true name of any of the peoples whom we propose to group under the term 'Shona-speaking people' and further, that it lies under strong suspicion of being a name given in contempt by the enemies of the tribes. It is pretty certainly a foreign name, and as such is very likely to be uncomplimentary. It is true that the name 'Mashona' is not pleasing to the natives, but that may simply be because it is a group name imposed from without, and ignoring all true tribal distinctions. Certainly no people in the country claim the

name Mashona as their tribal name, and each would prefer to be described by the proper name of his particular group. (quoted in Brutt-Griffler 2002:82).

The dialectal/"ethnic" names were just as contrived: Some, like Ndau, were derogatory terms used by raiding communities, and others, like Korekore and Zezuru, were drawn from topographical features. Since the colonialists were not merely giving names to existing identities but actually creating them, the problem did not lie with nomenclature. Although the Shona peoples possessed many common cultural traits, they did not have a sense of belonging to a common ethnic identity: "Between the Shona culture as a whole, and the local chiefly group there existed no intermediate concept of ethnicity" (Ranger 1989:121).

Shona, like other "indigenous" languages produced by colonial administrations,[1] was designed to constrain fluid identities within colonial contexts to facilitate European rule. The missionaries' goal was religious conversion, requiring as a matter of expediency that they learn the language at the earliest juncture possible, create written versions, and translate their religious propaganda (see Fabian 1986). The first round of language codification they undertook was aimed simply at facilitating their cultural imperialist project, for which, somewhat ironically, indigenous languages were best suited. For their part, the colonial authorities were motivated mainly by a desire to cheapen the costs of colonial rule, for which uniform standards across

---

[1] ChiShona is not unique as a constructed language. Similar processes occurred in numerous cases throughout southern Africa and the British empire elsewhere. Missionaries in South Africa and eastern Transvaal forged Tsonga, Ronga, and other languages out of diverse speech forms, creating both new and linguistic and political identities (Harries 1989). In Nigeria, missionaries from neigh- boring Sierra Leone codified a diverse group of languages under the name Yoruba, itself a Hausa word not too familiar to those whose language it purportedly denoted. On the other hand, colonial officials opted to make separate languages of Zulu and Xhosa, although the two were as close as the languages unified in other cases.

the missionary-constructed "dialects" were necessary because they reduced the number of written languages in which materials had to be produced, colonial agents trained, and education conducted. In none of the colonial projects were the needs or aspirations, and least of all the cultural heritage, of Zimbabweans even considered. Indeed, it was just precolonial Zimbabwean society, including its cultural heritage, that was being deconstructed and displaced by the processes that led to the creation of Shona and its dialects.

The effects of this standardization project on language use had to be profound. Apart from the influence of a written standard more or less arbitrarily decreed, processes of language change today bear the unmistakable traces of the politically motivated decisions of missionaries and colonial officials. For instance, Kalanga, though mutually intelligible with the dialects of Shona, was, for reasons of geographical proximity, classified and treated as a dialect of Ndebele. Since Kalanga speakers would therefore be educated in standard Ndebele rather than Shona, spoken Kalanga has inevitably become more remote from Shona dialects and ever closer to Ndebele.[2]

Awareness that the emergence of indigenous languages represented a consequence of colonialism remained present among the Africans for whom the newly distinct, codified, and standardized languages/dialects were henceforth to serve as mother tongues. They expressed this consciousness in the names THEY gave to the languages they were being assigned to speak. For example, the variety of chiShona associated with European missionary evangelical work in Zimbabwe was generically referred to as *chibaba* 'the language of the priests'. More specifi-

---

[2] Note that the opposite is also the case: Speakers may regard speech forms that are not mutually intelligible as constituting the same language. For instance, the Chagga people at the foot of Mount Kilimanjaro in East Africa regard themselves as speaking the same language, although linguists can identify at least three mutually unintelligible languages there (Batibo 2005: 2).

cally, depending on the geographical region in which the missionaries were working, they might call it "Church Manyika Language" (Chimhundu 1992). Similarly, in the Republic of the Congo, since the term "Kituba" associated with the colonial state was a colonial invention, it was referred to as *kikongo ya leta* 'Kikongo of the state' (l'etat) (Mufwene 2001:176).

The resulting languages, named, codified and standardized by colonial agents, were then assigned to southern Africans in rather arbitrary ways as part of what Brutt-Griffler 2002 calls the CONTAINMENT POLICY of limiting the spread of English, often for purposes of undertaking education in the "mother tongue" together with the pragmatic demands of colonial administration. While the set of assumptions on which the language endangerment movement operates includes the notion of the imposition of English as part of a European policy of linguistic imperialism (Phillipson 1992), the colonial reality in Zimbabwe was ironically one of the European imposition of these European-generated versions of African languages. These "vernaculars" became the basis of the primary education that was alone available to the vast majority of Africans. These written languages—produced as much by colonial agency as by southern Africans, and bearing at times little resemblance to the spoken language of the region's peoples—became, in effect, mother tongues in search of speakers.

What is Shona today?
What is called *chiShona* comprises today a very complex linguistic construct and legacy of its colonial pedigree.[3] It is something more than a written language (of the type represented by Arabic) but something less than a standard language as such standards emerged, for example, in early modern Europe (though it is sometimes described under either category). Like

---

[3] The general trend in southern African linguistics is to use the word "Shona" as an adjective to refer to the speakers of the language, and "chiShona" as a noun to refer to the language and the culture.

those sociolinguistic categories, chiShona is a language primarily acquired in education and used in and for institutional purposes, while the various missionary-constructed dialects, though they have essentially lost their written standards and functions, remain in everyday usage.

Two additional factors complicate this sociolinguistic picture. First, language boundaries retain, if not exactly their precolonial shape, at least some- thing of their precolonial fluidity. As such, the attempt to capture, as *Ethnologue* and national censuses do, the contours of language use on dialect maps and via tables setting out the number of speakers of each dialect render a misleading and largely meaningless picture of language use in Zimbabwe. If anything, it more reflects statist (in this case, via a postcolonial policy that essentially reproduces the colonial) attempts to impose order for purposes of governance on an inherently unstable linguistic terrain. Second, much everyday interaction and primary language socialization outside (and increasingly, perhaps, within) formal schooling takes place not in either written chiShona or even in the codified dialects but increasingly in urban vernaculars like chiHarare (cf. Childs 1997, Mufwene 2001).

"ChiShona" in this article refers to the written standard language, a stable system but one that is something of an ideal variety realized primarily as a literary style, based largely on ChiZezuru, the dominant dialect of the capital city, but with some aspects taken from the other four main language varieties or dialects, ChiKaranga, ChiManyika, ChiNdau, and ChiKorekore. The dialects of ChiShona are mutually intelligible. While the written standard is stable, the spoken versions are quite unstable.

The urban African context and language use: a sociohistorical note on Zimbabwe and Harare
In this section, we turn to an examination of language use in urban contexts in Harare, Zimbabwe. Zimbabwe, like many

other African countries, is made up of many indigenous groups along with a significant number of Africans from other parts of southern Africa, notably Malawi, Zambia, Mozambique, and South Africa. The ethnic divisions are further complicated by a legacy of racial divisions, which separates off those of European and Asian descent and those of mixed ancestry (so-called Coloreds) (Muzondidya 2002). Zimbabwean politics and scholarship have tended to focus on the relations between the dominant ethnic and racial groups—the Shona, the Ndebele, and the whites—to the exclusion of the African immigrant communities (Muzondidya 2002). In this article we depart from this tradition and focus in part on the use of urban vernaculars by Zimbabweans of Malawian origin.

Zimbabwe's capital and largest city, Harare, has a diverse population of some 1.2 million, including a relatively large immigrant community from Malawi. In the 1950s they made up almost 60% of the people who worked for the City Council. There was a second wave of immigrants from Malawi in the early 1980s after Zimbabwe gained its independence.

Any understanding of language shift necessarily begins in this urban context, since, like much of the rest of the world, Zimbabwe has been undergoing rapid urbanization that has brought different language groups together in a small geographic space. Moreover, though it is sometimes assumed that urban and rural areas are cut off—the former constituting sites of language shift, and the latter sites of ethnic language maintenance (e.g., Nettle & Romaine 2000)—the economy of migration that links them means that their linguistic fates are inextricably intertwined. The phenomenon of cyclical migration is neither new nor restricted to Zimbabwe. For example, a tradition exists of the young "leaving for adventure" to experience work and life elsewhere during the seasonal break (Canut 2001). What occurs in the towns and cities, therefore, has profound ramifications in nonurban contexts as well. Given the patterns of rural-urban migrations, both permanent and transient, the analysis of rural language use given in our data (extract 4) is an indispensable complement to studies of urban language use.

Drawing on the assumptions of the dominant/indigenous binary that is constructed as the exclusive lens through which language shift must be interpreted, it has been assumed since colonial times that, as "Westernized" areas, urban spaces are sites in which ethnic African or Asian languages give way to European languages. Until recently there has been little interest in language shift that does not involve English or French, reflecting a belief that a shift that does not cross the dominant/indigenous divide can hardly constitute a case of real language shift. Indeed, if it did not involve some incorporation of English or French, some commentators would find nothing of interest in it whatsoever. It is, then, precisely in this type of language shift that the paradigmatic limitations of dominant vs. indigenous break down. For the vast majority of the profound language shifts taking place throughout Africa are precisely of this kind.

Within Zimbabwe's African urban space, "indigenous" languages have entered into new linguistic configurations in light of speakers' adaptive responses in the form of linguistic practice to their changing environment and the new communicative needs it presents (cf. Mufwene 2001). We have selected as our case study Harare, Zimbabwe, a city that linguistically exemplifies other African urban locations in three important respects:

> * social interactions take place in a multilingual environment;
> * they rest on the assumption that speakers are able to COMPREHEND a number of local languages and are willing to accommodate their interlocutors;
> * Harare embodies the pattern of migration to cities that brings people from different linguistic and socioeconomic backgrounds to the same urban space.

The linguistic results of these processes, known as URBAN VERNACULARS, are languages made up of discourse elements, lexical items, and syntactic forms drawn from a number of different languages. These ensembles have been reported in different parts of Africa, including Mali, Kenya, Congo, Zambia, South Africa and Senegal (Canut 2002), all of which have experienced extreme economic deprivation and political oppression.

The defining feature of urban vernaculars is not merely that they are mixed languages, but that their individual speakers may not necessarily be able to develop full competence in each of the languages that make up the amalgam (Njoroge 1986). For example, some chiShona speakers produce and use utterances of mixed chiShona and chiChewa but display very limited knowledge of chiChewa. It is not uncommon to hear chiShona speakers comically exchange greetings with chiChewa-speaking acquaintances, such as *Muri bwanji here aPhiri*? 'How are you Mr. Phiri?'. The speaker's limited competence in chiChewa in this example is evident at the phonological level. Standard chiChewa uses lateral /l/ where chiShona uses trill /r/, and it employs a high tone to mark the interrogative whereas chiShona uses the interrogative morpheme *here* 'yes/no'. Thus, put in standard chiChewa, the greeting above would be *Muli bwanji (aPhiri)*?

The widespread use and social importance of these urban vernaculars in southern Africa has been given market recognition, for example in their presence as a staple of television and radio programs, particularly those targeting youth. There has been, however, no similar institutional recognition, which has profound implications for educational policy. While urban vernaculars are the mother tongues of many urban children, children continue to be tested in "indigenous" languages that sound foreign to their users. It has been noted in the South African context that many serious problems arise from the teaching of standard Zulu in classrooms for Zulu children whose language repertoires vary greatly, and this is a challenge to Zulu teachers, who compare the teaching of standard Zulu to teaching in a foreign language.

A main reason for this discrepancy between actual language use and educational language policy is the reification of the colonial linguistic heritage of written standards that do not correspond to language-in-use. While official indigenous languages remain to a large extent mother tongues in search of speakers, urban vemaculars have been rendered spoken languages in search of legitimacy. Because the language rights and language endangerment movements have successfully reduced language policy to the unanalyzed categories of dominant vs. indigenous without sufficient historical or empirical investigation, they find themselves in the ironic position of defending the colonially imposed "standard indigenous languages" against those that more directly express the cultural legacy that is supposed to be preserved.

Language use in urban public transport.
Some 60% to 80% of Zimbabweans commute daily to work by small minivans or buses. Such daily commuting brings together speakers of a variety of languages and ethnic backgrounds, including Afrikaans, chiChewa, English, isiNdebele, chiShona, Portuguese, and Sotho. Encounters between drivers and passengers provide us with the opportunity to explore the dynamics of communication, and more specifically the use of urban vernaculars in a clearly delineated social and linguistic space (Rakodi 1995).

To understand the use of urban vernaculars among adults, we carried out an ethnographic study in the densely populated Harare suburb of Mbare, specifically in Zata Street, where the majority of residents are of Malawian origin. We identified families in which one of the heads of household was of Malawian origin but had lived in Zimbabwe for at least a decade, while the other was ethnically Zimbabwean. The informant was also expected to have had a job that required that he or she leave the family home and interact with the general public constantly. Through participant observation, we both recorded interactions within the family and followed the informants and, with their permission, recorded their interactions with non-family members as part of their professional and social life to see how the informants used urban vernaculars to negotiate their identities in different spaces. We observed five families, in which the husbands were all of Malawian origin and the wives ethnically Zimbabwean. The couples had been married for at least five years.

Below we report on the data collected for one subject, whom we will call "Mr. Phiri." This informant was born in Malawi and attended elementary school there and high school in Zimbabwe. When these data were collected on 18 June 2002, he was working as a bus conductor for a local company. At 6:30 a.m., as he is preparing to leave his rented house on Zata Street, Mbare, he converses with his ethnically chiShona wife (Ms. Phiri) about the transport problems facing the public:

(I) *chiChewa* is in italic; ***chiShona*** is in bold italic; **English** is in bold roman.
    1 Mr. Phiri: *Amai ndiri kupita kunchito.*
       'My wife I am leaving for work.'
    2 Ms. Phiri: *Zikomo **fambai zvakanaka**.*
       'It's all right, go well.'
    3 Mr. Phiri: *Antu ambiri masiku **ano**. Kulibe* **mabhazi**.
       'People are many these days. There are no buses.'
    4 Ms. Phiri: (nods in agreement)
    5 Mr. Phiri: *Antu amavhuta.* ***Vanopindira*** **makiyu**. *Antu ambiri masiku aino. Kulibe* **mabhazi**. *Antu amavhuta.* ***Vanhu vanopindira pama***queue.
       'People are restless. They jump the lines. There are many people who use public transport these days, yet there are very few buses. People become restless and jump the lines.'

6 Ms. Phiri: *Masiku ano zintu zikuvhuta.* **Hakuna**, *kulibe* **transport**.
'These days things are hard. There are no adequate buses.'

By line 5, both husband and wife are near the road; they bid each other farewell, and the wife returns into the house and the bus conductor walks to the main bus depot in Mbare, where he works.

In the intimacy of a private conversation within their family, this couple uses an amalgam of chiChewa and chiShona. Mr. Phiri's discourse comprises 28% chiShona, 58% chiChewa, 11% English, and 3% consisting of words belonging to both chiShona and chiChewa. Ms. Phiri's discourse consists of 30% chi-Shona, 60% chiChewa, and 10% English. Her chiShona is strongly marked by a chiZezuru accent.

The word *amai* in line 1 (which may mean either 'one's mother' or can be used to refer to 'one's wife') belongs simultaneously to both chiChewa and chiShona - in this case, specifically the chiZezuru dialect that is dominant in the Harare region. In line 3, Mr. Phiri responds initially in what may be classified as chiChewa before concluding the sentence with a chiZezuru word. In line 6, Ms. Phiri initially responds in chiChewa, but again concludes her response with a chiZezuru phrase. By drawing phrases that alternate between chiChewa and chiShona when saying there is no transport (**hakuna**, *kulibe*) she seems to emphasize the gravity of the poor transport situation by crossing language boundaries—using the chiShona word followed by its chiChewa equivalent. While Ms. Phiri's incorporation of an English word involves no morphosyntactic alteration, all of Mr. Phiri's utterances where English is the source language show significant morphosyntactic alteration. Thus, **mabhazi** 'buses' takes the form Shona plural morpheme + Shonalized (via vowel insertion at the end) English noun. He also uses two words derived from the English morpheme "queue": **makiyu** (Shona plural morpheme + Shonalized [via vowel insertion at the end] English noun); but also *pamaqueue* (Shona morpheme + non-Shonalized English noun).

The next excerpt finds the bus conductor at the bus depot in Mbare. He is now addressing passengers who are pushing each other to get into the bus, shouting at the top of his voice:

> (2) *chiChewa* in italic; ***chiShona*** in bold italic; **English** in bold roman; slang in normal roman. BC: bus conductor; Pf: female passenger.
>
> 1 BC (to passengers): **mapassengerz** *yimani* **mukiyu**, *mosatchita zatchigororo*.
> 'Passengers stand in a line, do not behave like hooligans.'
>
> 2 BC: ***Pindai tiende*** **muface**.
> 'Get in so that we may leave, my acquaintance.'
>
> 3 BC: ***Pinda tiende sisi***. 'Get in so that we may leave, my sister.'
>
> 4 BC: ***Handei*** **kuback seat**.
> 'Let us go to the back seat.'
>
> 5 Pf: *Hapana kwekuenda* **bhazi** *rakazara*.
> 'There is no more place to go to because the bus is full.'
>
> 6 BC: **One** asara! *pinda tiende* shasha. *Ngatisebedzane* **bigaz**.
> 'One left behind, get in so that we may leave, pal.'

Extract (2) illustrates the nature of language use in a public domain that takes the form of an amalgam of chiShona and English, a variety referred to as chiHarare (Chimhundu 1983). This spoken variety is used in everyday communication. Unlike the standard chiShona, chiHarare is quite unstable, often an admixture of ChiShona and English, plus switches and borrowings from other languages. ChiHarare is a byproduct of urbanization or cosmopolitanism.

The meaning of English words in such an urban vernacular at times radically differs from their meaning in Standard English. For example, the noun phrase ***mu*face** in line 1 combines the chiShona prefix ***mu*** + English noun **face**. In this context, it is used to mean 'my acquaintance'. A similar case is the word **bigaz** (English ***big***) (literally 'the senior one', in line 5). The phonological rules used in **bigaz** depart from those in Shona because it ends with a consonant when most Shona syllables end with vowels. The pattern of the chiShona prefix plus the the English noun is repeated frequently. For example, the phrase ***ku*back seat** in line 3 combines the chiShona locative ***ku*** + English noun **back seat**; ***ma*passengerz** is morphologically marked by double pluralization—a prefix drawn from chiShona and a suffix **-s**. *Zatchigororo* is analyzed as Chewa and Shona because the first part, *zatchigo*, is Chewa, but the second part, *-roro*, is Shona or Shonalized Chewa, since proper Chewa would use the lateral /l/ rather than the roll /r/, common in Shona.

Semantic alternation also takes place in the case of many words that chiShona speakers borrow from English. In Standard English, people talking about a soft drink clearly distinguish the container (bottle) from the contents. In everyday chiShona, when one says Unoda bhotoro ripi?, literally 'Which bottle do you prefer?', the speaker implies the content (e.g Coca-cola, Sprite) and not the container. The word kokokora 'Coca-cola' is also commonly used generically to imply any other type of soft drink.

Another striking feature of the combined chiShona and English discourse is the use of kinship and other terms suggestive of intimate relations when the crew refers to passengers. We observe this tendency in the bus conductor's use of *mu*face (line 1), *sisi* 'sister' (line 2), and *bigaz* 'the senior one' (line 5) (cf.

Mashiri 2002). From a linguistic perspective, the use of words such as *sisi* can be read as incorporation of abbreviated forms of urban discourse. The strategy of abbreviating English terms as they get incorporated into urban vernaculars made up of predominantly chiShona and English shows that the phenomenon we are dealing with is much more complicated than simple borrowing. In both urban and rural communities, the abbreviated forms are widespread. Examples of this process include the nouns *ma-vegi* 'vegetables', *ma-mini* 'miniskirts', *ma-exams* 'examinations', and *ma-phone* 'telephone'. The abbreviated expressions are often interchanged with the full forms, resulting in "double" plurals, chiShona plural prefix *ma-* (class 6) + English noun + English plural suffix. For example, *ma-vegi* is at times used interchangeably with *ma-vegetables*, *ma-mini* with *miniskirts*, *ma-exams* with *ma-examinations*, and *ma-phone* with *ma-telephones*. The double morphological forms illustrate the variation within urban vernaculars. The full form, when used in a social interaction, conjures up a more formal relationship with the addressee.

Although we are referring to some of these terms as abbreviated, it is not obvious that the users perceive them as such. It is also likely that some users of the abbreviated expressions may not have encountered the expressions in their full form in English. An abbreviated form may not necessarily be an elliptical form from the perspective of the users, particularly those with limited exposure to English. We thus do not know whether the users regard *sisi* as an abbreviated form of *sister*, or *ma-vegi* as an abbreviated form of *vegetables*.

In extract (3), the bus conductor is conversing with conductors from other buses. Mr. Phiri's Shona colleague Mr. Mazo teases the bus conductor, who does not seem amused by his jokes:

(3)
1 Mr. Mazo: *Aphiri bwera kuno.*

'Mr. Phiri, come here.'
2 BC: *Ndiri kubwera, mufuna kundijairira ndikubwera*
'My friend I don't like the way you are teasing me. I am coming.'

In this short sample, a Shona bus conductor addresses Mr. Phiri in Chewa, albeit a Harare or second-language variant of chiChewa that we may regard as "mock Chewa." While *Kubwera* is chiChewa, the syntax of *Ndiri kubwera* is Harare Chewa. The typical Chewa syntax is *ndikubwera*. Although Mr. Phiri responds in Chewa, he seems to feel offended, perhaps because he regards being addressed in Chewa in public among non-intimate acquaintances as disclosing an alien identity he was trying to mask. The attempt to cross over to a Chewa identity is not reciprocated by Mr. Phiri.

The use of chiHarare has social significance in a city where there is a relatively large number of speakers of other minority languages, particularly from Malawi, who are threatened with marginalization decades after their ancestors' migration. Thus, while Mr. Phiri's chiHarare in the private domain draws heavily on chiChewa, the situation is different when he is interacting with passengers in the public domain. His chiHarare seems to draw more on a combination of English and chiShona. In doing so, he both refuses to accept a socially ascribed Malawian ethnic identity (the foreign other) and claims the status he covets—not that of an ethnic Shona, nor even a Zimbabwean national, but a cosmopolitan urbanite. ChiHarare, which as a mixture of English and chiShona is distinct from both, allows him to do so. The emergence of such a tendency is also reported, for instance, in studies of urban language use in West Africa, particularly in Dakar in Senegal (McLaughlin 2001:170). This suggests that in analyzing language use in multiethnic contexts, we need to take cognizance of the ability of urban dwellers to move out of old ethnicities and create new identities centered on the urban experience (cf. Mufwene 2002).

Urban vernaculars and non-urban contexts: The impact of urban/rural migration.

Urban vernaculars have been studied and analyzed with respect to urban contexts almost exclusively. Given, however, the close interconnection of these two spaces that results from the high level of migration in the African context, we also collected data in a rural community to see to what extent urban vernaculars had spread to rural communities.

Although the term URBAN VERNACULARS might signal that they are limited to urban spaces, migration patterns in Zimbabwe allow language practice to be "transported" to some non-urban dwellers as well. As we stated earlier, some 60% to 80% of Zimbabweans travel to work in urban places. Many of them come from the areas surrounding the city, and some travel from non-urban places, in a nation that is approximately three-fifths rural. We were interested in how the local language practices of people of Malawian descent in non-urban places resemble those in urban Harare. The data from two informants, Mr. G and Ms. G, come from a community called Chiundura in the Midlands province of Zimbabwe, near the city of Kwekwe. The data are part of our ethnographic study carried out in Zimbabwe in the summer of 2002. The interviews with our informants were conducted in their house. The conversation was recorded on a late summer afternoon and was held in chiShona. Mr. G is a prominent subsistence farmer. He and his wife are in their early sixties. The interviewer was a former school principal, now a successful farmer in Chiundura, who therefore is familiar with the local context. The objective of the research project was to investigate the nature of language use in a rural domestic environment.

(4) R: Researcher; Mr. G. *chiShona* in italic; **chiNyanja** in bold italic; **isiNdebele** in bold; English in roman.
  1 R: *Munotaura mitauro mingani?*
    'How many languages do you speak?'

2 Mr G: *chiShona .. chiZezuru, chiNdevere, chiNyanja ne chirungu.*
    'Shona .. Zezuru, Ndebele, Nyanja, and English.'
3 R: *Munoshandisa rurimi rwipi?*
    'In which contexts do you use each language?'
4 Mr G: *chiShona* usually *mumba mangu muno, chiNyanja kana ndasangana neve ku Marawi. Ndinogona kuti* **maZuzuru sagula mowa**, *vechiNdevere tigere navo muno. Kanatichikwazisa maNdevere tinoti* **Livhuke njani**? *Chirungu kana ndaenda kutawindi. chiNdevere ndiri* good. *ChiNyanja ndakanaka. Chirungu ndinogona pandakangumira.*
'I usually use Shona here in my home, Nyanja when I meet people of Malawian origin. I can say, the Shona do not buy beer [at the beer halls] in Nyanja. I use Ndebele when I meet Ndebele speakers here in the Midlands. When we greet the Ndebele we say **Livhuke njani** ('How did you sleep?'). I use English when I go to town to sell my farm produce. My Ndebele is good. My ChiNyanja is fine. My English is good when one takes into account my level of education.'

Mr. G's language use exhibits fragments that belong to different languages. For example, he incorporates English adverbs to describe his knowledge of languages, as in *chiShona* usually 'I usually use Shona at home' and *chiNdevere ndiri* good 'my Ndebele is good'. In addition to identifying the languages he speaks and displaying some linguistic expressions from those languages, Mr. G evaluates his knowledge of those languages. He feels he is proficient in chiShona, isiNdebele, and chiChewa (chiNyanja), demonstrating his knowledge of the latter two with the incorporation of fragments. He describes his knowledge of English as good considering his level of education.

In addition to elements from English, he draws upon linguistic expressions particularly from chiNyanja, as if to display his knowledge of chiNyanja, and in *MaZuzuru sagula mowa* 'the Shona do not buy beer'. He uses this linguistic expression that he has most likely heard used by chiNyanja speakers when referring to chiShona speakers when they meet in pubs, describing their reluctance to buy beer. In the Ndebele greeting **Livhuke njani**? lit. 'How did you wake up?' the prefix /li-/ 'you plural' is a new phenomenon in Ndebele. Originally Ndebele had no honorific plural as is found in chiShona. While Shona distinguishes the use of the subject concords /wa-/ 'you singular past', as in *Warara sei*? 'How did you sleep?' and /ma-/ 'you plural past' in greetings, Ndebele does not. It uses /u-/ 'you singular' to express both singular and plural. Therefore, it is acceptable in Ndebele to greet an adult with **Uvhuke njani**? Yet it would be e considered rude in Shona to greet an adult using the singular subject concord (*wa-*). The use of /li-/ as demonstrated by Mr. G. is not limited to chiShona speakers but is becoming quite acceptable, especially among urban Ndebele speakers.

It is interesting that when he lists chiShona as his first language, Mr. G quickly corrects himself to say *chiZezuru*. Later, he reverts to calling it chiShona in describing what contexts he uses it in. In the same description, he switches again to the use of *maZuzuru* where he might have been expected to use *maShona*, though in this case the choice is ascribed to the chiChewa speakers he is, in effect, quoting. That he does not feel constrained to overrule their naming of his ethnic identity—and that he himself is as comfortable using the one as the other in interacting with a fellow chiShona speaker—suggests that the collective Shona identity has not entirely supplanted that of the Zezuru, even among prominent members of this rural community. The association of chiShona with chiZezuru may in part reflect the historically dominant role that chiZezuru plays in the construction of chiShona. But it also strongly suggests that he is laying claim to the cosmopolitanism that his occupation entails, since he references his use of English when he goes into town. Indeed, his lengthy response to the question of where he uses the languages he is proficient in, complete with phrases from each language as if to confirm his claim to his listener (a former educational official), foregrounds his sense of his performing multiple identities—of being a cosmopolitan, though of rural residence, who goes into town, joins friends at the beer hall, and lives in a multilingual world.

Mr. G's linguistic repertoire differs from that of Ms. G. Their language is in part shaped by their social responsibilities and the social roles they play in the communities. Ms. G has no formal education and does not claim to have any knowledge of English. She plays, however, an active role in the education of her grandchildren, and she does so in chiShona by teaching them community values:

(5) R: Researcher; Ms. G.
   1 R: Adhiresi *yenyu ndiyani*?
      'What is your address?'
   2 Ms.G: *Handina kudzidza, handinzwe zvamuri kutaura.*
      'I am not educated, I cannot understand what you are referring to.'
   3 R: *Mungati munoziva chiShona zvakadiyi?*
      'How good do you think your Shona is?'
   4 Ms. G: *ChiShona ndiri* number one, *mbuya vakandi-dzidzisa vaitaura chiShona vana kana vabva kuchikoro ndinovadzidzisa zviragwe-kurumba handikusvika.*
      'My Shona is number one, my grandmother who taught me Shona was excellent. When the children come from school, I teach them riddles and proverbs—it is reckless to be in a hurry.'

Ms. G typifies the results of this study in that the language experience of our informants is not necessarily made up of complete language systems, but of integrated fragments that make up an inventory on which the speaker draws. For example, Ms. G in the sentence *ChiShona ndiri* number one, *mbuya vakandidzidzisa vaitaura chiShona vana kana vabva kuchikoro ndinovadzidzisa zviragwe—kurumba handi kusvika*, draws from standard Shona for the greater part of the sentence, English in the phrase 'number one', the Karanga dialect of Shona in the word *zviragwe* 'riddles', and the Ndau dialect in the proverb *kurumba handi kusvika*.

In her interview, she also indicates that she is familiar with chiNdau, another chiShona "dialect" spoken in the eastern part of Zimbabwe. She has learned and experienced chiNdau because her sister lives in eastern Zimbabwe where chiNdau is frequently spoken. Her language experiences are therefore partly shaped by her family and social relationships and the role she plays in the socialization of her grandchildren. She resorts to the use of proverbs when asked how good her Shona is. She keeps returning to the proverb *Mugona wepwere ndiye asina* 'the person who can bring up children is the one who doesn't have them', or she cites another proverb she uses when socializing her children about the dangers of being in a hurry (*Kurumba handi kusvika*, line 4).

Interestingly, she cites that chiNdau proverb and the Karanga word for 'riddles' to demonstrate how she educates her grandchildren in chiShon—that is, via dialects used in distant regions of Zimbabwe. This usage suggests that what interests her is not so much the transmission of the chiShona language as the knowledge she wishes to impart through its usage. Moreover, she describes her proficiency in chiShona with an English-like expression (though she may not know the origin of the words she employs). In this respect, Ms. G's language use is perhaps even more telling than that of her spouse. In response to questions that might have been expected to yield unmixed chi-

Shona, her first language, she not only displays the competence of a multilingual but also incorporates multilingual elements in her discourse. She disclaims knowledge of English when the interviewer asks her for her address (using the English loanword with chiShona phonetics and morphosyntax). There are, however, some English-like expressions that recur in her language production. For example, when she describes her family's social status in the village as the most prominent family, she uses the English phrase 'number one'. This seems to suggest that the idea of unmixed chiShona is extremely rare. Even the speech of non-educated speakers contains English-like expressions.

In any case, rural Zimbabweans do not perform pure, authentic, unmixed languages. Rather, their usage reflects the web of social relations in which they are enmeshed, crossing region, urban/rural, and ethnic lines. Though perhaps not to the same extent as in cities, language usage in rural areas nevertheless reflects the same cosmopolitan influences that have produced the urban vernaculars that establish urbanity.

In sum, individuals will develop comparable linguistic inventories to the extent that they share similar social and economic experiences, as the examples of Mr. G and Ms. G point out. The exact details of the linguistic inventories may vary depending on the individual's social and urban networks and, for example, her or his gender role in the speech communities. For Mr. G, knowledge of a language is defined as the ability to use and draw on "different" languages (Ndebele, Nyanja, and English) in interactions with people from different ethnic groups in his everyday life and as part of his occupational needs as a subsistence farmer. in his everyday life and as part of his occupational needs as a subsistence farmer. Even then, rural areas, whose residents are sometimes viewed as custodians of ethnic identity, present not a homogenous cultural/ethnic domain but a multilingual one in which language use indexes the ability to function in a changing socioeconomic environment. This already represents something of a transition to an urban environment in which performance of the urban variety indexes a coveted urban identity. Not cultural authenticity but social capital governs language use.

Discussion

A study of language use in Zimbabwe shows that speakers move with relative ease across language boundaries. For example, Mr. Phiri, of Malawian origin, may use an amalgam of Chewa, Shangani, and Nambya in intraethnic communication, with the interaction accompanied by song and dance, depending on the context (Makoni & Mashiri 2007). Though Malawians and other African immigrants in Zimbabwe tend to live in the same neighborhoods, as the case of Mr. and Ms. Phiri demonstrates, there is much interethnic marriage; hence, even these community interactions require multilingualism, as Mr. and Ms. Phiri's home use of an amalgam of chiChewa and chiShona illustrates. A short while later, we observe Mr. Phiri using an urban vernacular with other township residents in a situation in which he seeks to downplay his ethnicity as a marker and to foreground his urban identity. He may then use English in situations where he wants to stress his social status and education. For urbanites like Mr. Phiri, primary language socialization involves learning to interact in an amalgam of chiChewa and urban Shona/English (and occasionally Afrikaans), and learning how to deploy his linguistic resources depending on the nature and goal of the interaction. The communicative practices of Africans like Mr. Phiri are "composed of an ensemble of varying subsystems in contact and in the process of permanent transformation and evolution" (Canut 2002:39).

    This understanding provides an alternative account to the "dystopic vision of linguistic catastrophe" or language endangerment (Jacquemet 2005:1). Rather than suggesting that "indigenous" languages are in the process of extinction in African urban contexts, we show how speakers incorporate "indigenous" languages and the "dominant" one to move across different ethnic and social classes.

Within that movement, urban vernaculars form an important part of their linguistic repertoire. The Harare urban vernacular is a linguistic hybrid or amalgam similar to those found in other parts of Africa (Abdulaziz & Osinde 1997, Githiora 2002). It is important to note that such a linguistic description should not be construed to mean that the speakers themselves see their language use in this way. Thus, Mrs. G sees no contradiction in demonstrating her chiShona proficiency not only with elements of chiKaranga and chiNdau, but even with English. She focuses on the contextually appropriate meaning rather than on the dialectal or linguistic system it is taken from. Speakers do not inherit knowledge of the history of a language (cf. McLaughlin 2001:121). As with other languages, an intimate knowledge of the etymology of the language of everyday interactions requires specialized study. The term "hybrid" may also lead us to interactions requires specialized study. The term "hybrid" may also lead us to misconstrue the sociolinguistic situation. For example, speakers of linguistic hybrids may differ considerably in the nature of their linguistic repertoire. Ms. G has a different repertoire from her husband, Mr. G, as a consequence of their different social experiences.

Radical differences in repertoire are not restricted to urban vernaculars in Zimbabwe. For example, in Senegal, the urban vernaculars are made up of urban Wolof, French, and other Senegalese languages for some people, while for others the amalgam may be perceived as monodialectal, made up of urban Wolof alone. Consequently, the same amalgam may be said to belong either to a single language or to different languages simultaneously—a form of multivalency (Woolard & Schieffelin 1994). To describe the linguistic amalgams as code-switching might be inappropriate because some of the speakers may not have any substantial proficiency in the unmixed forms of the languages represented in the amalgams (McLaughlin

2001). Thus, in the case of Zimbabweans, if a speaker's production includes fragments from English, chiShona, and chiNyanja, this does not necessarily mean he is able to speak any of those languages separately.

Languages like chiHarare seem to derive from the shared social experience of living in a postcolonial urban environment. In order to survive in the African city, one has to improvise, and this improvisation extends to language use (McLaughlin 2001). Becoming urban means being able to adopt a new identity. For example, Mr. Phiri's language use demonstrates how he moves in and out of a Malawian-origin identity and adopts a Harare identity. Such a shift from one identity into another is not restricted to Harare. When addressed by a non-Malawian coworker in chiChewa, Mr. Phiri is offended by what he apparently views as the inappropriateness of such an ethnic essentialization of his identity in an urban, multiethnic space where an urban vernacular is more appropriate. He thus appears to see language use as context-specific. Similarly, McLaughlin 2001 writes that for many Senegalese,

> slipping out of one identity and into another as easily as if they were changing clothes ... is a common experience as they travel backwards and forwards to urban and rural areas. There is an awareness of the fluidity of identity as they speak Wolof in one way in Dakar as opposed to rural areas with some claiming that even their ethnicity changed when they were in the city: 'Quand je suis chez moi je suis Haalpularr, quand je suis a Dakar je suis Wolof' 'When I am at home I am Haalpularr, when I am in Dakar I am Wolof'. (2001:156)

Urban vernaculars may represent an attempt to redefine the public space in countries such as Senegal. At times they may even be construed as a challenge to the socioeconomic and ruling elite. It is thought, for example, that Sheng, an urban vernacular of Nairobi, Kenya, emerged and developed in the lower socio-economic classes in the Nairobi ghetto—a similar origin to that of Johannesburg, South Africa's Isicamtho. Sheng apparently spread owing to the influx of migrants into Nairobi in the early 1960s after Kenya had attained independence and was widely used by Kikuyu ex-Mau Mau, school dropouts (as Isicamtho is said to have evolved among prison inmates and township gangs). Sheng spread away from the Eastlands because of its widespread use in the informal sector, for example by shoe shiners, curio sellers, hawkers, and parking attendants. There is also some evidence that street children may have Sheng as their primary language. Whatever its exact origins, Sheng has spread widely in Nairobi. Young people, in particular, use it as their language of interaction. It dominates the discourse practices of primary and secondary school students. Sheng is, however, not strictly a youth language; adults also report using it. ChiHarare's use by persons of Malawian origin—often targets of anti-immigration sentiment—fits a similar pattern. In that sense, Mr. Phiri's preference to be addressed by co-workers in chiHarare is an assertion of the primacy of urban identity over national origin and ethnicity in contemporary Zimbabwe. Such a hierarchization of identities derives from the postcolonial socioeconomic and political realities of Zimbabwe (and other parts of Africa) discussed earlier.

The degree to which urban vernaculars are an integral part of urban life is apparent in their use in popular songs, in the routines of comics such as Boy Dakar in Senegal (Spitulnik 1988), and even in the news media. Because of the social significance of writing, the use of urban vernaculars in written form in particular may serve as a form of social legitimation.

Though urban vernaculars are intimately linked to the city cultures in which they emerge, to identify them as exclusively city-based (as the names chiHarare or Town Bemba imply) is misleading, given their presence in rural areas. Hence, as we have found evidence of chiHarare in rural Zimbabwe,

Bamako has also been found to serve as a lingua franca in rural Mali (Canut 2002). When used in rural areas, urban vernaculars tend to diverge considerably from "traditional" rural dialects (themselves possibly also a product of modernity, as in the case of the dialects of chiShona).

Conclusion

We have presented a historical account of the notion of "indigenous" language with the goal of refining the study of language endangerment. We suggest that the classification of languages into "dominant" and "indigenous" requires modification to include an understanding of languages as products of history. The analytical framework of language endangerment that often consists in dividing all languages into "indigenous" and "dominant" —and the misleading notion of linguistic diversity that accompanies it—actually serves to obscure significant processes of language shift in Zimbabwe and other African settings. The socio-linguistic significance of the development of languages like chiHarare is something that has not been contemplated in the language endangerment literature: In Zimbabwe, and perhaps in other parts of sub-Saharan Africa, urban identity trumps national, which standard chiShona might represent, or the colonial-constructed ethnic, which dialects might reflect.

Though it has been widely argued that English poses the greatest threat to the world's linguistic diversity because of its global power (Phillipson 1992, Nettle & Romaine 2000, Skutnabb-Kangas 2000), there is not much evidence of the emergence of monolingual English speakers of African origin as a significant factor in Africa, where English speakers remain bilinguals. In the most comprehensive survey of language shift on the continent to date, Mufwene (2002) concludes, "We should not overrate the importance of European languages regarding language endangerment." On the contrary, because English is not a lingua franca, indigenous lingua francas have developed to fill the void. Mufwene notes:

The new indigenous lingua francas (such as Wolof, Swahili and Lingala) have gained economic power and prestige, and have gradually displaced (other) ancestral ethnic languages. It is these that can be said to have endangered indigenous languages, to the extent that some rural populations have been shifting to the urban vernaculars, abandoning some of their traditional cultural values for those practiced in the city. (2002:175-76)

By bringing data from Zimbabwe, we have shown how local language practices signal the speakers' attempts to abandon easy ethnic classifications on the basis of one's "ethnic" language. Urban vernaculars like chiHarare provide such a means for Zimbabweans like Mr. Phiri.

A mechanical application of the dominant-encroaching-on-indigenous paradigm that has been a prominent feature of much of the language endangerment literature risks a reductivist interpretation of the rise of urban lingua francas like chiHarare. Such a view would focus exclusively on the admixture of lexis and, less often, structural elements of English within the emerging languages or existing languages as evidence that, in all cases of language shift, the direction is from indigenous to dominant. First, that overstates and overvalues the actual influence of English on indigenous languages, subsuming even cases in which English influence is nonexistent or minimal under the category of English dominance and encroachment. Such an approach actually trivializes the "indigenous" languages that are said to be the objects of preservation efforts, since it regards differences among them as unimportant in comparison to their overarching distinctness from "exogenous" languages—for example, in the notion of African languages as used in both Nettle & Romaine 2000 and Phillipson 1992. To say that language shift from one "indigenous" African language to another that is lexically and structurally English-influenced amounts to a shift from an indigenous language to English would be akin to arguing that English is really linguistically subsumed under the French that exerted an enormous impact on it—certainly far greater than the impact of English on African languages. Speakers of English-influenced vernaculars in Africa are no more anglophone than English speakers are francophone. Such arguments seem to construct the object of language preservation in terms of maintaining an impossible and nonexistent indigenous purity rather than variety, as though the real object were to protect indigenous languages from contamination rather than to preserve patterns of language use (cf. Mufwene 2001, 2002). In such terms, those speakers who shift to vernaculars are already lost to cultural purity, and so are really no longer indigenous at all—a self-contradictory argument that, if anything, only points to the crudely reductionist nature of the categories employed. Thus, the literature on language endangerment implicitly argues that if Europeans arbitrarily and artificially create standard, written versions of indigenous languages, that does not negate their character as authentic representations of "indigenous" society and culture that should be preserved. If, on the other hand, language contact does in Africa what it has done everywhere else—leave its mark on the lexis and structure of languages—then the languages so affected are dangerous to the linguistic processes (or language ecology) that produced them, along with every other natural language.

The point of this article is certainly not to question the social status of English. On the contrary, it is to point to a hitherto largely ignored and rather unexpected effect of withholding it from speakers of African languages: It accelerates a language shift disguised by the employment of political rather than linguistic analytical tools and categories. The effects are not, however, limited to the realm of language endangerment; they are more significant and tangible for the speakers involved. Even so seemingly simple a principle as mother-tongue-medium education is complicated by this circumstance. It leads to the ironic phenomenon in many parts of Africa, so far entirely ignored by the language rights movement, that "mother tongues" as they are used in schools are less and less the home languages of the students educated through them. What is euphemistically labeled "mother-tongue education" thus becomes a vehicle for mother tongues in search of speakers. It is strange that language rights advocates have apparently ignored this violation of the basic tenets of mother-tongue education, to which African sociolinguistics has increasingly called attention (cf. Childs 1997). To be sure, to criticize it would call attention to the point Mufwene (2002) has made about the real threats to the indigenous languages they seek to protect: that they are threatened not by English but by urban vernaculars. They would then essentially have to alter the way they have theorized indigenous vs. dominant languages. They would have to give greater attention to the tendency toward language change in multilingual settings. When the complexities of such linguistic contexts are restored, the neat and tidy political narrative of language endangerment gives way.

This study adds to the growing body of evidence that language use in many parts of Africa is undergoing a process of transformation from a function of ethnic affiliation to one determined more by degree of urbanization, adding to that the caveat that we need to see the urban/rural divide as more of a continuum. As we have demonstrated, the results of this process are not accurately described in terms of a reduction of linguistic diversity, a notion that relies on a very static perception of language use and ignores language change. Even if the officially recognized "indigenous languages" of Zimbabwe were somehow to disappear (though none is actually endangered), the result would not be a reduction in the complexity of language use. On the contrary, speakers in Zimbabwe possess a remarkable range of linguistic competencies that represent a form of linguistic diversity that has hitherto received too little consideration.

* The authors would like to thank Xingren Xu for his technical support during revision of this article.

References

Abdulaziz, Mohamed H., & Osinde, Ken (1997). "Sheng and English: development among the urban youth in Kenya" *International Journal of the Sociology of Language* 125: 45-63.

Batibo, Herman (1992). "The fate of ethnic languages in Tanzania. In M. Brenzinger (ed.), *Language Death: Factual and Theoretical Explorations with Special Reference to East Africa*, (pp. 85-98). Berlin:Mouton de Gruyter.

Batibo, Herman (1998). "The fate of the Khoesan language of Botswana" In M. Brenzinger (ed.) *Endangered Languages in Africa*, (pp.267-284). Koln: Rudiger Koppe.

Batibo, Herman (2001). "The endangered languages of Africa: A case study from Botswana" In L. Maffi (ed.), *Language Knowledge and the Environment: The Interdependence of Biological and Cultural Diversity*, (pp.311-324). Washington: Smithsonian Institution Press.

Batibo, Herman (2005). *Language Decline and Death in Africa: Causes, Consequences and Challenges*. Clevedon: Multilingual Matters Press.

Bradley, David, & Bradley, Maya (eds.) (2002). *Language Endangerment and Language Maintenance*. London: Routledge.

Brutt-Griffler, Janina (2002). *World English: A Study of Its Development*. Clevedon: Multilingual Matters Press.

Canut, Cecil (2002). "Perceptions of languages in the Mandingo region of Mali: Where does one language begin and the other end?" In D. Long & Dennis Preston (eds.),

    Handbook of Perceptual Dialectology, (pp.31-41). Philadelphia: John Benjamins.

Childs, G. J. (1997). "The status of Isicamatho, an Nguni-based urban variety of Soweto" In Arthur Spears & Donald Winford (eds.). *The Structure and Status of Pidgins and Creoles*, (pp.341-370). Philadelphia: John Benjamins.

Chimhundu, Herbert (1983). "Early missionaries and the ethnolinguistic factor during the invention of tribalism in Zimbabwe" *Journal of African History* 33:255-64.

Chimhundu, Herbert (1992) "Standard Shona: myth and reality" In Nigel Crawhall (ed.), *Democratically Speaking: International Perspectives on Language planning*, (pp.77-88). Johannesburg: National Language Project.

Crystal, David (2000). *Language Death.* New York: Cambridge University Press.

Fabian, Johannes (1986). *Language and Colonial Power: The Appropriation of Swahili in the Former Belgian Congo, 1880-1938.* Cambridge: Cambridge University Press.

Githiora, Chege (2002). "Sheng: peer language, Swahili dialect or emerging creole?" *Journal of African Cultural Studies* 15:159-81.

Harries, Patrick (1989). "Exclusion, classification and internal colonialism: the emergence of ethnicity among the Tsonga" In Leroy Vail (ed.), *The Creation of Tribalism in Southern Africa,* (pp. 82-118). Berkeley and Los Angeles: University of California Press.

Jacquemet, Marco (2005). Transidiomatic practices: Language and power in the age of globalization. *Language and Communication* 25:257-77.

Makoni, Sinfree (2003). "From misinvention to disinvention of language: multilingualism and the South African Constitution" In Sinfree Makoni et al. (eds.), *Black Linguistics: Language, Society, and Politics in Africa and the Americas*, (pp.132-153). Clevedon: Multilingual Matters Press.

Makoni, Sinfree & Mashiri, Pedzisai (2007). "Critical historiography: Does language planning in Africa need to postulate the existence of languages as part of its theoretical apparatus?" In Sinfree Makoni & Alastair Pennycook (eds.), *Disinventing and Reconstituting Languages*. Clevedon: Multilingual Matters Press.

Mashiri, Pedzisai (2002). "Shona-English code-mixing in the speech of students at the University of Zimbabwe" *Southern African Linguistics and Applied Language Studies* 20:245-262.

MacGonagle, Eve (2001). "Mightier than the sword: The Portuguese pen in Ndau history" *History in Africa* 28:169-86.

McLaughlin, Fiona (2001). "Dakar Wolof and the configuration of an urban identity" *Journal of African Cultural Studies* 14:153-72.

Mamdani, Mahmood (1996). *Citizen and Subject: Contemporary Africa and the Legacy of Late Colonialism*. Princeton: Princeton University Press.

Mudimbe, Valentin Y. (1988). *The Invention of Africa: Gnosis, Philosophy, and the Order of Knowledge*. Bloomington: Indiana University Press.

Mufwene, Salikoko S. (2001). *The Ecology of Language Evolution*. Cambridge: Cambridge University Press.

Mufwene, Salikoko S. (2002). "Colonisation, globalisation and the future of languages in the twenty-first century" *International Journal on Multicultural Societies* 4:165-197.

Muzondidya, James (2002). "Towards a historical understanding of the making of the coloured community in Zimbabwe, 1890-1920" *Identity, Culture and Politics* 3:73-97.

Nettle, Daniel, & Romaine, Suzanne (2000). *Vanishing Voices: The Extinction of the World's Languages*. New York: Oxford University Press.

Njoroge, Kimani (1986). "Multilingualism and some of its

implications for language policy and practices in Kenya" In Alan Davies (ed.), *Language in Education in Africa*, (pp.327-353). Edinburgh: Centre for African Studies, University of Edinburgh.

Phillipson, Robert (1992). *Linguistic Imperialism*. New York: Oxford University Press.

Phillipson, Robert (1999). "Englishisation: One dimension of globalisation, English in a changing world" *AILA Review* 13:17-36.

Phillipson, Robert (2003). *English-Only Europe? Challenging Language Policy*. London: Routledge.

Rakodi, Carole (1995). *Harare: Inheriting a Settler-Colonial City: Change or Continuity?* New York: John Wiley.

Ranger, Terence (1989). "The invention of tradition in colonial Africa" In Eric Hobsbawm & Terence Ranger (eds.), *The Invention of Tradition*, (pp.211-262). Cambridge: Cambridge University Press.

Skutnabb-Kangas, Tove (2000). *Linguistic Genocide In Education or World Wide Diversity and Human Rights?* Mahwah, NJ: Lawrence Erlbaum.

Spitulnik, Debra (1988). "The language of the city: Town Bemba as urban hybridity" *Journal of Linguistic Anthropology* 8:30-59.

Trail, A. (1995). "The Khoesan languages of South Africa" In Rajend Mesthrie (ed.), *Language and Social History: Studies in South African Societies*, (pp.1-18). Cape Town: David Philip.

Woolard, Kathryn, & Schieffelin, Bambi (1994). "Language ideology" *Annual Review of Anthropology* 23:55-82.

III

In the beginning was the missionaries' word: The European invention of an African language: The case of Shona in Zimbabwe

The Notion of inventing African Vernaculars

The notion of invention or narration (Bhabha 1990) or imagination Anderson (1983) has occupied a central place in cultural studies, particularly among analysts working in the areas of ethnicity, national identity or traditional legal systems. Ranger (1989, 1993) is one of the scholars within this tradition, and his work on the invention of ethnicity in Zimbabwe is central within this tradition. Paradoxically, Ranger himself is spearheading an attempt to modify the notion of invention. Unfortunately, his recent attempts to modify the construct of invention only serve to strengthen his original ideas about the values of invention of cultural formations. In this paper I explore the implications of the concept of invention in the light of Ranger's original ideas particularly as articulated in his seminal work on the invention of ethnicity in Zimbabwe.

The upshot of Ranger's original ideas about invention has been that some of these cultural formations such as ethnicity and traditional legal systems are seen as a product of colonial ideology. Part of the objective of introducing a cluster of related terms — invention, narration and imagination — was to "rebut primordialism and the related, but not identical, realist assumption that ethnic groups existed unproblematically in some out there space" (Fardon 1996:115).

Language specialists, particularly those working in African languages, have been slow to take full advantage of the concepts of invention in the discourses about African vernaculars. The notion of invention foregrounds the historicity of the social conditions in which African vernaculars were created. One of the aims of my paper is to demonstrate some of the severe constraints imposed on our thinking about African vernaculars resulting from this ahistoricity. The notion of invention foregrounds the historicity of the social conditions in which African vernaculars were created and by extension draws attention to the manner in which they were (un)systematically constructed. In other words, missionaries were not sin-free in their creation of African vernaculars.

Another merit of the notion of invention is that it draws attention to the notion of agency and by extension the product of that invention, the languages created by the missionaries with the assistance of local converts. Missionaries played a crucial role in the specification of the speech forms subsequently regarded as African languages, with Africans playing the role of 'laboratory assistants'. The laboratory assistants were mainly African missionary converts. David Mandisosdza, Joseph Nyamurowa and Paul Marlyanga were some of the prominent missionary converts who were working with American Methodist missionaries. They provided the vocabulary and the missionaries the orthography and grammar (Ranger 1989).

The collaborative process resulted in a specification of African dialects/vernaculars. The term 'specification', although elegant and ostensibly neutral and objective, does not adequately capture the vast range of sociolinguistic processes which were set in motion; it arguably masks the reality. It is a sugar-coated pill. Perhaps Mühlhäusler (1990) 'reducing' languages to writing is a more frank description. Although Mühlhäusler uses the term when describing the situation in the Pacific area, the process of reducing languages with the accompanying consequences is applicable to the southern African region. Fabian (1983), in an extended study of colonial language classification, shows how missionaries in their urgent need to communicate, made a set of crucial decisions about which dialect to privilege, what orthography to use.

In Zimbabwe the decisions to reduce speech forms to writing did not result in a production of distinct languages but of distinct dialects. It is, however, to the credit of the missionaries in Zimbabwe that, as Chimhundu (1992) points out, the missionaries realised that the speech forms which they were dealing with were one language, a realisation which was not necessarily always shared by all the missionaries working in different parts of Africa. For example, today the Zulu and Xhosa are divided by a common language in part because of the competing interest and rivalry of missionaries. Although the missionaries working in Zimbabwe realised that they were dealing with one language their work magnified differences between the dialects: each missionary station became associated with a distinct dialect.

> Missionary linguist created discrete dialect zones by developing written languages centred upon a number of widely scattered bases. The American Methodists at Old Umtali (Mutare), the Anglicans at St. Augustine's and the Mariannhill fathers at Trashill together produced Manyika; the Jesuits at Chishawasha, near Salisbury (Harare), produced Zezeru; the Dutch Refomed Church at Morgenster produced Karanga. Differences were exaggerated, obscuring the actual gradualism and homogeneity of the real situation. And once these forms had been codified, they were then expanded out from these missionary centres by means of the mission out-school

networks until specific dialects zones had been created. (Ranger 1989:127)

The different missionaries were working in 'peak dialects' (Chimhundu 1992:83) — those areas exhibiting the greatest differences between each other.

Philosophically, the missionaries were motivated by positivism in their bid to classify speech forms into mutually exclusive categories. The 'boundaries' metaphor (Fardon and Furniss 1994) was driven by a Western-dominated perception of language. The boundaries metaphor about language was the underlying philosophical view in the specification of speech forms into separate dialects. The boundaries metaphor contrasts with the 'frontiers' metaphor in which lines between dialects or languages are permeable (ibid). Makoni (1996) describes the process of classifying speech forms into separate dialects/languages as 'boxing'.

Boxing led to a magnification of differences between dialect. The creation of these boxes set in motion a process of cultural feedback and consequent focusing, resulting in exaggerated differences between the dialects. Subsequent users of these dialect creations were slow to realise the full impact of these creations on the formation of regionally-based identities. Ranger (1989), for example, describes the animosity which teachers from the Mutare and Makoni districts encountered when teaching outside the Manyika district; an animosity linguistically legitimated in part by the differences between the texts from other missionary stations. Differences between the dialects were exaggerated and perhaps sociolinguisticaly legitimated through linguistic scholarship which became dialect based (dialect nationalism): Dembetembe worked on Korekore, Mkanganwi on Ndau, Pongweni on Karanga. This type of research is an excellent example of dialect-bound nationalism. Anderson (1983) in *Imagined Communities* argues persuasively that print-capitalism created unified languages where there had been oral multiplicity.

Ranger is however right to draw attention to the fact that in the case of Zimbabwe the opposite is the case.

Print-capitalism created distinct and competitive communities. The earliest drive towards harmonisation in Zimbabwe was sponsored by the white settler state and capitalists enterprises in their attempts to create standard Shona. The motivation was to facilitate the political and economic exploitation of Africans, not to serve their interests; a point which I return to later in the paper as I outline the various senses of the word harmonisation in the history of Shona.

It is through popular culture and music that what I call a liberating Shona is beginning to emerge, particularly in the urban settings such as Harare; a form of language use which Chimhundu describes as the "general-spoken variety of the capital" (1992:87). The emergence of a liberating urban vernacular is, however, not peculiar to Zimbabwe.

There is increasingly compelling evidence about the emergence of creolised African speech forms in urban settings all over the African continent (Laitin 1992; Street 1993). The process might have reached its acme in some urban settings in South African cities through the emergence of Iscamatho (Ntshangase 1995) which although initially associated with gangsters and youth culture has been degangesterised as it begins to be associated with a type of urban identity and panethnicity (Makoni 1996).

In vogue but vague and vain: additive bilingualism
I have serious doubts whether the terms additive and subtractive can accurately capture the complexities of the African multilingual simation (Makoni 1993). While in an immigrant situation, acquisition of a second language may result in a loss of the mother tongue (Fillmore 1991). The situation is different in African contexts where English and African languages are used in different domains.

This should not be construed to mean that African multilingual situations are best described as additive. In Africa second languages are not learnt out of choice but for instrumental purposes. In the Cummins research, learning of the second language was out of choice. The learning of French by English mother-tongue speakers in Canada was a voluntary one by a dominant English community. Africans do not learn English out of choice and neither are they the dominant group when dominance is defined in terms of political power and economic influence, although they are demographically in a majority.

Notions of additive bilingualism when applied to Africans learning English reinforce the position of English as a dominant language. The subtext of the additive model in Africa is that when African speakers have reached a 'threshold level' they can acquire English. In this case additive bilingualism is an argument for delaying the introduction of English. What is interesting, however, is that additive bilingualism is interpreted in a single direction. Proficiency in an African language has to be consolidated for the acquisition of a second language to take place. African languages are therefore being subordinated to the interests of English, implicitly reinforcing the status of English. It is the subtext of notions of additive bilingualism which has led Itumelang Mosala (1997) to suggest that unless such concepts are handled carefully they will simply reinforce the dominant position of English.

Paradoxically, additive bilingualism may stand a chance of succeeding as a theoretical explanation if English, the dominant language, is used as a basis for the acquisition of African languages. This is because most English speakers approach the task of learning an African language when they have the reached the so-called 'threshold level', unlike African speakers whose proficiency in the pan-ethnic varieties is not recognised, and who are still in the process of developing expertise in standardised versions of their mother tongues (what I refer to as their steptongue).

The process of boxing

Another advantage of the construct of invention is that it draws attention to the how. It is the how that I now turn to by looking at grammar books and dictionaries. The process of reducing African speech forms to writing had vast sociolinguistic implications. The popular perception is that the codification resulted in a creation of a sense of reverence for the written word. My aim here is to foreground some of the less well-known sociolinguistic processes.

Following Jeater (1994), I identify a number of features which are an intricate part of the process of vernacularisation. The grammar books did not aid any meaningful communication between English and Shona speakers. The phrases for translation and the vocabulary used reflected settler and missionary ideology. The phrases were useful for talking about Africans and not for engaging with them in any egalitarian communication. Christian missionaries were keen to understand African cosmology in their own terms. Consequently, terms describing African cosmological views which were inconsistent or clashed with their perception were marginalised and a negative value attached to them. Colonial Shona (still I must hasten to add used in contemporary Zimbabwe) "distanced the converted elite from the world views of the vernacular population". Not only were the missionary educated alienated from the perspectives of the vernacular population, but "the vernacular distorted and silenced, vernacular participation in the concepts used to describe human physiology were so different from local views that this frustrated moves to get local people involved in developmental projects" (Jeater 1994).

Robinson (1991) accurately stresses at a micro level little or no attention has been paid to the effects of language choice on rural development, to such an extent that Phillipson (1992) talks about the "invisibilisation of language in developmental projects". The argument should be more sophisticated than that; it should be borne in mind that simply opting for African vernaculars does not automatically challenge the settleristic thinking encoded in these languages. In actual fact the exact opposite can happen: settler and missionary ideology can be remorselessly perpetuated under the guise of vemacularisation.

Urban or mission educated Zimbabweans generally find it difficult to understand rural Shona and find it extremely difficult to understand some of its concepts. The vernacular Shona does not successfully communicate ideas from either the African or European perspectives. Popular arguments about the inevitable desirability of using African vernaculars in education and developmental projects fail to recognise the extent to which African vernaculars are heavily colonised, hence my suggestion that contemporary Shona is best described as colonised Shona. The battle for independence is simply not won by opting for African vernaculars over English as normally articulated in the decolonisation literature (Ngugi 1997). What is required is a sophisticated realisation of the imprint of colonial thinking on African vernaculars by taking full cognisance of some of the contemporary manifestations of current uses of colonial Shona. From UNESCO to the multicultural lobby the potential negative effects of learning through vernaculars is not addressed as it is assumed that it is cognitively and emotionally advantageous that a child learns through such a medium, overlooking as it does the colonised images encoded in such versions of African vernaculars.

Such media do not constitute the mother tongues of African speakers but what can be called steptongues. The term steptongue was first used by Gupta (1994) in her description of English language usage in Singapore but is readily applicable to the African continent because of the disconcerting differences between the codes used as medium of instruction in the classroom and those used by the students outside the class.

Harmonisation

The notion of harmonisation in southern African studies is associated with the arguments of Nhlapo and more recently reinvigorated by Alexander. Nhlapo first raised the argument in the 1940s and 1950s when he argued that the Bantu languages should be unified at least in the written form into two major languages. One group would consist of the Nguni languages — Ndebele, Zulu, Xhosa, Swati — and the other would be made up of the Sotho group — Tswana, Northern Sotho and Southern Sotho. The aim of this section of the paper is not to respond to issues about harmonisation by citing examples from Zimbabwe, but to demonstrate how difficult it is to systematically and coherently respond to debates about harmonisation because of the various senses in which the concept is used, and to draw attention to the way the concept has been handled in the case of Shona in Zimbabwe, a country in which debates about harmonisation are not contentious. One of the earliest attempts at harmonisation of Shona was an attempt by the Southern Rhodesian government to create standard Shona, motivated by the government's desire to use African vernaculars to serve its secular purposes. The religion-designed and competing dialects did not serve its purposes well. The attempts to harmonise the various dialects were also supported by capitalist enterprises interested in reaching as wide a market as possible. The issue which becomes quite clear historically at this time is that the promotion of African vernaculars was designed to serve the interests of colonial governments and capitalism. The argument that to use vernaculars will be in the interests of local Africans is a recent manifestation of vernacular argument. It is important to notice how the promotion of African languages was implicitly calculated to undermine the interests of speakers of those languages.

The second sense in which harmonisation has been used in the history of Shona relates to the different forms of spelling. Because of the regional activities of the missionaries there was a great diversity in spelling. The use of different orthographic standards by competing missionaries is a common practice. In some cases the orthographic standards would be so radically different as to make it difficult for people using the 'same' language to use similar texts (Mühlhäuser 1990).

Conclusion

It is generally well known that the spread of 'European languages' was one of the consequences of European imperialism. What is less well known, however, is the effect of the work of missionaries in the construction of African languages. The written African languages which they created were 'new' in many respects both in their potential and limitations and until recently those who were promoting African vernaculars, particularly Shona, were doing so for their own purposes. It is these selfish interests which have in part led to the word 'vernacular' assuming a negative connotation.

References

Anderson, Benedict (1983). *Imagined Communities: Reflections on the Origin and Spread of Nationalism.* London: Verso.

Bhabha, Homi K. (1990). *Nation and Narration.* New York: Routledge.

Chimhundu, Herbert (1992). "Early missionaries and the ethnolinguistic factor during the invention of tribalism in Zimbabwe" *Journal of African History* 33 pp.87-109.

Fabian, Johannes (1983). "Missions and the colonization of African languages: developments in the former Belgian Congo" *Canadian Journal of African Studies / Revue Canadienne des Études Africaines* Vol. 17, No. 2, pp. 165-187.

Fardon, Richard (1996). "Crossed destinies: the entangled histories of West African ethnic and national identities" in L. De la Gorgendiere, K. King and S. Vaughan et al. (eds), *Ethnicity in Africa: roots, meanings and implications.* Edinburgh: University of Edinburgh Centre of African Studies.

Fardon, Richard and Graham Furniss (1994). *African Languages, Development, and the State.* New York: Routledge.

Fillmore, Lily Wong (1991). "When learning a second language means losing the first" *Early Childhood Research Quarterly*, 6, pp.323-346.

Gupta,Anthea Fraser (1994). *The Step-tongue: Children's English in Singapore.* Clevedon (UK) & Philadelphia (PA): Multilingual Matters. (Multilingual matters, 101)

Jeater, D. (1994). "'The way you tell them': ideology and development policy in Southern Africa." Paper delivered at the Twentieth Anniversary Conference, Paradigms Lost, Paradigms Regained. University of York.

Laitin, D. (1992). *Language repertoires and state construction in Africa.* Cambridge: Cambridge University Press. (Cambridge Studies in Comparative Politics)

Makoni, Sinfree (1993). "Mother-tongue education: a literature review and proposed research design" *South African Journal of African Languages* 13(3) pp.89-94.

Makoni, Sinfree (1996). "Language and identity in Southern Africa. In L. De la Gorgendiere, K. King and S. Vaughan et al. (eds), *Ethnicity in Africa: roots, meanings and impli-cations.* Edinburgh: University of Edinburgh Centre of African Studies, pp.261-275.

Mosala, Itumelang (1997). "Auditing academic practices in South African tertiary institutions". Transcript from an interview conducted by the South African Academic Development Audit Project, Johannesburg.

Mühlhäusler,Peter (1990). "Reducing Pacific language to writing" In *Ideologies of language.* ed. by John E. Joseph and Talbot J. Taylor, pp.189–205. London: Routledge.

Ngugi wa Thiongo (1997). "Moving the centre." Paper presented at the conference, English Teachers Connect. University of the Witwatersrand, July 1997.

Ntshangase, Dumisani Krushchev (1995). "Indaba yami i-straight: language and language practices in Soweto. In Mesthrie, R. (ed.), *Language and Social History: Studies in South African Sociolinguistics*. Cape Town & Johannesburg: David Philip Publishers. pp. 291-297.

Phillipson, D. (1992). *Linguistic imperialism*. Oxford: Oxford University Press.

Ranger, Terence O. (1989). "Missionaries, migrants and the Manyika: the invention of ethnicity in Zimbabwe." In L. Vail (ed.), *The creation of tribalism in Southern Africa*. London; Berkeley and Los Angeles: James Currey. pp.118-151.

Ranger, Terence O. (1993). "The invention of tradition revisited." In Terence Ranger and Olufemi Vaughan (eds.), *Legitimacy and the state in Twentieth Century Africa*. Oxford: St Anthony; London: Macmillan.

Robinson, Clinton D. W. (1991). "Language use and language attitudes: Communicating rural development in Africa." In Paul Meara and Ann Ryan (eds.), *Language and nation: Papers from the annual meeting of the British Association for Applied Linguistics held at University College, Swansea, September 1990*, pp.73-90. [London]: British Association for Applied Linguistics.

Street, B.V. (1993). "Culture is a verb: anthropological aspects of language and cultural processes." In D.Graddol, L.Thompson and M. Byram (eds.), *Language and culture*. Clevedon, Philadelphia: Multilingual Matters, pp.23-44.

IV

The pragmatic import of pronominal usage in chiShona discourse
(with Pedzisai Mashiri)

Abstract
This article discusses the pragmatic significance of chiShona pronouns by examining the use of different pronouns: personal, enumerative, and demonstrative, and by demonstrating their address and referential value and social meanings. Two important issues are addressed. First, we demonstrate that a purely grammatical analysis of pronouns, which emphasises the internal analysis and the anaphoric function of pronouns, fails to capture the complexity of pronominal usage in ordinary conversations. Second, the discourses that we analyse in this article demonstrate how in particular communicational contexts, specific speakers use pronouns to index referents other than the ones conventionally associated with a particular pronominal form in an analysis based on grammatical analysis. For example, besides its generic self-reference, the first person pronoun may be used to refer to a second or third person. The second person pronoun, apart from having a second person reference, can be used as a second first or third person reference. The third person may, apart from its conventional reference, be used to mean

either the first or second person. The pronoun switches also involve indirectness, reflecting a wide range of social meanings which have politeness implications.

Introduction
In this article, we demonstrate the pragmatic significance of chiShona pronouns or pronominal categories by examining how they alternate and vary in terms of address, and the social meanings which these variations and alternations realise.

The term pronoun and derived terms such as pronominalisation have long been part of the metalanguage of traditional grammarians. "The term has been used in the grammatical classifications of words to refer to a closed set of [nominal] lexical items that can substitute for a noun or noun phrase" (Mühlhäusler & Harré, 1990: 9). The notion of 'closed set' implies that in human languages only a small, definite repertoire of pronoun forms is found in each case. However, "such sets differ enormously in complexity and range of discrimination"; there are languages "with a mere handful of pronouns and others with as many as 200" (ibid.). Most writers on pronouns further distinguish subclasses of pronouns such as personal, possessive, demonstrative, indefinite, and so on and also describe pronominal systems in terms of person, number and gender. Table 1, below, shows the classification of chiShona personal pronouns according to person and number:

Table 1: Classification of Shona personal pronouns in terms of person and number, with possessive stems, demonstratives and agreement morphemes

Person	Singular					Plural				
	Pronoun	Poss. Stem	Dem	AM-Pre/Fut	AM-Past	Pronoun	Poss stem	Dem	AM-Pre/Fut	AM-Past
1st person	Ini	-ngu	-	Ndi-	Nda-	Isu	-du	-	Ti-	Ta-
2nd person	Iwe	-ko	-	U-	Wa-	Imi	-nyu	-	Mu-	Ma-
3rd person	Iye	-ke	Uyu/uyo	A-	A-	Ivo	-vo	Ava/avo	Va-	Va-

Several linguists emphasise the syntactic function and status of the pronoun in a noun phrase or in a sentence. Leech and Svartvik (1975: 275) define pronouns as 'words that can function as a whole noun phrase (e.g. in being subject or object of a clause) or as the head of a noun phrase. Many of them act as substitutes or 'replacements' for noun phrases in the context'. The process of substitution referred to in Leech and Svartvik's definition is pronominalisation. Many linguists perceive pronominalisation as a mechanical process used in producing mere surface variants of underlying structures. Hence, in the original Chomskian version of transformational grammar pronouns were not located in deep structure, but introduced transformationally.

Semantically, traditional grammarians assert that pronouns provide information about "who is speaking and who is listening" (Grimes, 1975: 71), and about whom or what they are speaking. Leech and Svartvik (1975: 57) define the pronoun we as "stand[ing] for a group of people including the speaker". This definition implies that we has the same reference in every context. This is a kind of one morpheme equals one meaning principle which we seek to question.

In this article, we will illustrate how chiShona pronouns, like pronouns in other languages, perform diverse roles and functions depending on the communicational contexts in which they are used. Taking another perspective, Reichenbach (1966) remarks that pronouns are pointers of variables that perform two basic functions: anaphoric and deictic. Duranti (1984) notes that in addition to looking at their referential functions, linguists should also look at the work pronouns do in defining the role of a given character in a story, as well as the judgements being made about the character in the story. Specifically he argues that Italian subject pronouns are devices through which speakers define main characters in a narrative and/or convey empathy or positive affect towards certain referents. Speakers/Authors, on the other hand, use demonstratives to define inanimate objects, minor characters, and people with whom they show no empathy.

We will also show how chiShona interactants sometimes use pronouns to index referents that differ from the person conventionally associated with a particular form. Kahananui and Anthony (1970), Wills (1977) and Head (1978) discuss the use of one pronoun to index another (for example, using the first person to mean the second person) when referring to or addressing someone. Kahananui and Anthony, for example, argue that the use of the first person dual inclusive in Hawaiian is considered a polite form of address for greeting an individual. For his part, Head (1978: 172) notes that the use of the first person plural to refer exclusively to the referent to show similarity of interests with the referent occurs in many languages, notably English, German, Swedish, Danish and French.

We will also show that in chiShona, as Obeng (1997) has shown with regard to Akan (largely spoken in west Africa), pronouns in conversation often violate certain grammatical [syntactic] rules and involve changing and shifting their prototypical meaning as described in conventional grammars. This change or shift in reference is in part attributable to sociolinguistic and pragmatic factors, which formal grammars tend to exclude.

The data which forms the basis of the analysis in this article show that the simplicity of grammatical pronominal paradigms can not successfully capture the complexity of pronoun use resulting in a loss of awareness of the pragmatic significance of pronouns in ordinary conversations. Further comments on the limits of a grammatical approach will follow the analysis of the data on specific instances of pronoun use.

Recent pragmatic consideration of the way in which European, especially English pronouns are actually used in context "indicates that pronouns are far from categorical, and indeed, their interpretation is mediated by a range of social and personal factors producing a range of possible uses and interpretations" (Wilson, 1990: 45). Much of the contemporary work was stimulated by Brown and Gilman's (1960) work on French, German and Italian, which Hodge and Kress (1988: 40) describe as an exemplary analysis with implications for "many other semiotic codes". We would argue, however, that the context of pronominal usage that both grammatical pronominal paradigms and the

Brown and Gilman based studies involve undervalues conversations. For that reason they are not relevant to this study.

chiShona conversationalists use several devices to define characters or participants in an ongoing conversation. Among these discourse tools are the use of pronouns. As the data used in this study demonstrates, conversations are "populated with a cast of actors, present and absent, whose explicit characterisations and implicit known identities give shape and meaning to the talk" (Malone, 1997: 43). In a study of conversations among members of a food cooperative, Labov (1980 cited in Malone, 1997: 43) argues that collections or categories of people are often indexed in implicit ways by references to group membership, past activities or characterisations, times or places, or plurals hidden in singulars.

Given the potential complexity of interactional reference alluded to above, how do conversationalists know or think they know to whom reference is being made? Speakers and hearers seem in most cases to know who is being spoken to or about and are able to get on with their conversations without frequent need for clarification. Proponents of the conversational analysis approach (CA) would argue that "this knowledge is neither the result of some external institutional order which provides rules to follow" (Wilson, 1991: 27 in Malone, 1997: 43), nor does it result from a cognitive model possessed by each talker. It is the interaction order with its concomitant demands of self-presentation and sense-making that provides a framework within which such practical knowledge is possible.

Contrary to CA analysts, our data will show that "the institutional external order", the culture of the society in which the interactants are members, sometimes constrains the speaker's choice and use of pronouns in a conversation. Mashiri, Mawomo and Tom (2002) show of chiShona as does Obeng (1997) of Akan that some interactive rules or conditions (e.g. in African societies) may require the use of indirect or ambiguous reference. The participants' shared or assumed knowledge:

'unspoken and unstressed' (Ellis, 1992) also determine pronominal use. Obeng sums it up well in his statement that '[u]se of indirectness, as well as the mechanism for understanding indirect speech acts, depends in part on mutually shared background information and on the cultural background of the discourse participants'.

The collection of data for the study

The qualitative data that form the basis of this study came from two sources: (a) transcripts of 15- to 20-minute natural conversations, and (b) transcripts of semi-structured personal interviews. We recorded thirty conversations in all, twenty six of these in Harare in 2001 and the remaining four in the town of Norton (40km west of Harare), in 2002. Although this study is based on urban chiShona, the observations made have general relevance to the chiShona both sociolinguistically and pedagogically. We were attempting to demonstrate the differences between the chiShona as described in chiShona grammar books and the emerging variety as used in urban Zimbabwe (Makoni and Meinhof 2003, Makoni and Mashiri 2007). All the interactants were unaware at first that they were going to be recorded. However, when we later informed them of the proposed recordings, they consented to being recorded on condition that their identities were disguised, and the data were used for academic purposes only. We conducted 10-minute interviews with eight chiShona speakers between the ages of eighteen and sixty-five. Five of the interviewees were selected from the interactants engaged in conversations recorded earlier and the other three were colleagues. Both men and women were involved.

The data from the interviews complemented the conversations. Hence, the questions were derived from the patterns of pronominal usages observed in the conversations. They were centred on the reason(s) behind the pronominal choices and switches, what messages were spoken to the addressees or implied in the references and what situations the speakers considered as 'unspeakable'.

In our discourse analysis we paid particular attention to the range and types of pronouns used, the role relationships between the speaker and the addressee or referent (where the speaker is not the referent) and the situations in which the discourses occurred. We also observed the situation in which the conversations occurred and the role relationships between the interlocutors since these were directly relevant to what was said. We considered the background information such as the identity of the interactional participants, the situational context of the discourse and the purpose of the interaction. We also paid attention to the content and form of the message, its purpose, manner, tone and effect and the interpretation the other participants give on the basis of shared knowledge and other previous encounters. Lastly, our intuition and inside knowledge of chiShona language and culture enhanced our insights into the communicational events. In the discussion that follows, we use the first names of the participants only to disguise their identity.

Before examining the non-conventional uses of chiShona pronouns in ordinary conversations and the social meaning deriving from these uses, we will briefly describe how pronouns are said to function grammatically in chiShona.

Standard functions for Shona pronouns

The following examples show how pronouns serve their expected functions according to a grammatical model. Consider Example 1 and Example 2:

>1. Martin: Ini ndinoda mukadzi anosevenza.
>   (I prefer a woman who is formally employed.)
>
>   Tariro: Unoda iye here kana kuti unoda mari yake?
>   (Do you love a woman as an individual or you love her for her money?)

2. Vanhu vomuno muZimbabwe vane tsika chaizvo. Hatina basa neMother's day nokuti tinoda vanamai vedu nguva dzose. Tine zviyerwa zvinotirambidza kuvarova kana kuvatuka.
(We Zimbabweans are very courteous people. We do not value Mother's day since we show love to our mothers all the time. In our culture there are taboos that discourage beating or berating one's mother.)

In 1, Martin, aged 21, and Tariro, aged 20, students at the Catholic University in Zimbabwe are engaged in a social discussion during a literature class. In Martin's utterance, the pronoun *Ini* (I) refers to the first person singular, the speaker and it functions as the subject of the sentence. The *u-* (you) in the string '*Unoda iye here kana kuti unoda mari yake?*' (Do you love the woman as an individual or you love her for her money?) also functions as the subject of the sentence, but *iye* (she), the third person singular pronoun functions as the object of the sentence and determines the possessive stem of the modifier of the noun *mari* (money) in the object noun phrase *mari yake* (her money). In other words, the pronouns in the utterances in 1 perform their expected functions grammatically.

Example 2 is part of an interview on general cultural issues that the researcher had with Jonathan, aged 45, a high school teacher. In this example, the third person subject concord /pronoun *va-* (they) refers (back) to the noun phrase *Vanhu vomuno muZimbabwe* (Zimbabweans) which, functions as the subject of the sentence. The subject concord/pronoun *ti-* (we) in '*Hatina basa...*' (We do not value...) also performs its normal or conventional function – inclusive first person plural pronoun. Although there is an intersentential pronominal switch from third to first person in Example 2, this appears to be a typical switch that does not interfere with the ordinary/referential meanings of the respective pronouns.

In the remaining part of this article, we will focus on data that reflects how interactants' use pronouns to index referents that differ from the person typically associated with a particular form and reflect contextually determined meanings which cannot be successfully captured in a grammatical model of pronouns.

Data analysis
First person reference
In this section we will examine how the first person singular and plural chiShona pronouns derive their multiple meanings from the contexts in which they are used. Malone (1997: 58) stresses the interdependence of meaning and situation: "the indexicality of talk, its unalterable connectedness to a particular situation, is played out in pronoun choices which create alignments between talkers and their topics and their hearers". This implies that the relationship between the speaker and the hearer(s), the topic and the situation of talk, among other things, are significant in enhancing our understanding of a pronoun's social or pragmatic meanings.

First person singular
In traditional grammar, the first person singular pronoun *I* refers only to the person who uses it, that is the speaker. The data analysed in this study reflects the complexities of pronoun use in conversations. Consider:

3. Ndiri kuda ma*assignments* **angu** nhasi nokuti ndinoda kuamaka pa*week-end*.
   (Please hand in my [= 'your'] assignments today so that I can mark them over the week-end.)

4. Hapana zva**ndi**chagona kuita **nde**ga ipapa. **Ndi**kawana a**ndi**simudzawo aka**ndi**isa pamushana ndizvozvo. Upenyu hwakaona mukwasha!

(I am [= 'She'] now bed-ridden. I now rely on the good will of others for taking me out to enjoy the sun and back into the house.)

5. 1. Zvinhu zvakaoma mazuva ano. Zvako zvokuswera uchiti, '**Ha**n**di**dyi
2. manhuchu **ini**', he-e, 'handidye chingwa chisina bhata', wotozvirega.
3. Ini handichazvikwanisa zvokuti chingwa mangwana mangwana. Kamwe
4. chete pasvondo kana tazvigonawo tazvigona.
(The cost of living is now very high. Your petty excuses that 'I [= 'you'] don't like *manhuchu* and I also dislike bread without butter' have got to stop. I can't afford to buy bread every day anymore. Once a week is the best I can do.)

The use of the first person singular pronoun, its subject concord or possessive form in examples 3, 4 and 5 above is not self-referential. We recorded Example 3 in a High school classroom. This utterance is used by a teacher to direct students to submit their assignments on that particular day. Some students probably attempt to give excuses for not being able to meet the deadline; hence, the teacher uses the first person possessive pronoun *ngu-* (mine), to index the second person plural pronoun *nyu-* (yours), to stress his authority, rights and duties to direct the students' actions and the students' lack of power to challenge the command.

This is so since in African [chiShona] culture, the teacher-student relationship is an asymmetrical one; the teacher is older and more knowledgeable than the students. The teacher is expected to be in control, "to preserve an appropriate distance from students, and to instruct and inform the students" (Holmes, 1983: 97). In fact, the surface structure of the utterance that the teacher uses conforms to the form akin to a type of English directives Ervin-Tripp (1976: 29) calls "personal need or desire statements" directed down-wards to subordinates primarily. Such directives start with the phrase, "I need....". Changing from the prototypical use of second person plural to first person singular is a way of "asserting, maintaining, and perhaps increasing power" (Pearson, 1988: 79).

Example 4 is an extract from an interview that the researchers had with Angela, aged 36, who is nursing her younger sister living with AIDS. Since Angela narrates her sister's ordeal to the researcher with the sister as a co-present referent, she employs what Mashiri, Mawomo and Tom (2002: 228) refer to as 'pronoun substitution or pronoun mismatches' to save face[1] in a face threatening situation. The speaker uses the first person singular subject concord /ndi-/ (I) to refer to the third person (her sister, in this case), while ostensibly referring to herself.

The utterance in Example 5 is one of several instances of such utterances observed in conversations involving varied and mixed interlocutors where the speaker uses the first person pronoun or its subject concord /ndi-/ (lines 1 and 2) to refer to the hearer. Urban (1989 cited in Malone, 1997: 63), calls a pronoun used in direct [and indirect] quotation, as in Example 5, quotative *I*. The quotative I here takes the form of what Goffman (1974: 534) calls 'say-fors' or mimicry. In this case the speaker

---

[1] Pronominal substitution is one of several and varied 'off-record' linguistic politeness strategies (Pan, 1995: 465) that are used in different cultures to save face. Brown and Lewinson (1978) and Goffman (1987) employ the notion of face to refer to "the public self-image that people want to claim for themselves" (Chen, 1991: 113) in interaction. Face is something that must be constantly attended to in social interaction, since it can be lost, maintained, or enhanced. Details of what face involves are not given in this study. However, being 'off-record' in the case of the utterance in Example 2 implies that the speaker used pronouns stylistically to avoid embarrassing or hurting the referent. The ambiguity or implicitness created by this strategy provides a high disclaimer of performance. When words attract a high disclaimer of performance it means that a speaker can use them with immunity or impunity in potentially threatening situations such as the one involving someone living with HIV AIDS.

is 'saying-for' or acting out as the hearer or addressee in a mannered voice.

The use of the auxiliary verb /ti-/ (say), in line 1, before the quotation syntactically marks the boundary between reference to the speaker and reference to the hearer between what the speaker says and what the hearer said. It introduces an embedded quote in which the speaker is mimicking another person. The prosodic markers such as '*he-he*' (what-not), (line 2) clearly reveals that he is putting on another persona. The use of this prosodic marker reflects a change from a normal to a marked voice quality to suggest that a different person is doing the speaking. In the present example, as in many others in our data, syntactic and prosodic devices are used simultaneously. The pragmatic import of the use of the quotative *I*, in Example 5 is sarcasm and caricature. In this case the speaker derides the hearer's behaviour with the objective to influence and shape social behaviour. While the first person pronoun used in Example 5 refers to the second person, there are instances in the data which may refer to the third person singular. Extracts in which the quotative *we* is used are illustrated in the next section.

The use of the first person singular, then, in interaction makes it referentially more complex than the self-referentiality as described in a strictly grammatical description of chiShona. It becomes a resource that speakers can use to do a variety of interactional work, including dramatising the personae of others by imitating their voices to articulate social meanings while saving the 'face' of the person being spoken about.

First person plural
As in the previous section, our concern in this section is the speakers' manipulation of pronouns, in this case the first person plural, within various social contexts. We are interested in the speakers' selectional choices in referring to themselves and others and the distributional range of the first person plural pronoun. Our assumption is that the individual choices and the

distributional range of pronouns may indicate how they treat the meaning of the first person plural pronoun in each context of use. In other words "the proportional use of certain pronouns may itself affect the interpretation (meaning) of certain pronouns for certain speakers" (Wilson, 1990: 56).

Table 1 shows that the chiShona first-person plural pronoun is *Isu* (we). This, like all the other pronouns in Shona, and like in other languages, occurs in a sentence or in discourse as noun phrase (NP). Hartmann and Stork (1972: 155) defines an NP as "a word or a group of words with a noun or pronoun as its head and functioning as the subject, object or complement of a sentence". When a pronoun appears in a sentence, overtly or covertly, as subject, it is followed or substituted by a pronominal subject concord that varies according to the tense of the verb (see Table 1, above) and by an object concord, when it functions as an object.

The data analysed here shows that the chiShona first person plural pronoun has a wide range of non-conventional referencing possibilities within everyday talk. Before we demonstrate the choices made and the social meanings implied in the varied uses of the first person plural pronoun we should explain the exclusive/inclusive distinction. Consider the following examples:

6 (a) Nga**ti**nyararei tiri muimba yaMwari.
(Please, let's be silent, we are in church.)

(b) Jerry: Ari kuti chiiko muface uyu?
(What is this fellow talking about?)
Rungano: Ndinofunga kuti **ti**ri kungobatwa kumeso chete ini. Iwe uri better sha, **isu** vamwe zvakatodzvanya.
(I think we are simply being fooled. You seem to be managing better than some of us friend, who are in precarious situations.)

Example 6(a) involves a church minister at a congregation in Highfields (a suburb in Harare) who directs members of his congregation to be silent during a worship session. In this context the directive meant that only the congregation but not the minister himself, should be silent. Hence, the *ti-* here excludes the speaker although compliance with the directive would be to his benefit. Describing the use of the English exclusive *we*, Mühlhäusler and Harré (1990: 173) say, "the principle function of the directive *we* is to get others to perform an action that is in the speaker's (and his group) own interest". Goffman (1981) has argued that the use of forms like the exclusive *we* serves to distance the speaker ('animator') from what it is that is being said.

However, discussing instances of pronominal use comparable to Example 6(a), Mashiri (2003: 122) stresses that the use of the exclusive *ti-* gives the addressee(s) an impression of the speaker's inclusion in the action ensuing from the directive. This means that the directive is perceived as a face-threatening action (FTA) that requires the use of some mitigating device. In fact, in Example 6(a) the mitigation is emphasised by adding the accounting statement, '*tiri muimba yaMwari*', hence, shifting the real author (speaker) of the directive to God. Mitigation is also evident in the speaker's preference to using the hortative formative *nga-* (let) followed by *ti-* to the direct imperative form, *Nyararai* (Be quiet please.). The context forces the minister to employ the exclusive pronoun with mitigating devices in order to manage the addressees' emotions. The speaker's identity as a religious leader, the church setting that demands piety and egalitarianism, and the cultural rules of respect influence the minister's pronominal usage.

Now let us take Example 6(b) where Jerry and Rungano are discussing a local politician's speech broadcast on television. In this case it is clear that *ti-* (in boldface) refers to both the speaker and the addressee, thus it is inclusive. The *ti-* in this case refers to Jerry and Rungano's shared situation at the moment of making the utterance. When Rungano uses *ti-*, he assumes that he is speaking for Jerry as well. However, Rungano's use of *isu (vamwe)* in the second line shows a referential shift in the same utterance. At this stage Rungano no longer speaks for Jerry, but includes some unspecified others. Thus, the *isu* creates and calls attention to a new identity boundary. Commenting on the use of the American English *we*, Malone (1997: 65) says, "*We* has shifting sets of referents of greater or lesser inclusiveness, and is a prime example of one of the ways speakers can shift their 'footings', creating new alignments with others, in the course of very brief stretches of talk".

Although the pronoun *isu* in 6(b) could refer to Rungano and the unspecified other, we observed in other contexts that the first person plural pronoun, when used this way could also be self-referential. In this case, the first person plural stands for the first person singular pronoun as in the Example 7 below:

> 7. Mandisa: Mune chokutaura here panyaya iyi mukoma?
> (Would you have anything to say on this issue brother?)
> Mutape: **s**u vamwe ha**ti**po panyaya dzenyu. Itai zvamafunga.
> (Do not drag us (= 'me') in your mess. Do as you please.)
> Mandisa: Hazvinzarwo mukoma! Chivi hachidzoreranwi.
> (Calm down brother! Two wrongs cannot make a right.)
> Mutape: **Ti**siye zve**du**!
> (We (= 'I') have no interest meddling in your affairs.)

The form of first-person plural that Mutape uses approximates what Head (1978: 165) calls the 'plural of modesty'. The effect here of using *isu/ti-* (we) is one of disassociation with a certain idea, position or affiliation and to index a negative emotional disposition. There are however other examples in the data which reflect how the speakers may reveal how they are aligned with particular ideas through their use of pronouns.

We also observed that some speakers employ the first-person plural pronoun to refer to themselves when they relate general experiences that in fact apply to them personally. We observed such usages in social conversations involving mixed groups of workmates in terms of age, sex and rank, often held during lunch breaks in the industrial sites. Example 8 is the contribution of Beauty, aged 29, to one such discussion:

> 8. **Isu** madzimai **ti**nooneka setisina kuzvibata nguva dzose. Ukangosekererana nemunhurume zvonzi wava kutodanana naye. Munhu anogona kutorambirwa izvozvo.
> (We (= 'I') women are always viewed as people of loose morals. Any friendly interaction with a man is misconstrued as an illicit relationship. Some men divorce their wives on account of such allegations.)

A follow up interview with Beauty established that she herself is, in fact, enstranged from her husband because of her suspected infidelity. Nevertheless, the discourse style represented in Example 8 is not unique to the speaker in this particular conversation. In Example 8 the speaker relates her own experience in an indirect way. By using the first-person plural pronoun, she associates herself with a much wider class of women (who become victims of gender stereotyping), downgrading her own experience to incidental status of the discourse, phrasing it as something that could or would be anybody's.

The analysed data shows that at times speakers use the first person plural pronoun instead of the first person singular pronoun to show the relationship between the speaker and the other person (s) implied in the *we*:

> 9. **Isu** hatifungi kuti zvine basa kuendesa mwana kukireshi inotaurwa Chirungu. **Ti**nodada nomutauro wedu. M*aattitudes* chete ndiwo anonetsa vanhu vatema.
> (We (= 'I') do not believe that it's necessary to send a child to an English speaking crèche. We are proud of our language. In fact, Blacks tend to have an attitudinal problem.)

> 10. Highlanders **ta**kairakasha pahome payo chaipo nezuro.
> (We (= 'they') thoroughly beat Highlanders on their home ground yesterday.)

Example 9 is an extract from a recording of a discussion on raising children by a group of Christian newlywed couples group. The speaker, Richard, aged 37, sits with his wife Tendai, aged 32 and glances occasionally at her as he speaks. Although Richard gives his own opinion, his *isu* (we) refers to him and Tendai. Hence, the *isu* in Richard's utterance serves an integrative function. According to Weiner and Mehrabian (1968), personal reference is used to establish verbal and social immediacy, with *we* pronouns signalling greater psychological inclusion (or integration of identities) and *I/you* pronouns establishing greater separation of self and other. Commenting on the functions of language in marital relations in Western society Ellis and Hamilton (1985) and Fitzpatrick, Bauman and Lindaas (1987) classify couples, which use *we* pronouns as 'interdependent', stable and homogenous and place high value on togetherness and sharing. Since the current study has not extensively analysed marital conversations, we do not have adequate evidence to test the applicability of these observations to the chiShona [Africa] context. It is clear, however, that the use of the first person plural pronoun in such situations as exemplified by Example 9 above implies a level of intimacy which is consistent with the research done by Ellis and Hamilton (1985) and Fitzpatrick and Lindaas (1987) research.

In Example 10, the ta- (we) also serves an integrative function, but of a different nature. In this example the first person plural pronoun refers to the third person plural (representing the Highlanders players). By using the we pronoun the speaker (the sports fan) shows his commitment to 'his' team, although he did not participate in the game personally.

Another example of usage with a similar effect is found in Example 11 below:

> 11. Svondo rakapera **ta**kadzidza chii zviya nezvechirwere chomukondombera?
> (What did we (= 'you') learn about HIV/AIDS last week?)

We recorded Example 11 in a junior high school class. The teacher is referring to a previous class she gave. The pronoun *we*, in this case represented by the subject concord *ta-* refers to the students and does not include the teacher. By using the pronoun the teacher simply expresses her commitment to the successful instruction of her students.

We also observed how the first person plural pronoun could be used to refer to the secondperson singular. Consider Example 12 and Example 13:

> 12. Riri sei gumbo re**du** nhasi ambuya?
> (How is our (= 'your') leg today granny?)

> 13. Nga**ta**idyeika mwanangu. Chidyai vamwene. Honai ini ndiri kudya. Oo, chiti kabu kabuki zimhandara.
> (Let us (= 'you') eat my child. Please eat mother-in-law. See, I am eating. Look, eat quickly my big girl.)

The use of the first person plural pronoun in Example 12 is in the context of a follow-up visit by an old woman to a medical doctor. This form of pronominal use is an example of the so-called 'nursery *we*' (Laberge & Sankoff, 1980, Mühlhäusler & Harré, 1990). Laberge and Sankoff suggest that the 'nursery *we*' is used in English when doctors and nurses or other caregivers express their strong commitment to patients or children they are responsible for. However, the data for this study seem to show that besides commitment, the speaker's use of the pronoun in such instances also connotes compassion and solidarity with the addressee.

The data analysed in this study show that the use of the first-person plural pronoun in address is common in the language used in caretaker speech/baby talk (Head, 1978:172). According to (Head) 'baby talk', reference may be either to both the speaker and the addressee, in order to encourage participation by the latter in a mutual activity, or only to the addressee, as a means of showing interest or may serve as a directive. This variable range of inclusiveness makes the use of the first person in addressing small children ambiguous.

We observed that chiShona speakers use the first-person plural pronoun when addressing small children, whether reference is to both the speaker and the addressee or to only the latter. When referring to both, the speaker and the addressee, the parent or caregiver, acting as the speaker, participates in the activity in question in a phony voice in order to to encourage the child to perform the activity. When Chenai, aged 32, instructs her daughter to eat her food in 13, the former takes only two spoons of porridge and lets her daughter finish the rest. The address form *mwanangu* (my child), the social honorific *zimhandara* and the relational honorific *vamwene* (mother-in-law) complement the illocutionary force[2] of the pronoun by adding the social

---

[2] This concept is attributable especially to Speech Act theory (Austin, 1962; Searle, 1969) and is relevant here because of our emphasis on the intentional nature of a communicative activity. Trudgill (2003: 125) devines an illocu-

meanings of closeness, affection and patronage (Mashiri 2004), resulting in the child eating all her food.

One other use of the first-person plural pronoun similar to the 'baby talk' that we observed is when parents, Sunday school teachers and Pre-school teachers order small children, in a polite manner, to stop certain actions:

> 14. Hati**ti**ambi **ti**chirova vamwe *and* kana **ti**chida kuenda ku*toilet* **ti**nokumbira kuna *auntie*.
> (We (= 'you') should not beat other children. When we (= 'you') want to visit the toilet, we (='you') ask the teacher's permission.)

The utterance in 14 is part of a statement that a pre-school teacher for a beginners' class at a private crèche in Harare gave to the children in her class in 2002. In an interview, the teacher, Tecla, aged 39, says that while she made this utterance as part of the routine classroom discipline reminders, she was, in fact, indirectly issuing an order to one particular boy who was in the habit of pinching other children and going to the toilet without asking for permission. We observed that the use of indirect directives shown in Example 14 is most common among children under the age of six. Tecla notes that a direct, firm and stern-sounding directive could negatively affect the delinquent child both psychologically and socially. The use of the first-person pronoun in 14 is used, first, to deal with a case at hand, but as Torode (1976: 93) reminds us, "this use of *we* is not [only] located within the present situation-at-hand, it is portrayed within a realm whose time-span transcends any particular spatially and temporally bounded occasion".

Our data also show how speakers use the first person plural pronoun to indirectly refer to a co-present referent (third person) both the speaker and the addressee assume to be a non-

---

tionary force of a speech act as "the effect, which a speech act is intended to have by the speaker".

speaker of Shona or a passive bilingual. The pronoun is used as a referent term in gossip involving the core-referent. Consider Example 15:

> 15. Baba ava vanonetsa. Izvozvi zva**ti**ri ipapa **ti**ri kusapura asi **ti**ri kusapotwa neUN. Basa nderokungosweroteedza ndari yemuZimbabwe.
> (My friend, this is a problem student. Currently, we (= 'he') are due to write supplementary examinations, despite that we get full funding from the United Nations. How can he do well when he spends time boozing in Zimbabwean bars?)

Example 15 features James, aged 38, a lecturer at the University of Zimbabwe who describes a foreign student's academic problems and social behaviour to the researcher. The use of the first person plural pronoun in Example 15 is exactly the same as that of its singular form in Example 4, which we noted as an instance of pronoun substitution or mismatch. The figurative nature of this discourse style makes the utterance in Example 15 inaccessible to non-native speakers of Shona. This style enables the speaker and the addressee to exclude the co-present referents from the discussion and to gossip about or insult them freely. In Example 15, the reference term *baba* (father), modified by the demonstrative *ava* (this), reflects a derogatory tone that connotes the referent's immature and irresponsible behaviour contrary to that expected of a father-figure denoted by the noun *baba*.

In the last example, we show Shona speakers' non-self-referential use of the first person plural pronoun in narratives or utterances that involve direct or indirect quotation similar to the use of the first-person singular pronoun illustrated in Example 5. The quotative *we* may refer to more than one addressee (numerical plural), the addressee and unspecified others associated with him/her, the addressee alone or overhearers who have no association with the addressee. This kind of ambiguity (seen in Example 15) is also evident in Example 16:

> 16. Imi vanaChamu munoswera muchizviti 'Tiri mawar vet, tiri mawar vet', yet ndimi maiva vanamujibha. Pamwe pakarwiwa hondo yacho maiva musati mambozvarwa futi!
> (People like you Chamu who go around saying, 'We (= 'you') are veterans of the war of liberation, we are veterans of the war', were probably just war collaborators. It's also possible that the war was fought before you were born.)

Besides the deriding and sarcastic tone of the mimicry, the referent ambiguity in the quotation makes it possible for the speaker to attack overhearers who would not be ratified addressees. In Example 16, Gerald, aged 41, makes these comments to Chamu, aged 37, during a friendly chat at a friend's wedding party attended by members of their social circle. Membership of the gathering gives Gerald the licence to speak freely without risking an altercation with anyone or being quoted out of context.

Second-person pronoun

In ordinary use the second person refers to the person addressed by the speaker. As Brown and Levinson (1987) suggest, when a speaker refers to a hearer as 'you', that hearer is an 'addressed recipient', a 'target' of the speaker's words. But, as the data for this study will show, the second person has a wide range of interactional uses that can index alternation of person to convey social meanings. Hence, the data analysed in this section will reveal that the second person pronoun can be used as a marked address pronoun and can be allocated to first, and third person, as well as the more generic second person.

Use of the second person as a marked address pronoun
chiShona grammars for both linguistic purposes and for second language learners (see e.g. Chimhundu and Mashiri, 1996, Brauner, 1995, Erickson, 1988 and Fortune, 1980) have typically described the unmarked forms of the second person pronoun. According to Brauer (1995:34), grammatically, the second person singular is usually used for one person and the "second person plural has two functions: address to a majority of persons and honorific plural form for one person". The explanation for this categorisation is sociolinguistic in nature. Both the social distance and the relative social status between interlocutors determine the speaker's choice for either the singular or plural [honorific]. Boxer (1993: 105) writes:

> Whereas the relative social status is viewed primarily in a vertical sense of higher or lower status, social distance differs from this concept in that it refers to the horizontal relationship between participants in a speech sequence. While the former has to do with one's social position in a community owing to age, occupation or level of power, the latter has to do with the level of friendship/intimacy between interlocutors. These are two variables having the potential of interacting and/or overriding each other, depending on the context of the interaction.

Some researchers have viewed the social distance scale as a continuum (e.g. Boxer, 1993; Holmes, 1990; Wolfson, 1988) in line with Wolfson's theory of social distance termed the 'The Bulge'[3]. In the continuum, we would find complete

---

[3] When we examine the ways in which different speech acts are realised in actual everyday speech, and when we compare these behaviours in terms of the social relationships of the interlocutors, we find again and again that the two extremes of social distance – minimum and maximum – seem to class forth very similar behaviur, while relationships which are more toward the centre show marked difference' (Wolfson, 1988: 32).

strangers at one extreme and intimates at the other end, with friend and acquaintances nearer to the middle. 'The categories of 'strangers', 'friends', and 'intimates' are not discrete categories but are points along the continuum' (Boxer, 1993: 104). Social distance and social status would interact where speakers comply with the Shona rule that a speaker is expected to address a hearer using the second person honorific pronoun if the latter is an acquaintance or a stranger who occupies a higher social status than the former. However, social distance may override social status where the interlocutors are intimates, hence their pronominal choice is determined by other contextual variables other than age or other forms of social status.

The data presented here will show that the patterns of language use characterised above disregard the speaker's creative usage and violation of conventional grammatical or cultural rules in order to achieve social meaning or pragmatic intent. An example of a marked use of the second person singular address pronoun can be seen in the following conversation between an adult married woman aboard a commuter omnibus and a teenage bus conductor:

> 17. Conductor: Ambuya seberai uko umwe agare.
> (Lady could you please move over to create room for one other person.)
> Woman: Silence and no movement.)
> Conductor: (Angrily) **Imi** ambuya **imi** seberai ku*side* uko. Maita seiko?
> (I am talking to you lady, please push over that side. Is there a problem?)
> Woman: Ndinosebera kupi kwacho? Iyo *seat* iyi yakazombogarwa nevanhu *four* kupi kwacho?
> (I do not see any space to push over to. Isn't it strange that you want the four of us to sit here?)
> Conductor: Moving closer to the woman) **Iwe uri**

aniko **iwe**? Uri *girlfriend* ya*driver* here kana kuti uri hure? Unoda kushamisira kunge uri mumota mako sei? Kana usingakwane buruka tione! Uri kupedza nguva yedu.
(You, what authority do you have to challenge me? Are you the driver's girl or just a prostitute? Why do you behaviour so arrogantly as if you are in the comfort of your personal car? If you have problems pushing over, then out you go! You are wasting our time.)
Woman: (Silent as she gets down).

In his first and second utterances the conductor uses the unmarked forms of address for the adult female stranger. The kin term *ambuya* (mother-in-law) and the second person plural pronoun *imi* (you) express the politeness/respect expected between strangers in service encounters. The shift from the second person plural to the singular pronoun *iwe* (you), and from the kin term of respect to insulting labels, such as *hure* (prostitute) shows the conductor's anger and desire to embarrass the woman for refusing to co-operate with him or comply with the bus rules. The encounter in Example 17 is not unique. Similar uses of the second person singular to addressees whom speakers are normally expected to give the honorific (either because the addressees are strangers to or are older than the speaker(s) or both) were observed in other service encounters, especially those involving queues and gatekeeping such as medical health-centres, registry offices, supermarkets, and banks.

Use of the second person for reference to the speaker/first person
In Shona the use of the second person pronoun to refer to oneself is widespread. Example 18 will help to make this clear.

18. **U**nodoedzawo kufadza murume asi hapana ano**ku**oona. Ndaneta tete. Murume wangu anorova.
(You (= 'I') try everything possible to please your (my) husband but he does not notice you (me). I am fed up auntie. My husband is abusive.)

The context captured in this example is that of Ruth, aged 33, narrating her experiences with her abusive husband to her aunt. In this case it is clear that the second person subject concord *u-* (you) and the object concord *ku-* (you) in '... *anokuon*' are actually intended to refer to the speaker herself. At issue in Ruth's utterance is her own experience with her abusive husband. But, by using the second person proforms she assimilates herself to a much wider class of women, downgrading her own experience to incidental status in the discourse, phrasing it as something that could be anybody's (Laberge & Sankoff, 1980: 281). The pragmatic effect of using the second person pronoun to mean the first person in this case is to evoke sympathy and solidarity and to legitimise the speaker's subsequent action or decisions. While the *you* in Example 18 seems to refer to the speaker only, the one used in Example 19 tends to be rather ambiguous. James, aged 29, a graduate high school teacher relates his financial situation to the researcher in an interview:

19. Ndiri *graduate teacher* asika **u**noshaya mari ye*rent* chaiyo **iwe u**ne *degree* iroro.
(I am a graduate teacher yet you (= 'I') can not afford to pay my rentals in spite of the degree.)

Example 19 shows how a speaker may choose to refer to himself in the second person rather than in the first person. The ambiguity referred to above relates to the possibility of the second person in this example to refer to the speaker only or the speaker and others like him, possibly including the addressee. In this case 'you' has been allocated to first and third person as well as the conventional second person. Support for this position has been implicitly noted in the work of Laberge and Sankoff (1980). The use of 'you' in this case is what Laberge and Sankoff and Wilson (1990) call 'situational insertion' (p. 280). "Situational insertion" argues Wilson, involves "the conversion of one's own personal experience into experiences which might be, or can be, shared by the addressee" (p.56). This kind of generalisation has the effects of locating the speaker in a potentially repeatable activity or context (Laberge & Sankoff, 1980: 281).

There are also instances where the second person indexes the first person plural. Consider the utterance in example (20) which we recorded from the sentiments of one male member of the Association of University Teachers (AUT) of the University of Zimbabwe to a member of the University Council at a salaries dispute meeting in 2003:

> 20. *It's not like* tinoda kuenda pa*strike. The question is* **u**noita chii ne$400 000,00 mazuva ano? Ukabhadhara *rent* nokutenga chikafu, ko *tranport*? Unopedzesera wakweretaka kuti **u**wane mari ye*fees* muna *January*!
> (It's not like we want to strike for the sake of it. The question is what do you (= 'we') buy with Z$400 000,00 these days? You (we) can only pay rent and buy some groceries and remains with no money for travel expenses. One has no option but to borrow money to pay children's school fees in January!)

Here *u-* is repeated a number of times and in no case does it seem to legitimately refer to the addressee, the second person singular or plural. Instead, because it refers to the speaker as well as the hearer(s), it seems to mean 'all of us'. This use of the second person implicitly refers to an indefinite reference.

Indefinite second person
Malone (1997: 69) notes that, "When a speaker uses the indefinite second person, he or she generalises about experiences that presumably relate to the whole group". Let us consider Example 21 (a) and 21(b):

> 21 (a) Kana **u**chida kuchengetedza murume mufadze paura. Muitire zvose zvaanoda. Zvema*women's rights* hazviite mumba.
> (If you (= 'one') want to keep your husband, cook good food for him. Do everything to make him happy. Women's rights are not applicable in the home.)

> (b) **Munhu** kana **u**chinoroora rega kubva **wa**zviratidza kuti **u**ri shoroma. Ukada kuenda nepajero **u**nozochema. Chide vakaziva kuti uri ku*UK*! Vanotoda kana *5 million* chaiyo yerusambo.
> (A person who goes to pay bride-wealth should not make it obvious that he is rich. Once the in-laws see you (= 'one') driving a Pajero to their home, they will raise the bride-wealth. Pity you (one) if they discover that you work in the United Kingdom! They might ask for Z$5 million for rusambo.)

A female research assistant recorded Example 21 (a). It forms part of Marian's, (aged 47), speech to young women attending a baby shower and we recorded Example 21 (b) from an informal discussion on gender issues by male colleagues at a construction site. Although one could say that the *u-* (you) concord Marian uses refers primarily to the bride, it could also index a hypothetical activity open to anyone, that is, how to keep a husband happy in a married relationship. In this case, as in many others, it is fairly clear that the 'indefinite agent' serves as a rather transparent guise for the speaker's own experience and opinions.

As is shown in Example 21 (b), there are many instances where the term *munhu* (person), (equivalence of the English pronoun *one* and French *on*), is used with the indefinite second person. Like the English pronoun one and the French pronoun on, (Laberge and Sankoff, 1980: 280) the Shona noun *munhu* is often used in Shona speech as a kind of pronoun to generalise, to avoid the problems of simply talking about personal experiences. This seems to be the distancing technique where the speaker does not want to make a personal statement but creates a separate persona and attributes his/her feelings to that persona. This technique results in reference ambiguity and, by so doing, allows assertions of greater generality and in some cases the "formulation of morals and truisms" (Laberge & Sankoff, 1980: 280). This is precisely what Marian does in Example 21 (a) where *munhu* is understood to be the headword of the sentence '*Kana [munhu] uchida kuchengetedza munrume mufadze paura*', and the speaker in Example 2 (b) does with *munhu* in his utterance '*Munhu kana uchirooora...*'.

Besides foregrounding morals, a lower status speaker can also use the indefinite pronoun to indirectly refer to a co-present referent of a higher social status to avoid embarrassing the referent in public. Similarly, an equal status speaker can use this pronoun to achieve the same effect. We observed the use of a second person pronoun to indirectly refer to a third person higher status referent, either when the referent is a co-present or in the presence of overhearers who could act as whistle blowers. At a construction site Mako, aged 26, an assistant to the builder indirectly ridicules a plasterer Mupositori, aged 38, for habitually borrowing money from him without paying him back, by treating an equal status colleague, Patrick, aged, 25 as a pseudo addressee:

22. Patrick: **Ndi**powoka mari yesadza Mako.
    (Mako, could you please lend me (= 'him')
    money to buy sadza.)

> Mako: Ndini bengi ra**ko** ini? Kana **u**chida chinja birth certificate rake woti ndini baba vakoka nevana vako vava vazukuru vangu. Kusina mai hakuendwi Patrick.
> (Am I your (= 'his') bank? If you want to depend on me so much why don't you have you birth registration changed to reflect me as your father and your children's grandfather. You have to learn to be selfreliant Patrick.)

We discovered that both the first person pronoun *ndi-* (I), that Patrick uses for self-reference, and the second person pronoun – *ko/u-* (you), that Mako uses to refer to Patrick, ostensibly refer to the third person, Mupositori. The non-verbal communication cues from the context made the interpretation of this pronominal shift simple. It became obvious from Mupositori's angry look and the overhearers' gazes and giggles that the speaker's message was meant for Mupositori and not Patrick. The indirect use of the second person singular pronoun to imply the third person in the above discourse provides an insight into the social relationship between the interlocutors. Specifically, it tells us that the interlocutors are friends, who know each other very well or are of equal status.

The discussion in this section has revealed that the second person pronoun has ranges of meanings and reference: it can refer to a single addressee; it can refer to a set of more than one addressee; or it can refer to an abstract category of people that do something or has something done to them.

Third person
Besides referring to people being talked about, rather than talked to by the speaker and addressee in talk, the third person pronoun performs other pragmatic functions in discourse. Jesperson (1924), Head (1978) and Openg (1997) discuss, in detail, the use of the third person in self-address. Jespenson (1924: 217) notes

that writers' use of the third person in self-reference in autobiographies is sometimes considered a form of modesty. It may also be self-effacement to convey the impression of absolute objectivity. This, argues Head (1978), implies greater distance than does the more commonly used first person. Head (ibid: 172) further remarks that in a natural conversation, "use of the third person for self-reference is more likely to occur when the speaker is also addressed in the third person by those with whom he is communicating". Furthermore, Head points out that while in several other languages the use of both the third person singular and plural is attested (especially in differential situations), in English, the use of the third person in self-reference occurs in the singular.

The data surveyed for this study shows that although the third person singular is more widely used in Shona, both the third person singular and plural are used to index the first person and the second person.

Third person used to mean first person
In Shona, the third person enumerative singular pronoun *mumwe* (someone) and/or its subject concord, *a-* (she/he) or the generic honorific plural *ivo* (and/or its subject concord *va-*) (they), may be used to index the first person only in reference. We cite two extracts to help substantiate this claim:

> 23. Unoswera uchipedzera mari mumahure ako zvako uchikanganwa kuti une **umwe munhu** anoda kudya. Haunyari!
> (You waste all the money on your prostitutes forgetting that there is someone (= 'me') who needs food. You are not even ashamed of yourself!)

> 24. Tendekai: Baba, baba chimukai munonditengera
>   pfuti yangu.

>(Father, father, could you please wake up so that you can go and buy me a (toy) gun.)
>George (baba): Ndazvinzwa Tendi. Chirega kudaro *daddy* **va**kaneta. Tichazoenda *later*.
>(Ok Tendi. Leave daddy (= 'me') alone, he (= 'I') is tired. We will go later.)

Example 23 is an extract from Maud's (aged 35), complaint to her husband for neglecting her and spending all the family savings on other women. In this utterance, Maud refers to herself as *mumwe munhu* (someone). This use of the generic third person to mean first person is also found in Akan (Obeng, 1997) and French (Grevisse, 1964). The generic third person is deliberately used to draw the husband's attention to the fact that he is being selfish by wasting the family resources on other women and has ignored his responsibility of taking care of his wife. Shona cultural norms require a man to take care of his wife [and children] adequately. Neglect, is therefore a breach of the wife's cultural rights. In the above example, then, the speaker expresses self-pity or the fact that she is being deprived of what is her cultural right. The indirect style that the speaker uses is such a common convention that there is no ambiguity as to whom the third person enumerative pronoun refers.

Example 24 features an extract of a conversation between Tendekai, aged 4, and his father George, aged 29, in George's bedroom. George had, earlier on promised to buy Tendekai a toy gun from a local shop. In this context Tendekai enters his father's bedroom in the morning to remind him of his promise by asking him to go and buy the gun. The reply that George gives is not unusual. But, "it is certainly not explicable by reference to the standard grammatical paradigm" (Malone, 1997: 44). Why would someone refer to him/herself in the third person? According to prescriptive grammarians, people should not use language that way. Hence, only an interactional explanation that focuses on the pronoun's reference to the speaker's identity or status and the rights and obligations that go with it, can offer a plausible answer to the question raised above.

First, when George uses the third person pronoun to refer to himself he implies his institutional role as father, which allows him to claim certain rights. Second, this self-reference becomes a resource for refusing politely to honour the child's request. In Shona society, as in many other cultures, refusals are not preferred responses to requests, and hence must normally be accompanied by accounts to justify or mitigate the refusal (Heritage, 1984, Mashiri 2003a) as a way of saving face. Here George's refusal to his son's legitimate request not only involves reference to his institutional [kinship] status and its implied rights, and an explanation of why his refusal is being made ('*Daddy vakaneta*'), but may also be seen as a distancing in which a third person, rather than *I*, marks the refusal. The use of the third person pronoun in Example 23 and Example 24 is clear evidence of the 'creative indexical usage' (Silverstein, 1976) of pronouns in Shona.

Third person used to mean second person
Our transcripts reveal that the use of the generic third person enumerative pronoun (also referred to as 'quantifier pronouns by Leech and Svartvik, 1975: 163) to indicate the second person is widespread in Shona society. The most common contexts of use are those involving intimates: parent-child, siblings, lovers and friends. The excerpt in (25) involves Panashe, aged 5, misbehaving in the house in the presence of visitors. The mother, Vena, aged 36, repeatedly orders him to stop misbehaving but Tadiwa is unmoved by the order. Finally, Vena issues a threat:

    25. Vena: **Mumwe munhu** ane pari kumuvava chete!
            (Someone is itching for a beating.)
            [=Stop misbehaving or I will smack you!]

Vena uses the generic third person enumerative pronoun, *mumwe* [*munhu*] (someone) to mean *iwe* (you). Given the context that Panashe is the only child (misbehaving) in the house and the Shona socialise their children to behave themselves in the presence of elders or visitors, there is no ambiguity with regard to the referent. Vena uses the generic third person pronoun for two reasons. First, Shona values do not allow a parent or caregiver to openly reprimand or threaten a child in the presence of visitors, lest the threat is interpreted as being indirectly targeted at the visitors. This is so since the Shona, like other African peoples, believe that a FTA may be addressed to a psuedo-epicentre, usually a child, a dog, a cat, or any pet, rather than to the real addressee (Obeng, 1999: 83). Since the referent is only a child, the indirection is prompted not by the relationship between mother and child, but by the mother's relationship with the visitors and the need to protect her public self-image that is "emotionally invested and cannot be lost, maintained or enhanced, and must be constantly attended to in interaction" (Brown and Levinson, 1978: 66).

Second, the use of the third person generic pronoun is for distancing or avoidance. In the context in which it is used, it suggests that Panashe's behaviour is so detestable that he is not worthy to be addressed by name and moreover addressing him by name would give him the undue recognition and attention that he does not deserve.

A similar context was the use of the same pronoun by Tsitsi, aged 25, to discourage her fiancé, Fanuel, aged 27, from drinking in excess at Tsitsi's cousin's wedding ceremony:

26. Tsitsi: Uchiri kunwa here sha?
    (Haven't you had enough dear?)
    Fanuel: (Speaking loudly) Handiti muchato here
    Tsitsi, rega ndimbonwa *a bit more*.
    (This is a happy occasion Tsitsi, let me take some more.)

Tsitsi: **Vamwe vanhu** makuda kuonererwa!
Someone is now trying to show-off
[=You are now trying to embarrass me.]

Since Tsitsi and Fanuel are still dating, cultural values do not allow the latter to lose his public image in the presence of Tsitsi's family. Since Fanuel has an avoidance relationship with members of Tsitsi's family, Tsitsi is responsible for controlling his behaviour in this context. The situation is emotionally delicate hence; Tsitsi uses the plural form, *vamwe vanhu* (some others), in this case, to hide Fanuel's identity by avoiding the singular form, *mumwe munhu* (someone) and his name. However, both the addressee and the overhearers are still able to infer who the referent is. Such uses of the generic third person could be said to be fully consummated and sufficient for referent identification (Ashby, 1992).

We observed that the generic third person could also be used in a superior-subordinate relationship. A female secretary, aged 28, checks on her boss, aged 37, who is in the habit of forgetting to charge his cellular phone:

27. *I know* kuti **mumwe munhu** akanganwa kuchagisa
    phone.
    (I know that someone has not remembered to charge his phone)
    [=I know that you have not remembered to charge your phone.]

Instead of using the second person honorific plural *imi/ma-* (you), the secretary uses *mumwe munhu* (someone). This pronominal shift enables the speaker to politely ridicule her superior without risking a reprimand.

Demonstrative pronouns
Studies on demonstratives have often been limited to their anaphoric characteristics and functions. Leech and Svartvik's (1975: 58) categorisation of demonstratives as 'pointer words': back pointing (i.e. they can point to something mentioned earlier), forward-pointing (i.e. they can point to something mentioned later) and outward-pointing (i.e. they can point to something in the context outside language) clarifies this point. Referentially, demonstratives are classified into those that identify 'something near the speaker (either physically, in terms of space or time, or psychologically' and those that 'identifies something not so near the speaker' (Leech & Svartvik, 1975: 58).

The data surveyed for this study show that Shona speakers use demonstratives as reference terms in place of the referents' names. What we found interesting is that only those demonstratives Leech and Svartvik say identify something near the speaker are used, except that in the usages we observed, the issue of physical proximity is insignificant. Primarily speakers use the singular form *uyu* (this), to refer to equal status referents and the plural (honorific) form *ava* (these), to refer to superior referents. Consider examples 28 (a), (b) and (c):

28 (a) Researcher: Muri kurongei nezve*accomodation*?
(What plans do you have for housing?)
Tandi: Hapana but tine stand yatakatenga ava vachiri vapenyu.
(Nothing specific, but we own a stand that we bought when this one (= 'He') was still alive.)

(b) Sorry shamwari *I delayed you*. Ndanonotswa ne**ava**.
(I am sorry friend for delaying you. I was held up by this one (= 'him')).

(c) Tami: Unosvika kumba nguvai ne*Friday*?

>(What time do you get home on Friday?)
>Simon: Ndichaona kuti ndasvika *by 6.30* asi ndicha-mbonopika **uyu** Ku*college*.
>(I will make sure I am home by 6.30, although I have to pick this one (= 'she') first from college.)

Example 28(a) is an excerpt of an interview that the researcher had with Tandi, aged 29, a family friend, about her housing plans since the death of her husband, (b) was uttered by a woman, aged approximately 25, to a friend who waited for outside their house and Example 28(c) is part of a conversation the researcher's former students, Tami, aged 26, and Simon, aged 26, had at a bus terminus. We noted from these examples and many others that the speaker only uses the demonstrative for a referent known by both the speaker and the addressee and that the demonstrative is meant to hide the identity of the referent. Tandi's use of *ava* (this) to refer to her deceased husband also seemed to have a distancing and/or avoidance effect. The tone of the voice and the facial expression of the woman cited in 28(b) show that she used *ava* (these) to denigrate and scorn her husband.

In an interview, Esther Chivero, a fellow linguist at the University of Zimbabwe, noted that "When this demonstrative is used between husband and wife it normally shows a negative attitude towards the referent. Either the husband is being referred to as such because he is authoritative and demands respect or there is no intimacy between them that warrants use of the other's first name". Esther's explanation reveals that the use of the honorific plural *ava* either connotes genuine respect or scorn. The demonstrative *uyu* (this) that Simon uses in 28(c) is commonly used by intimates, although our data show that students and junior workers also use it to derogatorily refer to a teacher or superior. The underlying factor in all these usages is that the interlocutors are intimates/friends or acquaintances who share sufficient knowledge to disambiguate the referents of the demonstrative. The creative use of demonstrative in interaction enables interlocutors to engage in private conversations in public places.

There are cases where interlocutors may use commentary demonstratives such as *iri* (class 5), *ichi* (class 7), *idzi* (class 10) and *aka* (class 12) [this +NEGATIVE]. We noted that *idzi* is also used to refer to a person whom the speaker or both the speaker and the addressee view positively, or specifically, admire or empathise with. It is clear from the data that speakers of all sexes, ages and social classes only use any of these demonstratives when speaking to an intimate about a referent they both know and view the same. Depending on the conversational context, these commentary demonstratives are preferable because, to some extent, avoid face threat. In fact, the commentary demonstratives seem to be more ambiguous and anonymous than the ordinary ones, hence are more effective pragmatic devices.

Conclusion

In this article we have discussed the pragmatic significance of chiShona pronouns focussing specifically on the different personal pronouns, enumerative pronouns and demonstrative pronouns and illustrated how in some communicative contexts, specific pronouns are used to mark different persons. We addressed the general problem with the grammatical paradigms, the question of pronouns as linguistic signs, that is, entities in which constant form is paired with constant meaning. The case of the componential treatment of pronouns by structuralist linguists illustrates the problems in identifying tokens of the same form. The problem is considerably more difficult with meaning, where "the establishment of de-contextualised 'literal' meanings of pronouns run into problems for the very reason that the meaning of pronouns is text- and context-derived" (Mühlhäusler & Harré, 1990: 58). Hence, we have illustrated with numerous data, that the same pronoun form express a number of different meanings since meaning is situated in a particular context. As Malone

(1997: 75) noted, pronouns are "irredeemably interactional markers and their use is ruled by interactional rules primarily and grammatical rules only secondarily".

Besides the first person reference, the first person pronouns (singular and plural) and or their agreement concords can be used to index a second or third person reference form. Such pronoun shifts function in various communicative categories; for example, stressing authority, asserting and maintaining power, caricaturing, creating alignment, solidarity, showing commitment and compassion. Based on our data, therefore, pronoun switches involving the first person also help express what is otherwise unspeakable. This function of the pronoun switch, says Obeng (1997: 218), has implications for psycholinguistics. It reveals that fact that, "through pronoun switches, [interlocutors] can communicate their emotional state through a form of indirectness that is transparent enough for an addressee to understand but strong enough to prevent direct confrontation".

When the second person pronoun is used to index the first person it connotes a wide range of meanings. In Example 19 and Example 20, for instance, the second person indicates solidarity and shared experience, whereas in Example 18 it refers to a hypothetical activity and has a generalising effect.

The third person, apart from its ordinary usage, may be used indirectly to mean either the first or second person, especially when warning or threatening someone, hide the addressee's identity or communicating a face-threatening act. We have also discussed the use of the demonstrative pronouns in place of personal names with a distancing/avoidance effect. Sometimes demonstrative pronouns are used to hide the identity of the referent in primate discourse or to denigrate the referent. Throughout, we stressed the relevance and interplay of linguistic, sociolinguistic and pragmatic factors in determining the various uses of pronouns.

From the discussion presented in this article, it is clear that the knowledge of grammatical rules is not adequate for a proper understanding of pronoun usage. The discourses discussed in this study reveal that with respect to pronoun usage, we could argue that rules of social behaviour take precedence over rules of grammar.

In conclusion, following Hymes (1962), Lyons (1982: 58) notes that natural languages are primarily designed for use in face-to-face interaction hence; any analysis of natural language should take the speech event or context of the utterance into account. We therefore hypothesise that the choice of a pronoun depends on a speaker and the relationship between the speaker and the addressee or the referent, as well as the context of interaction. This discussion does not necessarily advocate the subordination of the morphosyntactic characteristics of Shona pronouns (or those of any other language) to their functional features. As Obeng (1997: 219) reminds us, an integration of the pragmatic, morphosyntactic, and discourse or social connotations of these pronouns will yield a considerable understanding of the behaviour of pronouns in a language.

References
Ashby, W. (1992). "The variable use of on versus *tu/vous* for indefinite reference in spoken French" *French Language Studies*, 2: 135-157.
Austin, J.L. (1962). *How to Do Things With Words*. Oxford: Clarendon Press.
Boxer, D. (1993). "Social distance and speech behaviour: The case of direct complaints" *Journal of Pragmatics*, 19: 103-125.
Brauner, S. (1995). *A Grammatical Sketch of Shona*. Köln: Rudiger Koppe Verlag.
Brown, R. & A. Gilman (1960). "The pronouns of power and solidarity" *American Anthropologist*, 4(6): 24-29.
Brown, P. & S.C. Levinson (1978). "Universals in language usage: Politeness phenomena" In Goody, E.N. (Ed.),

Questions and Politeness: Strategies in Social Interaction. Cambridge: Cambridge University Press.

Brown, P. & S.C. Levinson (1987). *Politeness: Some Universals in Language Usage.* New York: Cambridge University Press.

Chen, V. (1991). "Mien Tze at the Chinese dinner table: A study of interactional accomplishment of face" *Research on Language and Social Interaction,* 24: 109-140.

Chimhundu, H. and P. Mashiri (1996). *Taurai chiShona: Beginners' Workbook.* Kadoma: Juta Zimbabwe.

Dembetembe, N.C. (1987). "The structure and function of the noun phrase in Shona" In Pongweni, A.J.C. & J. Thondhlana (Eds), *The Role of Linguistics in Communication for Development. LASU Conference Proceedings,* Harare: University of Zimbabwe: 82-97.

Duranti, A. (1984). "The social meaning of subject pronouns in Italian conversation" *Text,* 4 (4): 277- 311.

Ellis, D. and Hamilton, M. (1985). "Syntactic and pragmatic code choice in interpersonal communication" *Communication Monograph,* 52: 264-278.

Ellis, D.G. (1992). "Syntactic and pragmatic codes of communication" *Communication Theory,* 2: 1-23.

Erickson, D. (1988). *The Morphology and Syntax of Shona: A Lexical Approach.* Unpublished D Phil thesis, University of Washington.

Ervin-Tripp, S. (1976). "'Is Sybil there?': The structure of American English directives" *Language in Society,* 5: 25-66.

Fitzpatrick, M.A., I. Bauman & M. Lindaas (1987). "A schematic approach to marital interaction" Paper presented at the International Communication Association, Montreal.

Fortune, G. (1980). *Shona Grammatical Constructions, Part 1,* Harare: Mercury Press.

Goffman, E. (1967). *Interaction Ritual: Essays on Face-to-Face Behaviour.* Harmondsworth: Penguin.

Goffman, E. (1974). *Frame Analysis.* New York: Harper Colophon.
Goffman, E. (1981). *Forms of Talk.* Oxford: Basil Blackwell.
Grevisse, M. (1964). *Le bon usage.* Gembloux, France: Duculot.
Grimes, J.E. (1975). *The Thread of Discourse.* The Hague: Mouton.
Hartmann, R.R.K. & F.C. Stock (1972). *Dictionary of Language and Linguistics.* London: Applied Science Publishers.
Head, B.F. (1978). "Respect degrees in pronominal reference" In Greenberg, J.H. (Ed.), *Universals of Human Language 3, Word Structure.* Stanford: Stanford University Press: 150-211
Heritage, J. (1984). "A change-of-state token and aspects of its sequential placement" In Atkinson, M.J. & J. Heritage (Eds), *Structures of Social Action: Studies in Conversation Analysis.* Cambridge: Cambridge University Press: 265-273.
Hodge, R. & G. Kress (1988). *Social Semiotics.* Ithaca, New York: Cornell University Press.
Holmes, J. (1983). "The structure of teachers' directives" In Richards, J.C. and W. Schmidt (Eds), *Language and Communication.* New York, London: Longman: 89-116.
Holmes, J. (1990). "Politeness strategies in New Zealand women's speech" In Bell, A. and J. Holmes (Eds), *New Zealand Ways of Speaking English.* Clevedon, Avon: Multilingual Matters: 252-75.
Hymes, D. (1962). "The ethnography of speaking" In Gladwin, T. & W. Sturtevant (Eds.) *Anthropology and Human Behaviour.* Washington DC: Anthropological Society of Washington: 13-53.
Jesperson, O. (1924). *The Philosophy of Grammar.* London: Allen and Unwin.
Kahananui, D.M. and ANthony, A.P. (1970). *Let's Speak Hawaiian.* Honolulu: University of Hawaii Press.
Larbege, S. and Sankoff, G. (1980). 'Anything you can do'. In

Sankoff, G (ed.), *The Social Life of Language*. Philadelphia: University of Pennsylvania Press: 271-293.

Leech, G. and Svartvik, J. (1975). *A Communicative Grammar of English*. Harlow, Essex: Longman.

Lyons, J. (1982). *Language and Linguistics*. Cambridge: Cambridge University Press.

Makoni, Sinfree & Mashiri, Pedzisai (2007). "Critical historiography: Does language planning in Africa need to postulate the existence of languages as part of its theoretical apparatus?" In Sinfree Makoni & Alistair Pennycook (eds.), *Disinventing and Reconstituting Languages*. Clevedon: Multilingual Matters Press.

Malone, M.J. (1997). *Words of Talk: The Presentation of Self in Everyday Conversation*. Cambridge: Polity Press.

Mashiri, P. (2003) "Managing face in urban public transport: Polite request strategies in commuter omnibus discourse in Harare" In Makoni, SB & Meinhof, U.H. (eds), *Africa and Applied Linguistics: AILA Review*, 16: 120-126.

Mashiri, P. (2004). "A sociolinguistic interpretation of the social meanings of kinship terms in Shona urban interactions" *Southern African Linguistics and Applied Language Studies*. 22(1-2), 27-42.

Mashiri, P.; Mawomo, K.; & Tom, P. (2002). "Naming the pandemic: Semantic and ethical foundations of HIV/AIDS Shona vocabulary. *Zambezia*, 29 (2): 221-234.

Mühlhäusler, P. and Harré, R. (1990). *Pronouns and People: The Linguistic Construction of Social and Personal Identity*. Oxford: Basil Blackwell.

Obeng, S.G. 1997. "Indirectness in pronominal usage in Akan discourse" *Journal of Language and Social Psychology*, 16 (2): 201-221.

Obeng, S.G. (1999). "In future if I buy a dog, I'll call it 'Okyeman-is-ungrateful': Indirect responses to potentially difficult communicative situations: The case of Akan dog names" *International Journal of the Sociology of Language*, 140: 83-103.

Pan, Y. (1995). "Power behind linguistic behaviour: analysis of politeness phenomena in Chinese official settings" *Journal of Language and Social Psychology*, 14(4): 462-481.

Pearson, B. (1988). "Power and politeness in conversation: Encoding of face-threatening acts at church business meetings" *Anthropological Linguistics*, 30(1): 68-93.

Reichenbach, H. (1966). *Elements of Symbolic Logic*. New York: Free Press.

Searle, J.R. 1969. *Speech Acts*. Cambridge: Cambridge University Press.

Silverstein, M. (1976). "Shifters, linguistic categories and cultural description" In Basso, K. H. and H.A. Selby (Eds), *Meaning in Anthropology*. Albuquerque: University of New Mexico:11-15

Torode, B. (1976). "The revelation of a theory of the social world as grammar" In Harré, R. (Ed.), *Life Sentences*. Chichester: Wylie: 87-97.

Trudgill, P. (2003). *A Glossary of Sociolinguistics.* Oxford and New York: Oxford University Press.

Wiener, M. and Mehrabian, A. (1968). *Language Within Language: Immediacy, a Channel in Verbal Communication*. New York: Appleton-Cetury-Crofts.

Wills, D.D. (1977). "Participant deixis in English and baby talk" In Snow, C. & C. Ferguson (Eds) *Talking to Children*. Cambridge: Cambridge University Press: 271-296.

Wilson, J. (1990). *Politically Speaking: The Pragmatic Analysis of Political Language*. Oxford: Basil Blackwell.

Wolfson, N. (1988). "The bulge: A theory of speech behaviour and social distance" In Fine, J (Ed.), *Second Language Discourse: A Textbook of Current Research*. Norwood, NJ: Ablex: 21-38

V

Is Zimbabwean English a type of new English?

Abstract
The concepts of interlanguage and "new Englishes" have generated a considerable amount of interest in applied linguistics and language teaching. This paper is divided into parts; the first part argues that the variety of English used in Zimbabwe by African users of English is a type of interlanguage, and not a type of "new Englishes" for two main reasons. The second section of the paper attributes interest in "new Englishes," in part, to sentiments generated by the subtle influence of British colonial language policy. It argues that there are powerful sociolinguistic and practical factors in Zimbabwe which militate against the standardisation of an interlanguage in the presence of a more prestigious, full-fledged native speaker variety.

Introduction: Interlanguage
The term interlanguage (IL) was introduced by Selinker (1972). It basically refers to a learner language. "The learner language is viewed as an independent social and psycological phenomenon ... It is not a defective version of something else: a chrysalis is simply a chrysalis, not a deformed or defective butterfly" (Phillipson. 1991: 61). A number of other competing terms have also been proposed, but none of them are as widely used as the Selin-

kerian term of IL. Corder (1967, 1971) proposed the terms "transitional competence" and "idiosyncratic dialects." Nemser (1971) opted for "approximative system." The terms cited above, in spite of some subtle differences in meaning, are all basic descriptions of a "learner variety" or a "language learner language" (Ellis. 1985; Klein, 1986).

There are at least two factors which potentially shape the nature of an IL: the environment within which the second language is acquired, and the influence of the mother tongue. The latter manifests itself in at least two ways. First, as transfer, or, as it is more recently called, cross-linguistic influence (Sharwood Smith, 1991). Secondly, differences in language background affect the magnitude of the language learning task (Corder, 1985). For instance, a learner coming from a language background which is typologically different from that of the target language will be faced with a much bigger learning task, than one coming from a background typologically similar to the target language. Ellis (1986), reviewing the literature on the role of instruction in Second Language Acquisition (SLA), suggests that the setting, i.e., formal and naturalistic environments, affects the rate and not the route of second language development.

Although ILs are susceptible to a number of diverse influences which include the setting and cross-linguistic influence, "every learner variety, no matter how elementary and inadequate it might be, constitutes a system in itself" (Klein. 1986: 57). Unfortunately, at present, the exact characteristics of this system have not yet been fully worked out (Davies, et al., 1985).

Both ILs and adult grammars are systematic. They, however, differ in the degree and type of systematicity which they exhibit. For instance, an adult native speaker's grammar may be systematic because of the presence of a number of linguistic forms which function as variants of the same form. A second language speaker's IL may have fewer variants of the same form, but still may be systematic. In some extreme cases. it is even doubtful whether much insight is gained by describing a learner's IL as systematic, particularly if the same form is used in a number of diverse contexts. For example, if someone knows one expression and only one expression, for example "sumimasen (excuse me)" in Japanese, and if that person uses it correctly and systematically, it does not necessarily mean that person has systematic knowledge of Japanese and that this language system is like that of an adult native speaker. Variability in IL can also be non-systematic, i.e., random. The main proponent of random variation is Ellis (1985, 1987, 1988). Theoretically, the existence of random variation accords with what is known about ILs, particularly their instability. Instability creates conditions which are conducive for random variation, while at the same time the violation through redundancy of basic principles of IL development limits the scope of random variation. Empirically, the case for free variation is weak because most of the evidence comes from cross-sectional studies. Longitudinal studies — paradoxically not of free variation, but of systematic variablilty, because random variation can only be established as a consequence of research into systematic variability (Makoni, 1991). Random variation is not peculiar to IL, it is also found in adult grammars. However its status. even existence, in adult grammars has also been challenged (Downes, 1988).

Adult grammars and ILs may also differ in their psychological properties. Adjemian (1976) claims that permeability is a unique property of IL. It is because of the IL's permeability that "it is easily influenced by the speaker's mother tongue forms (transfer) and by the over-generalisation and incorporation of target language forms" (Preston, 1989: 105). Unfortunately. Adjemian does not clarify whether it is the IL competence, performance, or indeed both which are open to "invasion" (Sharwood Smith, 1991). Contrary to Adjemian, studies into dialectology demonstrate that the uniqueness of permeability to an IL is a "fiction" (Preston, 1989).

Permeability engenders an atmosphere of instability in an IL. The instability manifests itself in variable IL production, and indeterminate grammatical intuitions. "Indeterminacy may be defined in broad terms — as the absence of a clear grammaticality status in the speaker's competence" (Sorace, 1990). The absence of a clear grammaticality status results in a constant revision of rules particularly at an intermediate level of proficiency. At an elementary level, second language intuitions may be indeterminate not because rules are being constantly revised, but from the absence of any sort of knowledge of a particular grammatical form. Such type of indeterminacy may be fairly widespread in ILs which are at an elementary stage of development.

The emergence of new englishes: a brief historical note
"New Englishes" are a historical consequence of British colonialism. They, however, differ from dialects of English such as American English, Scottish English, etc., in that the latter are widely used by native speakers, while the "new Englishes" are used by non-native speakers. English, like other European languages and notably French, spread to different parts of the world, partly, if not mainly, because of European colonialism. The end of the colonial period did not, however, signal the end of the use of "colonial languages."

The retention of what was formally a colonial language in independent African and Asian countries partly accounts for the emergence of "new Englishes." Contrary to what might be expected, the continued used of French in former French colonies has not resulted in the emergence of "new Frenches" in Francophone countries, such as Togo, Senegal and the Ivory Coast. The concept of "new Frenches" is not widely accepted as the idea of "new Englishes" (Davies, 1986), for reasons which will become clear later in the paper.

Psycholinguistic and sociolinguistic approaches to il and new englishes

Broadly speaking, approaches to IL studies are of a psycholinguistic nature. The studies aim at documenting the universal IL characteristics. Descriptions of "new Englishes" are sociolinguistically oriented. They are about properties which are typical of each new variety of English. Such description is thought to help alter the status of "new Englishes." Through studies of IL African linguists seek to achieve what British and American linguists have achieved through their description of non-standard dialects. Stubbs (1986: 20) expresses the point quite emphatically when he says: "Descriptions of social reality become persuasive as soon as people become aware of them." For example, the attention that linguists have given to non-standard dialects of English, community languages in Britain, and British and American sign languages has changed the status of these languages." Sometimes these linguistic endeavours were specifically made "to attack the notion that the language varieties are in anyway 'primitive'." But can description become "prescription due to dissemination?" As Stubbs put it, "there is no such thing as pure research on language and society."

The scholars of IL want to promote "new Englishes" to a level comparable to that of dialects like Australian English and New Zealand English. The movement to classify "new Englishes" as dialects of English is strengthened by a number of factors. For example, some of the "new Englishes," are used in a wide range of domains and have a long history of use in their respective communities. Omodiaogbe (1992) for example, claims the English language has been in use in Nigeria for at least 150 years. It is also claimed that there is no substantial native speaker influence on the varieties. However native speaker influence in the "new Englishes" is not lost. The native speaker has been disembodied and technologised. They are heard through institutions such as the B.B.C. and the Voice of America. The "new

Englishes" are under a much stronger influence from native speaker speech than was the case previously.

It has also been frequently claimed that "new Englishes" should be accorded a status comparable to that of the other dialects of English because there are more non-native speakers of English than there are native speakers (Bloor & Bloor, 1990). Crystal (1988) puts the number of English native speakers at about 350 million. The number of non-native speakers ranges from 300 to 1000 million. The "numbers game" is part of what Quirk (1989) cynically calls "liberation linguistics." The "numbers game" is designed to appeal to the democratic sentiments of the academic community, because, as the argument goes, if there are as many non-native speakers as there are native speakers, then non-native speaker have as much right to English ownership as the native speakers do. In spite of the powerful nature of the "liberation linguistics" argument, one wonders how the putative number of speakers of English was arrived at, because census figures which may be the potential source of such information in Africa are notoriously unreliable. Furthermore. those who happily cite the number of non-native speakers of English do not identify the minimum level of proficiency one has to acquire before being counted as a user of English.

The following section addresses the question whether the "new Englishes" should be described as ILs or as dialects of the English language, and whether the Zimbabwean English variety is a new English.

Some of the key properties of new Englishes
Platt & Weber (1980) and Nelson (1988) identify three main criteria which must be fulfilled before a variety of English can be "localised." They are:

> (1) The language should be developed through the educational system. It should be taught as a subject and at times used as a medium of instruction. As a rule there

should be no native speakers who act as the target of language learning.

(2) The language should be used for a wide range of purposes including, but not restricted to, letter writing, the writing of creative literature, parliamentary debates and media reporting.

(3) The language should exhibit "localised" features in pronunciation, sentence structure and the lexicon.

The requirements posed by Platt and Weber, and Nelson to be fulfilled before a variety is "localised," are a combination of socioliguistic and linguistic criteria. The first and second criteria above, focus on the role of the language variety at a national level. The third criterion is liguistic because it focuses on the characteristics of the code as reflected in the speech of non-native speakers. The assumption is that the linguistic features differ systematically from those of the target language and, more importantly, that the differences are sufficiently significant to warrant the variety being called a separate language.

I will now critically examine some of the criteria which have been proposed for the "localisation" of English. The aim of the examination is to establish whether the variety of English used in Zimbabwe is still an IL or is on its way to becoming a type of "new English."

The fact that English is taught as a subject and is the medium of instruction in Zimbabwe (Ngara, 1982; McGinley, 1989) partially fulfills the first criterion for the "localisation" of English. But the key criterion is that the target of language learning should be non-native speakers. The native speaker occupies a crucial role in both linguistic and applied linguistic research (Davies, 1982). In "localised" varieties, the norms of accuracy and appropriacy are not those represented by the native speakers of English, and their current role in establishing norms of usage in those countries is claimed to be insignificant. This is exactly the opposite of the situation in Zimbabwe. In Zimbabwe the number of native speakers of English is small relative to the entire population. McGinley (1989) estimated the number of native speakers of English in Zimbabwe at approximately 100,000 in a population of eight million. Even though the native speakers are in a minority, they are powerful enough to provide a set of norms which are used as reference points by the Black majority in language learning and other social aspects of life as well.

The sociolinguistic power of whites, which to a large degree stems from their economic strength, is reinforced by an increasing number of black middle class children who are ethnically African, but use English as their mother tongue; The presence of an increasing number of black and white as native speakers of English suggests that, in future. Zimbabwean English will refer to the variety of English used by Zimbabwean speakers of English. Unlike in Nigeria and Ghana, where the terms Nigerian English and Ghanaian English refer to the English used by second language users, and not native English speakers. Sociolinguistically, the variety of language which is the target of second language learning is that of the group with the most economic power. There is more than a grain of truth in the oft-quoted statement attributed Max Weinrich that a "language is a dialect with an army and a navy." In Zimbabwe, the variety of English spoken by non-native speakers of English cannot be called Zimbabwean English because it fails on the native speaker test.

Before a variety can be "localised" it must be used for a wide range of purposes, including but not restricted to, creative writing, parliamentary debates and the media reporting. Superficially, the variety of English used in Zimbabwe by second language users can be described as "localised" because it meets the above criterion. All the daily newspapers are in English in Zimbabwe. A close analysis of the domains within which English is used suggests that its use is largely restricted to formal institutional settings. Shona and Ndebele are the two main indigenous languages. The majority of Zimbabweans speak Shona as a mother tongue. Ndebele speakers need Shona more than

English because 80% of the population are Shona speakers and the chances of any contact, other than in formal contexts, for the Ndebele speaker with an English native speaker are low. The domains within which English is replacing the African languages to any noticeable degree in rural Zimbabwe are almost non-existent. Fears of linguicide (Spolsky, 1990) in rural communities may be unwarranted. The exception might be the black urban middle class which has been discussed above. If the sociolinguistic contexts within which English is used are restricted to institutional settings in the urban areas, the situation is radically different in the rural areas in Zimbabwe, where English is best described not as a second language (ESL), but as a foreign language (EFL). In the ESL/EFL divide thus corresponds to an urban/rural dichotomy. In light of the Zimbabwean experience, an experience which is likely to be repeated in many African countries, it might be more useful to talk of ESL/EFL situations and not countries. Unfortunately, the categorisation of situations as either EFL or ESL is complicated by the fact that, in some contexts, an ESL situation may be recategorised as EFL, depending on the ideological persuasion of the analyst. For instance, the director of the Inter-African languages Organisation of African Unity labels English and French everywhere in Africa as foreign languages to emphasise their colonial nature (Mateene, 1985, cited in Phillipson, 1991).

In the rural areas, because of the homogeneity of the local population, very little English is likely to be used or heard. In urban areas English may be heard over the radio and is used in the media. In the rural areas, radios are rare, television known but hardly seen, and videos, virtually unknown. The circulation of newspapers does not normally extend to rural areas. The homogeneity of the rural population, and the absence of technologies, such as radios, means that the rural population's exposure to English is confined to the classroom. Because English is a foreign language in rural Zimbabwe, it is not possible to argue that there is an emerging variety of Zimbabwean English there.

If there is an emerging variety, its use might be restricted to formal institutional settings in the urban areas. Even in the urban centers, there are strong reasons to be skeptical about the emergence of the new variety, because of the powerful effects of norms established and maintained by the native speakers of English.

Le-Page & Tabouret-Keller (1985) characterise speech communities as either diffused or compact. Compact speech communities, according to Preston (1989), regard the language variety they use as unique and not as negative part of another variety. Compact non-native varieties, such as Nigerian English and Ghanaian English, have developed highly "localised" norms because they have been in use for a long period, at least 150 years, as Omodiaogbe claims, in the case of Nigeria. Conversely, speech communities which do not accord a unique status to their variety of language partly because they have not used the variety for a long time will have diffuse norms, a situation which is characteristics of most EFL contexts including a large part of Zimbabwe. It is, however, difficult to see how the degree of compactness or diffuseness can be empirically measured.

Because of the restricted range of functions which English serves in rural and urban centres in Zimbabwe, it is doubtful that second language users of English in that country will have highly focused or compact norms. The Zimbabwean non-native variety, therefore, does not meet the key requirements for "localisation."

There are systematic differences at lexical, syntactic and phonological levels between the standard English and the variety of English used by non-native speakers in Zimbabwe. Phonologically, there are some sounds which are differentiated in standard English as in *head* and *heard*. The /e/ and /a/ vowels in the preceding words are undifferentiated in the English of non-native speakers of Shona. Syntactically, there is a tendency to use the present progressive in Zimbabwe where Standard English speakers use the simple present. For example, "I am not hearing," for, "I can't hear."

These characteristics are not peculiar to Zimbabwe, but are found in many ILs all over the world. Differences in pronunciation and vocabulary also operate at a dialectal level. Lass (1987) recently documented differences among Scottish English, standard English and African English in terms of vocabulary and pronunciation (South African English does not refer to the English used by "blacks" but by the white community which has English as a mother tougue, a situation which closely parallels that of Zimbabwe).

The Scottish and standard English are not two separate languages because the former may be pronounced with a Scottish accent and the latter with a received pronunciation accent. Differences at syntactic and lexical levels exist even within native speakers of the same dialect, and indeed, even within the same native speaker. The differences at a dialectal level have not led linguists to postulate the existence of different languages for each speaker. Spolsky (1980) forcefully argues that "there seems to be no more justification for postulating radically different languages for individual speakers of the same language who also deviate from one another in systematic and unsystematic ways (Spolsky, 1989: 35).

Another criterion which has frequently been evoked to justify the existence of institutionalised varieties of English is their stability. Stability, as pointed out earlier in this paper, is the loss of variability. It has been argued that all languages are unstable. Diachronic variability is testimony to this instability. Learner varieties are characteristically more unstable than adult grammers (Ellis, 1986). Therefore, if the variety of English used in Zimbabwe is to be considered as "localised," it must be empirically demonstrated to be more stable than an IL and as stable as any other full-fledged grammers.

The Makoni (1989) study shows that the use of English in Zimbabwe is variable at elementary, intermediate and even advanced levels of proficiency. The variability is attributed to a number of factors:

(1) the linguistic structure being investigated,
(2) the degree of plannedness of the discourse,
(3) the type of elicitation instrument used (Advanced second language users were variable in acceptability judgement tasks, suggesting that although their production was stable they had not yet attained stability at a competence level. Stability at a competence level is a prerequisite for localisation).

An examination of some of the reasons behind current interest in new Englishes

The aim of this section is to examine the hidden agenda behind current interest in "new Englishes." The reasons are an interesting mixture of history, sentiment and practical considerations.

I. *British and French Colonial Language Policies*

Historically, some of the reasons for the current interest in "new Englishes" can be attributed to the nature of British colonial policy as it related to languge. The French and Portuguese pursued a policy of direct rule which placed emphasis on colonial languages, leaving little room for the development of African local languages. The British, on the other hand, pursued a policy of indirect rule. Although the policy distinguished between the coloniser and the colonised, it encouraged the use and development of local languages (Wardhaugh, 1987). There is no "big jump" from the acceptance of local languages to the encouragement of the use of local varieties of English as a dignified area of applied linguistic research (Davies, 1986). The acceptance of localised varieties is a logical consequence of indirect rule, in as much as the reluctance to regard Senegalese or Togolese French as a direct outcome of French policy. The French insisted that the only variety of French which can be regarded as "true

French" is the one legitimated by the French Academy. The notion of "new Frenches" has not envolved because of the French "intolerance of dialects and xenophobic national linguistic purity" (Phillipson, 1991: 89).

II. *Localisation*

Localisation is a powerful factor in most African countries after independence and it operates at a number of different levels. It is most evident at the level of staffing or training as newly formed African govenments seek to replace expatriate staff with locally trained personnel. Similarly, the policy of localisation may be operational at a liguistic level as well, when scholars seek to achieve a level of liguistic independence commiserate with their political independence (Ferguson, 1988).

But there is one crucial difference which is usually quickly forgotten between localisation of staff and linguistic localisation. In education, generally, it is possible to train an apprentice to a degree of sophistication comparable with that of the expert, thus making the presence of the expert redundant particularly, if he/she is a foreigner. The situation is different in second language use, where, as a rule, a majority of learners fossilise before reaching native speaker competence (Davies, 1982). It is thus difficult to "localise" a second language in a way in which other areas of expertise may be indigenised.

III. *The Teaching Force*

The third factor which may stimulate interest in "localised" varieties arises from the indigenisation of the teaching force. Zimbabwe, for instance. has expanded its educational system tenfold since independence in 1980. The rapid educational expansion has meant that a majority of the pupils learning English are taught by non-white speakers whose level of proficiency is so low that they cannot be said to control the target language to any respectable degree. One way of rendering the variety of language the teachers used socially acceptable is to claim that the teachers are using a localised variety of English, hence the teachers are experts of that variety. Consequently, a comparison of the local variety with standard English is either aimed at giving validity to the limited proficiency or is a vote of confidence in the functional adequacy of a "restricted" code. My fear is that it is more of the former than the latter.

IV. *Pedagogical Implications*

In order for the local variety to be used as a teaching model, it has to be standardised. The standardisation will include the production of grammar books, textbooks, dictionaries, etc. Practically, whether the local variety is standardised will depend not only on whether it is more prestigious than the language used by the English native speaking community, but, more importantly, whether there are sufficient human and material resources for the standardisation to take place. The decision is an economic one, but it has clear sociolinguistic implications. With inflation currently running at above 20% and the country gripped in drought, there is keen competition for the limited resources. In such a situation, the government of Zimbabwe is unlikely to regard the standardisation of a local variety of English as one of its priorities when considering the allocation of its limited resources.

Conclusion

This paper has argued that the variety of English used in Zimbabwe is an IL, and not an institutionalised variety, such as Ghanaian English, Nigerian English, etc., because it has not yet been "localised" following the criteria:

(1) stability,
(2) native speaker norms, and
(3) degree of compactness within the speech community.

Nigerian and Ghanaian English ostensibly fulfill some, if not all, of the above criteria. The popularity of "new Englishes" is an indirect consequence of British colonial language policies, particularly its encouragement of the development of local "versions" of English.

References

Adjemian, C. (1976). "On the nature of the interlanguage systems" *Language Learning*, 26: 297-320.

Bloor, M. & T. Bloor (1990). "The role of English in resurgent Africa" *British Studies in Applied Linguistics*, 5: 32-44.

Corder, S. P. (1967). "The significance of learners' errors" *International Review of Applied Linguistics in Language Teaching*, 5: 160-170.

Corder, S.P. (1971). "Idiosyncratic dialects and error analysis" *International Review of Applied Linguistics in Language Teaching*, 9: 147-159.

Corder, S.P. (1981). *Error Analysis and Interlanguage*. Oxford: Oxford University Press.

Corder, S.P. (1985). *Introducing Applied Linguistics*. Harmondsworth, England: Penguin.

Crystal, D. (1988). *The English Language*. Harmondsworth, England: Penguin.

Davies, A. (1982). "Introduction to the special issue on language and ethnicity" *Journal of Multilingual and Multicultural Development*, 3(3): 153-160.

Davies, A. (ed.) (1986). "Introduction" in *Language in Education in Africa*, Centre for African Studies, University of Edinburgh Seminar Proceedings, No. 26: 1-17.

Davies. A., C. Criper, & A. P. R. Howatt (eds.) (1985). *Interlanguage*, Edinburgh: Edinburgh University Press.

Downes, W. (1988). *Language and Society*. London: Fontana.

Ellis. R. (1985). *Understanding Second Language Acquisition*. Oxford: Oxford University Press.

Ellis, R. (1986). "Developing interlanguage through fluency" *Focus*, 4: 23-39.

Ellis, R. (1987). "Interlanguage variability in narrative discourse. Styleshfting in the use of the past tense" *Studies in Second Language Acquisition*, 9: 1-20.

Ellis, R. (1988). "The effects of linguistic environment on the second language acquisition of grammatical rules" *Applied Linguistics*, 9(3): 257-274.

Ferguson, G. (1988). *Language Planning in Tanzania*. Unpublished Ph. D. thesis. University of Edinburgh.

Klein, W. (1986). *Second Language Acquistion*, Cambridge: Cambridge University Press.

Lass, R. (1987). *The Shape of English: Structure and History*. London: Dent and Sons Ltd,

Le-Page, R.B. & Tabouret-Keller, A. (1982). "Models and stereotypes of ethnicity and of language" in *Journal of Multilingual and Multicultural Development*, 3(3): 161-193.

Makoni, S. (1989). *Planning Variability in Second Language Acquisition*, Unublished Ph. D. thesis, University of Edinburgh, United Kingdom.

Makoni, S. (1991). "Arguments for and against free variation. *Edinburgh Working Papers in Applied Linguistics*, 2: 76-81.

Mateene, K. (1985). "Colonial anguages as compulsory means of domination, and indigenous languages, as necessary factors of liberation and development" In Mateene, Kalema, & Chomba, (eds.), *Linguistic Liberation and Unity of Africa*, Kampala: OAU Bureau of Languages, OAU/BIL Publication 6.

McGinley. K. (1989). "The future of English in Zimbabwe" *World Englishes*. 6(2): 159-164.

Nelson, C. L. (1988). "Why IVEs are not LOPOA's"

Unpublished paper presented June 1987, 22nd annual TESOL Convention, Los Angeles.

Nemser, W. (1971). "Approximative systems of foreign language learners" *International Review of Applied Linguistics in Language Teaching*, 9: 115-123.

Ngara, E. A. (1982). *Bilingualism, Language Contact and Planning: Proposals for Language Use and Language Teaching in Zimbabwe*. Mambo Press, Harare.

Omodiaogbe, S. A. (1992). "150 years on: English in Nigeria" *ELT Journal*, 46(1): 19-29.

Phillipson, R. (1991). "Some items on the hidden agenda of Second/Foreign language acquisition" In R. Phillipson, E. Kellerman, L. Selinker, M. Sharwood Smith, & M. Swain, (eds.), *Foreign/Second Language Pedagogy Research*, (pp. 38-52). Clevedon, England: Multilingual Matters.

Platt, T. & H. Webber (1980). *English in Singapore and Malaysia: Status, Features, Functions*, Kuala Lumpur: Oxford University Press.

Preston, D. (1989). *Sociolinguistics and Second Language Acquisition*, London: Basil Blackwell.

Quirk, R. (1989). "Separated by a common dilemma" *The Times Higher Educational Supplement*, 10(2).

Selinker, L. (1972). "Interlanguage" *International Review of Applied Linguistics in Language Teaching*, X: 209-230.

Sharwood Smith, M. (1991). "IL, conceptual confusions and new beginnings" In R. Phillipson, E. Kellerman, L. Selinker, M. Sharwood Smith, & M. Swains, (eds.), *Foreign/Second Language Pedagogy Research*, (pp. 92-103), Clevedon, England: Multilingual Matters.

Sorace, A. (1990). "Interdeterminacy in first and second languages, theoretical and methodological issues" In de Jong & D. K. Stevenson, (eds.) *Individualising the Assessment of Language Abilities*, (pp. 127-154), Clevedon, England: Multiligual Matters.

Spolsky, B. (1980). "Bilingualism and iliteracy"*Canadian Modern Language Review*, 37: 475-485.
Spolsky, B. (1990). *Conditions for Second Language Learning*. Oxford: Oxford University Press.
Spolsky, B. (1990). "English and endangered languages" Paper read at a conference on language in Venezuela, 1990.
Stubbs, M. (1986). *Educational Linguistics*. London: Basil Blackwell.
Wardhaugh, R. (1987). *Languages in Competition*. London: Basil Blackwell.

VI

Naming Practices and Language Planning in Zimbabwe
(with Busi Makoni and Pedzisai Mashiri)

Abstract
Studies of African naming practices focus almost exclusively on the meanings and etymology of names and details about the circumstances surrounding how such names are assigned. Such research has not examined the implications naming has for language planning, ideologies of language, and language shift. Focusing on names and naming practices in Zimbabwe from 1960 to 1990, this paper departs from this well-established tradition. The paper provides empirical evidence to show that naming provides significant insights into language planning, language ideology, language shift and the development of new varieties of English. It demonstrates the effects of non-Standard English on naming practices between the 1960s and 1990s and how this subsequently brought changes not only to the use of African languages, but also to use of names drawn from non-Standard English. This we view as an indication that the policy of promoting indigenous African languages is in sync with practice as ordinary citizens articulate their cultural practices in African languages. In addition, the promotion of English results in the spread not of standard English, but of nonstandard varieties of English in the area of naming.

Introduction
Research into the discursive construction of naming in Southern Africa is carried out largely in the linguistic subfields of onomastics and ethno-linguistics. In spite of the potential significance that a study of onomastics has for wider phenomena such as identity and language planning, it has remained, until recently, an area of marginal significance in linguistics (Joseph, 2004). Thus one of the major goals of this article is to analyse the nature of naming practices as a prism through which to conceptualise language planning. The article explores changes in naming between 1960 and 1990. Naming is susceptible to change. It is therefore conceivable that new naming practices have emerged as a result of the contact that Africans had with colonialism, Christianity, and Western education in the early part of the 20th century.

In sociolinguistics, a distinction is drawn between corpus planning and status planning (Fishman, 2004). Corpus planning is an instance of language standardisation manifested in the creation of new words, the modification of old ones, and the selection of words among competing forms (Cooper, 1989). Naming is largely an instance of corpus planning that involves the creation of new words and selection among alternative forms. A study of naming therefore brings into focus the distinction between corpus and status planning. The question a study of naming practices raises is: to what extent does status planning have a spill-over effect on corpus planning.

This paper analyses the nature of language planning in Zimbabwe from the perspective of naming of Africans between 1960 and 1990. Indeed, there is a vast amount of, and a continuously growing, literature on language planning in Africa, and on naming (see, e.g. Afful, 2005; Akinnaso, 1981; Alford, 1988; Bangeni & Coetser, 2000; Herbert & Bogatsu, 2001; Koopman, 1989; Suzman, 1994) but rarely has there been any systematic research into language planning carried out from the viewpoint of naming, particularly in Zimbabwe. An analysis of the naming practices of Zimbabweans is opportune, because of an increasing interest in the daily linguistic practices of ordinary citizens and their impact on language policies. Naming as an instance of language use sheds light on the effects of language planning on everyday language usage. This may lead to a development of models in which the common person is directly involved. Currently, the "common man – the 'consumer' of LP programmes – is present only by proxy, carrying the elite 'cross'" (Khubchandani, 1983: 149). It is mainly the educated custodians of languages who decide "what is 'good' for the masses, by virtue of their hold on the socio-political literary scene" (Khubchandani, 1983: 149). If research into naming opens up possibilities of including the common person in a serious anthropological sense, on their own terms, and not on the scholars', then there is a possibility that there might be closure on issues about status planning (Fishman, 1990).

The rationale in choosing the period from 1960 to 1990 is that each of these three decades reflect three different historical epochs in the history of Zimbabwe. The 1960s reflect the early years of nationalism, whilst the 1970s are characterised by the rise of African nationalism in which nationalists used African languages as part of military activities (Ranger, 1985). There are indications that there were significant changes in naming as suggested by Ranger when he writes:

> If in the 1930's no one in Makoni would have described themselves as 'Shona' by the late 1950's, when the nationalist movement came to the district, very many people thought in such terms. (Ranger, 1989: 243)

In this regard, the Shona language had become a powerful symbol of and instrument in the constitution of an ethnic idea in the rapidly modernising country.

Furthermore, the inclusion of names of those born in the 1970s is intended to explore the extent to which the nationalistic ideology had permeated Zimbabwean society and the degree to which this was reflected in naming.

The 1980s were marked by celebrations of many types of freedoms, political, religious, and cultural. Language was widely used to express these freedoms. Children born during this period were popularly referred to as 'born free' (Chitando, 1998: 116). During the colonial period, the Christian arena was dominated and monopolised by the main line missionary churches, for example Anglican, Lutheran, Wesleyan Methodist and Roman Catholic. Language use and naming practices tended to reflect the missionary discursive regimes. Politically-minded parents who spoke chiShona gave their children names such as *Rusununguko* ('Freedom'), or *Nkululeko* ('Freedom') in Ndebele and *Tongai* ('Govern') in Shona. Other parents who were affiliated to new Pentecostal churches gave their children pragmatic and creative names such as *Tineruvimbo* ('We have hope'), *Mutsawashe* ('God's grace') and *Petiri* ('God got us where we are').

In the Matebeleland region the celebration of the three freedoms was short lived as the North Korean trained Fifth Brigade popularly known as the Gukurahundi ('the storm that thunders') descended into the region and killed innocent civilians. The effects of this onslaught were also reflected in names of children born during that period. Names such as *Phephelaphi* ('where shall we go'), *Senzeni* ('what have we done'), *Soneni* ('what wrong did we do') and *Siphamandla* ('God give us strength to endure this torture') were prevalent. These names served as a meta-commentary on the repressive military regime that operated in the Matebeleland region.

The 1990s were a postcolonial period that, presumably, had a different language ideology, which has effects on language planning. The 1990's marked an amplification of invented binary distinctions between what is imagined as the imperial west, and the friendly eastern countries or what is termed by the Zimbabwean government as "the look east policy". In terms of language policy, this has translated into the formation of Confucian language centers in which local Zimbabweans are taught Chinese. (Local Zimbabweans have also responded by jokingly referring to Air Zimbabwe as *Air Zhim* and all products from China as *Zhungzhung*.) The discourses of language domination in Zimbabwe have become rather complicated by the potential emergence of Chinese as a possible competitor for space with English both commercially and academically as reflected in the setting up of Confucian centres.

Further binary distinctions were drawn between indigenous Zimbabweans and those defined as non-indigenous Zimbabweans, or those without a totem. A totem is imagined as a marker of cultural integrity in Zimbabwe. More nuanced distinctions were also made between indigenous Zimbabweans who had taken part in the liberation war and those who had not. Another set of new distinctions also emerged between Zimbabweans within Zimbabwe and those who are part of the diaspora. Zimbabweans outside the country were then regarded as *injiva* ('gold diggers'). In return Zimbabweans who are part of the diaspora view the name of Zimbabwe derogatively as an acronym for Zero Income Mainly Because All Brainy Workers Emigrated.

The period 1960–1990 thus enables us to examine the nature of language shift over three decades. Interest in language shift has been revived recently by continuing research into and public concern with language endangerment (Batibo, 2005; Makoni *et al.*, 2007; Mufwene, 2002; Nettle & Romaine, 2000; Phillipson, 2003; Skutnabb-Kangas, 2000). Scholarly concern with the nature of naming over three decades shows that some patterns become clearer over the *longue durée* (see Makoni *et al.*, 2007).

There are two main arguments in the literature with regard to language shift in Africa which have implications for language planning. First, it is stated that language shift is towards urban vernaculars rather than English (Abdulaziz &

Osinde, 1997; Childs, 1997; Githiora, 2002; Makoni et al., 2007; Spitulnik, 1988; Swigart, 2000). Secondly, it is suggested that the increasing domination of African languages by English constitutes a threat to the continued vitality of indigenous African languages (Batibo, 2005; Nettle & Romaine, 2000). In this article these claims are subjected to analysis in one clearly defined domain, i.e. personal names. However, language shift is narrowly defined as a shift in the choice of the language of naming.

On the other hand, research into language planning in Zimbabwe focuses on analysing either the changes or the continuities in the nature of language planning choices which colonial and postcolonial African governments made regarding English and African languages and the role both languages play in education and their current national status (Chimhundu, 1993; Mkanganwi, 1992; Roy-Campbell & Gwete, 1997; Viriri, 2003). In this paper, we explore the effects of these policies on naming in Zimbabwe. We analyse what this shows in terms of ideologies of language as part of a general interest in how, from a local perspective, people relate to and discursively construct this choice in the ways they name others. We investigate the changes in naming between 1960 and 1990 as indicative of Africans' attempts to balance interest in African languages and English while constructing their own identities simultaneously: a phenomenon relevant to language planning.

The paper concentrates on the sociolinguistic aspects of personal names as well as their discursive construction. It situates them within the broader theoretical views on language planning and ideologies of language or what Fabian (1986) calls critical historiography, that is research into historical changes in reflections about language. Of particular concern are those names Africans created and derived from known English lexical items used as words or compounds and then converted into proper names within African contexts of English usage. This is a process of linguistic derivation consistent with studies into New Englishes (Kamwangamalu, 1998; Magura, 1985). Examples of these include names such as *Belief, Sinfree, Eventhough, Sweetbetter, Kissmore, Conermore* (sic) and *Donemore*.

Most of these names appear dialectal and sound humorous, idiosyncratic and sometimes nonsensical and weird to non-Zimbabweans and English native speakers, but are consistent with the social and linguistic formations of New Englishes (Kachru, 1985). This paper demonstrates that these names are significant not only for their morphology and lexical meaning, but for the indexical and symbolic functions and the meanings they carry. The names embody individual or family social experiences, encode a message, express a wish, feelings, hope or prayer, and record something about the past or simply the parent's desires for the future, desires which are articulated through English. The meanings of these names are tied to their contexts; hence in some cases it may be difficult to understand them without the necessary background information supplied by the one who did the naming. Insight into the nature of the macro-context in which English is learnt helps us enhance the analyst's understanding of the meaning of the name (Brutt-Griffler, 2003).

The names discussed in this paper reveal how people, who at times had limited exposure to and fleeting encounters with English, appropriate it, consequently leaving an indelible mark on their socio-cultural experiences and sense of self. The crucial issue is that some of these individuals elect to record their intimate experiences in some form of English when they have other options. At times they use African languages or standardise them to render the names consistent with codified African languages. The fact that even the illiterate feel they have a claim to English, and want to be identified through a variety of English which they speak, is a far cry from feelings of being dominated by English. This underscores the importance of bringing into the picture the views of those who are directly affected by language policies, something which has not always been the case [see the arguments by Swigart (2000) and

Skutnabb-Kangas (2000); but see Canagarajah (2005) as an example of a bold move to incorporate local knowledge about language practices in non-Western contexts].

This paper is conceptualised as a contribution to language planning through an analysis of the study of ideologies of language in Africa (Blommaert, 2005; Makoni & Pennycook, 2007; Woolard & Schieffelin, 1994). Ideologies of language are contextual sets of beliefs about languages (Pennycook, 2007). The ways in which languages are constructed is never about language only, but also about how individuals are thought about in society and understandings about how "languages are always definitions about human beings in the world" (Woolard & Schieffelin, 1994: 55). In this particular article, ideologies of language are examined through naming in Zimbabwe from 1960 to 1990.

Analyses of the languages used in naming provide opportunities to explore the extent to which language policies have an impact on naming. An analysis of the naming practices is important as language planning shifts from top-down perspectives towards an understanding of how ordinary individuals react to language policies (Canagarajah, 2005; Mphande, 2006; Ramanathan, 2005; Summers, 2002).

Research into onomastics is not concerned with language planning. Similarly, language planning is not concerned with naming and identity (see Alexander, 1995; Ferguson, 2006; Kamwangamalu, 1998). By exploring the nature of language planning through naming, this article brings together three areas of scholarship typically kept distinct and separate in sociolinguistics: onomastics, the emergence of New Englishes, and language planning.

Background to the Language Situation in Zimbabwe
In order to situate the analysis of naming in Zimbabwe between 1960 and 1990 we begin with a brief description of the geography and history of Zimbabwe and a description of its linguistic

profile. This is followed by a description of the history of language planning in Zimbabwe from the perspectives of a number of agents: Christian missionaries, colonial governments, and nationalist movements and contemporary Zimbabwean government, all of whom have been involved in language planning in Zimbabwe.

Zimbabwe is a landlocked country with an area of 390,757 km2 (150,698 square miles), situated in the southern part of Africa between Victoria Falls and the Kariba dam to the north, and the Limpopo River to the south. It is surrounded by South Africa to the south, Botswana to the west, Zambia to the north, and Mozambique to the east. The 2002 national census gives the Zimbabwean population as 11,631,657. This is made up of Shona 71%, Ndebele 16%, other African 11%, Asian 1% and European 1% (Makoni *et al.*, 2006).

From the 12th century, the land now referred to as Zimbabwe was under the control of the Shona although they did not call themselves by that name. In 1827 the Ndebele conquered part of Zimbabwe and formed the state of Matabeleland. After Cecil John Rhodes (who gave Zimbabwe its former name Rhodesia) obtained a series of lucrative mineral concessions, the land fell under the influence of the British. In 1923 the Whites voted against the option of being incorporated into the Union of South Africa. In 1965 the Prime Minister Ian Smith declared Unilateral Independence from the British, a declaration which was regarded as illegal and unconstitutional. The period 1965 to 1979 was characterised by a war led by the nationalists. In 1980 in the newly named Zimbabwe, the Zimbabwe African Nationalist Union under the leadership of Robert Mugabe won after the first elections which resulted from the British-mediated Lancaster House Constitution.

The first decade of Zimbabwe (1980–1990) was characterised by attempts on the part of Africans to reconcile themselves to Whites politically, but the Whites still retained considerable economic influence over land, mining, and the commercial sector. Due to a series of short-sighted economic policies, poor governance, and pressures from powerful institutions such as the World Bank, the Zimbabwean state has been faced by a series of crises. The emergence of the Movement for Democratic Change (MDC) in the 1990s from a combination of civic and labour organisations heralded a new phase in Zimbabwean politics. The MDC posed the first serious threat to the dominance of a government formed by African liberation fighters. The Mugabe regime, within Zimbabwe and internationally, has managed to successfully split Black opposition against it through a powerful and astute deployment of an anti-imperialistic ideological offensive, while at the same time carrying out a "very specific, repressive class project" (Raftopolous 2006: 214) which conceals elite black accumulation of wealth and the compromising of human rights.

The redistribution of land has been projected by the Mugabe regime as a key marker of anti-imperialism, while his opponents have interpreted it as a reflection of its authoritarian politics. Debates in Zimbabwe are not only over land, but also over representation of its past, who is a Zimbabwean and who is not, what is indigenous and what is not. The rhetoric of the Mugabe regime has projected an essentialised view of race as central to African politics. The effects of the discursive regimes of race, indigeneity, anti-imperialism on language policy and language practices is an issue which still needs to be explored.

The official languages of Zimbabwe are English, chiShona and Ndebele, referred to in the Zimbabwean Education Act of 1987, amended in 2006, as 'main languages'. Black Zimbabweans are divided into two major language groups, namely Shona and Ndebele, but there are many other minority African languages – Lozi, Sena, Dombe, Nambya, Kalanga, Tonga, Sotho, Venda, Shangane, Hwesa, Chikunda, Doma, Tswana, Khoisan, Barwe, Fingo/isiXhosa – which are hardly ever written about (Hachipola, 1998; Mphande, 2006). The official languages are used as media of instruction even in situations in which these are not the first languages of the students. Teachers may also be deployed to schools in which they do not necessarily share a common language with the students, thereby rendering English the 'first' among equals in the languages of the state.

Although English is widely used in Zimbabwe it retains a class dimension not adequately captured in paradigms of New Englishes (Kachru, 1985). The localisation and spread of English is tied to the emergence of new class distinctions reflecting the importance of combining ethnic and class factors when analysing the macro-contexts within which English is acquired (Brutt-Griffler, 2003). Students who have English as a first language and an African language as a second language have higher social status than those who have an African language as a first language and English as a second language (Makoni et al. 2006). Those who have African languages as first languages and English as a second language disparagingly regard Black African students who have English as a first language as 'salads'.

Linguistic maps such as those produced by Ethnologue fail to capture the complexities of Zimbabwe's sociolinguistic situation in which a majority of Ndebele speakers also speak chiShona and English as additional languages. There is also considerable inter-ethnic marriage reflected in part in the use of names from different ethnic groups. For instance, names such as *Phumelele Makoni* and *Simangaliso Makoni* reflect interethnic origins in that *Phumelele* and *Simangaliso* are Nguni names whilst *Makoni* is chiShona. Similarly names such as *Tarisai Khumalo* and *Tendai Zondo* reflect the same phenomenon in that *Tarisai* and *Tendai* are Shona names whereas *Khumalo* and *Zondo* reflect Ndebele ethnicity. The relationship between naming and ethnicity is, however, complicated by the fact that in some cases people have names from an ethno-linguistic group which is not indicative of any intermarriage as both parents may be of the same ethnic group. For example, during data collection in 2006 in Victoria Falls, researchers encountered Rumbidzai who is ethnically Nambya and yet the name Rumbidzai is from chiShona.

Colonial and Post-Colonial Language Policy and Planning Practices

This section is a synopsis of language policies in Zimbabwe from the colonial era to the present. For an expanded analysis of language policies in Zimbabwe see Makoni *et al.* (2006). In colonial Zimbabwe, one of the major objectives of language policies was the development of a bilingual white colonial ruling class proficient in both English and at least one African language, as there were fears in many British colonies about Africans becoming fluent in English "because this erased one of the important markers of difference between indigenous and white populations" (Jeater, 2006; see also Mazrui & Mazrui, 1998: 141, who raise a similar point about Kenya). Post-colonial policies were initially formulated as an integral part of a nation-building project whose ultimate objective, albeit unsuccessfully, was to override ethnic, linguistic, and social class differences.

In order to overcome the problem of acquiring African languages without enhancing the status of Africans, it was necessary for colonial authorities to appropriate African languages. One of the steps in the appropriation of African languages is through linguistic standardisation.

The codification of these languages was carried out within a structuralist framework of language in which the individual identities of the language users are of secondary significance. This was done in order to establish an image of scientific objectivity in the construction of African languages (Errington, 2007; Irvine & Gal, 2001). Analysing naming practices is thus important for two reasons. It serves as a prism which has rarely been used in an analysis of the language of language planning in Africa because of the focus on cognitive and geopolitical issues. Theoretically, an analysis of naming is also important because it reintroduces into the analysis of the language of language planning a human dimension, thereby rendering language a human communicative activity and not only a cognitive *cum* neural entity.

When a human dimension is introduced into an analysis of the language of language planning, naming practices are consequently construed as 'acts of identity' (Haugen, 1971; Le Page & Tabouret-Keller, 1985). Language thus ceases to be a 'thing', an 'entity', but is transformed into a human communicative activity. The objectification of language leads policy makers to think in terms of who has languages, how many people can be persuaded to have them, or how people can be given these languages. Language is thus portrayed as if it is "akin to having access to clean water, fuel, or food" so that accessing them would produce cognitive and material benefits (Pennycook, 2004: 149).

A perspective that regards naming as central has implications for how language planning is construed. In such a perspective the goal of language planning is not the promotion of languages, but changing the political and economic status of individuals by enhancing communication between them. The promotion of language does not necessarily improve the social welfare of the speakers, as the South African story amply demonstrates as refl ected in the studies into poverty among Africans in South Africa (Buhlungu *et al.*, 2006). However, the converse may be true, i.e. improving the social welfare of people may indeed change the status of languages.

Theoretically treating naming practices either as 'acts of identity' (Le Page & Tabouret-Keller, 1985) or discursive practices may lead scholars to challenge the dichotomy between language structure and use (Joseph, 2006). It also prevents scholars from uncritically accepting the dichotomy between corpus planning (structure) and status planning (use) on the one hand, and on the other, encourages them to be sceptical of the tendency to endorse the view that corpus planning is technical, and status planning is political.

A large amount of the extant literature on language policy published during the colonial era in Zimbabwe emphasises the imposition of English on African languages (Mkanganwi, 1992; Viriri, 2003). And yet a more nuanced reading of the colonial language policies suggests that what was being imposed during the colonial era was not English on Africans, but European interlanguages of African languages on Europeans as reflected in the names of towns such as Umtali and Gwelo for Mutare and Gweru respectively. Linguistic description was therefore a political act. Through linguistic description, Europeans appropriated African languages as a prelude to the imposition of European variants of African languages on Africans under the guise of the promotion of indigenous language. Codification was a defensive act. African languages, even in their linguistic forms or structures, were political and discursive constructs although the orthodox view is to restrict the political dimensions of African languages to analysis of status planning and to regard corpus planning as apolitical and a technical exercise. But as Joseph (2006: 20) points out "Languages are political from top to bottom". If languages are political, the metalanguages used to describe them are equally political (Bauman & Briggs, 2003; Errington, 2007; Makoni & Pennycook, 2007) including their linguistic forms. An analysis of the naming practices is therefore not only an analysis of linguistic form but also of the politics of language, and therefore helps in comprehending the nature and character of the daily political decisions Africans made about language.

The tendency to create and promote African interlanguages out of the mother tongues of conquered peoples was a strategy which was also followed by previous African ethnic groups when they conquered other Africans. Despite the power and influence of the colonial regime, Africans still retained a strong sense of agency. This sense of agency enabled them to select, albeit within restricted limits, the nature and type of education they received, the languages through which they were taught, and indeed even the materials which were used in teaching them languages, particularly English (Summers, 2002). In some cases enterprising Africans set up, managed, and administered their own schools. This is evident from the story of Gonye who set up his own school at which he was a teacher, preacher and administrator in Masvingo in Zimbabwe (oral family narrative, 13 July 2006).

Naming Practices and Personal Names: A Literature Review
Naming is one area of study in both onomastic and ethnographic literature that has been extensively investigated (Lawson & Laimute, 1996; Lubisi, 2002; Moyo, 1996; Rapoo, 2002; Suzman, 1994). In Southern Africa research into naming is carried out in onomastics. It focuses on how places and people are named (de Klerk & Bosch, 1995; Mashiri, 2003; Moyo, 1996). The interest in naming geographical sites is stimulated by the ongoing changes in the naming of places and buildings in Zimbabwe. In fact, one of the most visible signs of political change is in the names of cities, roads and airports. For example, in 1980 the name Zimbabwe was officially used to refer to the country previously referred to as Rhodesia; there are a number of variants of Zimbabwe (*dzimbabwe, dzimbahwe*). The term Zimbabwe is a generic term for a stone dwelling. The name change to Zimbabwe is significant in language policy. It is significant because it signals an effort to assert the importance and official status of African languages, which as policy were meant to filter to ordinary Africans. Since *Zimbabwe* is a Shona term it reflects the extent to which Shona was *de facto* being made the 'superior' language by some Zimbabwean nationalists because it was the language being used in the name of the country, and the one through which the country was being imagined. It is therefore interesting from a language planning perspective that in spite of the superior status which Shona was being awarded, individuals still tended to use personal names, such as *Moreangels, Nevermore* and *Sweetbetter*, drawn from non-Standard English.

Recognition of African language names in preference to non-African names is also evident in the change of place names, especially names of towns soon after Zimbabwe attained its independence. For example, in Zimbabwe, the following name changes have occurred since 1980.

(1) Salisbury to Harare
(2) Gatooma to Kadoma
(3) Fort Victoria to Masvingo
(4) Wankie to Hwange

Similarly, in South Africa the name of the town Pietersburg changed to Polokwane while Naboomspruit changed to Bela-Bela after South Africa attained its independence in 1994. A number of other towns will also be affected, as their names will also be changed. The shifts in the above examples are characterised by a change to African languages, where a place name was in English. When the name was in an African language the shift is from a Europeanised version of African languages to an indigenised version of the name as shown by the shift from Umtali to Mutare, Wankie to Hwange and Tjolotjo to Tsholotsho.

Evidence of the use of Europeanised versions of African languages is critical because it demonstrates that it is simplistic to argue that British colonial rulers were always imposing English on Africans. In fact, what they were imposing were their own versions of African languages, as illustrated in the opening section of this paper. How Africans responded to European variants of African languages and their own Africanised versions of English through the naming practices which they adopted is the subject of this paper. The fact that there were European variants of African languages and these were perceived as such by Africans means that African languages were rarely regarded as single entities, but *each* language was regarded as variable, multiple, and conflictual. The unitary language is "not something given (dan) but is always posited (zadan) – and at every moment of its life it is opposed to the realities of heteroglossia" (Bakhtin, 1934/1981: 270). Thus, heteroglossia was always the norm (Bakhtin, 1934/1981).

Place names provide an important framework for language planning. The shift from European place names or Europeanised versions of place names to indigenised names of African languages reflects a shift in terms of policy towards African languages. Although the place names were officially in English or Europeanised versions of African languages, the Africans typically referred to the places using their African names. So Salisbury was always Harare amongst Africans, and Umtali was always Mutare as well. This suggests that the policy shift in naming was consistent with the language practices of ordinary Africans. Policy and practice were in sync after the changes as far as place names are concerned.

Discursive Construction of the Languages of Personal Names

There are two different strands of naming in African sociolinguistics, i.e. first, the linguistics of naming of languages and, secondly, the naming of individuals. The main focus of this paper is the latter, the naming of individuals. We will only comment briefly on the former, i.e. the naming of languages, to point to its relevance to language planning. The naming of languages is part of a project of 'governmentality' (Foucault, 1977) in which colonial governments develop encyclopaedic inventories (Fabian, 1986; Makoni & Mashiri, 2007). Some of these linguistic forms which were subsequently called 'languages' were not necessarily labelled prior to colonialism as "naming languages is an artifact embedded in the consciousness of Western formal education" (Makoni *et al.*, 2003: 3). The names given to African languages were not new, but had completely different meanings. For example, the terms *Korekore* and *Zezuru* were nicknames for highlanders and northerners that were subsequently used as ethnic labels. Naming contributed to a conflation of ethnicity and language proficiency, leading to circularity in definition: a Zulu spoke Zulu, a Yoruba spoke Yoruba (see Blommaert, 2005; Rampton, 1997). The study of the discursive construction of naming practices in Africa has enjoyed a lot of attention because of the interest in how "names and naming practices vary and reflect patterns of social organisation' (Herbert & Bogatsu, 2001: 2). In Zimbabwe, Pongweni's (1983) research into names is an important, groundbreaking study on the discursive construction of naming practices. However, while Pongweni's research is insightful, it has serious limitations. One of its limitations is that it is impressionistic. It does not address whether the language ideologies of African language speakers changed towards New Englishes over a historical period. From a methodological point of view Pongweni's study is also flawed. The analysis of the meanings of names is based on what the researcher thinks they mean without taking into consideration the voices of those who assigned the names. The data were also not collected systematically. The researcher randomly analysed names he came across and thought were interesting to him. In spite of the weaknesses of Pongweni's research this article is a continuation of his work.

Renewed interest in naming has focused on the ways in which naming interacts with aspects related to cultural change. As urbanisation and other colonial developments took their toll on African communities, many cultural practices were under pressure to survive in an environment often not conducive to their preservation.

Much has been written on the development of a Christian and colonial naming tradition in Africa. Consequently, the adoption of English names among Africans is attributed to the coercive power of Christianity and colonialism (Guma, 2001; Mathangwane & Gardener, 1998; Neethling, 2003; Saarelma-Maunumaa, 1996). Writing on perceptions of English names of Xhosa speakers, Neethling writes:

With the introduction of Christianity and education as practised by the mission schools to Xhosa speakers in the early 19th century, came a new development. English names were bestowed upon Xhosa children by the missionaries (at baptism) and by teachers (at school). These were often referred to as 'church' and 'school' names. (Neethling, 2003; 47)

Whilst Neethling (2003) identifies teachers and missionaries as name-givers, there are indications that community members act as name-givers as well. Suzman (1994) suggests that the identity of name-givers is "varied and extensive". In Zimbabwe white native affairs administrators and employers also re-named black Africans indiscriminately with certain English names. These names "served to tag black people as an imposition" (Bangeni & Coetser, 2000: 61). Because whites found African names difficult to pronounce, these tags facilitated communication between whites and blacks.

Discussions with different members of the communities in Zimbabwe indicate that naming is not confined to parents and guardians only. Anyone in the community can assign a name to any individual in the language of the namegiver's preference irrespective of its sociolinguistic status. This seems to be in sharp contrast with other Southern African ethnic groups. For example, Herbert and Bogatsu (2001) report that in South Africa, Northern Sotho and Tswana naming is confined to family members rather than extended to community members at large.

Naming may not only take place at early stages of the life course, but may occur at any stage across the lifespan. There are instances of individuals changing their names and naming themselves at later stages in their lives. This phenomenon seems widespread in most African and African American communities. Mphande (2006: 108) points out that "changing a personal name to suit the prevailing socio-cultural or political environment is nothing new in African history. Because they are a social commentary, names can be changed to indicate contemporary sociopolitical situations". In fact, a number of former combatants in Zimbabwe's war of liberation changed their names after independence. Thus, one former combatant who was assigned the name Hitler at birth changed his name to Chenjerai in 1980, shortly after independence.

The process of re-naming and self-identification suggests that Africans were and are not passive recipients of names imposed on them by a dominant system or by any other person. That Africans had a sense of agency in determining how they were named or gave themselves names is not to deny that this took place in a context in which they did not necessarily have full control of the socioeconomic contexts in which they lived. The act of naming oneself therefore reveals that naming and, in particular, names serve "as an indicator of broader social change and as devices for explaining and classifying patterns of domination and submission" (Alia, 1984: 34).

Although naming is a private act, its effects have public significance since, in a situation like Zimbabwe and possibly other African countries, it reflects the reactions to English. These responses to English have always been and continue to be an issue of major language planning concern since parents constitute one of the biggest constituencies directly affected by changes in language status. As a rule, their reactions are not taken into account in language planning decisions as these are based on impersonal macro-political, economic and cognitive factors. These factors rarely take into account onomastic factors because of a prioritisation of the arguments of the language activists rather than of those affected by the language planning decisions (Alexander, 1995). The continuation of an English onomastic tradition even among the illiterate reflects the tenacity of African parents' reactions to English. It also reflects the tenuous nature of the link between the discourses of the academy on language planning and the subaltern views about language. It is this widening gulf which needs to be reduced, in order to enable non-language experts to effectively take part in important decisions affecting their lives.

Discursive Construction of Personal Names and Surnames

Mphande (2006: 109), in drawing a distinction between personal names and surnames, sums up this distinction as follows:

> While surnames may refer to collective and more historical experiences, first, or given, names comment on more temporary social issues and are thus more relevant in deciphering the social atmosphere at a given time. Apart from indicating an individual's relationship with a physical and social environment, names are also statements about religion and the beliefs of the speakers and their relationship with the supernatural. Personal names thus provide a barometer for measuring changes in attitudes and moral codes at specific historical epochs.

This distinction between personal names and surnames is a postcolonial phenomenon. For example, most of the heroines of colonial rule in Zimbabwe are referred to by personal names only, for example Kaguvi, Nehanda (Pongweni, 1983). Because people belonging to the same clan share a surname, personal names are important for purposes of identity marking. However, while personal names are variable, in that the same individual may have different names, there may indeed be some limited variation in their use. For example, in some instances a totem may be used instead of a surname; thus, a *Makoni*, which is a surname, may be called *Nyati*, a totem; whilst a *Dube* would be known as *Mthembo*. Although totems or clan names can be used instead of surnames, their use is generally very restricted.

The extent to which surnames provide insight into language planning is limited, although in some cases surnames provide insight into differences in terms of the status of the languages in Zimbabwe. Mumpande (2006) enumerates a number of instances in which Tonga speakers had their surnames spelt wrongly on their national registration cards because of the limited proficiency in Tonga by either Ndebele or Shona government officials. The Tonga people construe this to be a violation of section 22 of the Zimbabwean Constitution which forbids discrimination on the grounds of race, ethnicity or language. The argument put forward by the Tonga is that if the Zimbabwean government seriously took into account the importance of minority languages such as Tonga then it would, at least, appoint government officials proficient in Tonga in the national registration offices. Interestingly, there are also instances in which Tonga surnames are changed to Ndebele voluntarily in order for Tonga speakers to pass for Ndebele as shown in the examples below (Mumpande, 2006: 25).

Tonga	**Ndebele**
Mudenda	*Dube*
Munsaka	*Ndlovu*
Muleya	*Tshuma*

That Tonga surnames are being changed to Ndebele reflects Ndebele hegemony because of the linguistic inequality between languages in Zimbabwean languages.

Africans use English names as personal names and yet rarely are English surnames used in Zimbabwe amongst blacks. However, among first generation Malawian Zimbabweans, the use of English personal names or common names as surnames is popular. These were either the names that were given to them by their white employers or, in some cases, they may have picked the names as a result of interaction with their employers or members of their employer's family. The names then became surnames for their children. As a result, there are ethnic differences in the propensity to use English non-standard names as surnames between, Shona and Ndebele and Malawian Zimbabweans.

Because of the consistency with which surnames have been used across generations among Zimbabweans, these will be excluded from the analysis of names in this paper.

In African languages personal names provide details about what the namers felt was important and the circumstances surrounding the child's birth (de Klerk & Bosch, 1995). They also describe the nature of the prevailing political and social contexts in which an individual is born. Drawing on examples from famous figures may best illustrate this point. Shaka, a famous Zulu King, was born out of wedlock and his mother had to hide the pregnancy. As the pregnancy advanced, it was rumoured that she had an incurable disease that made her stomach grow abnormally big. This disease was referred to as *isiShaka* ('an unknown incurable disease').[1]

Since naming in African societies plays a significant role in identity marking, analysing how the name is discursively constructed as a text and the language of the name is crucial. It provides insight into the namer's attitude towards the language of the name. Attitudes towards the language of the name are critical in understanding the possible effects of language planning. This is important, as namers are not limited to members of the immediate family. For example, Nelson Mandela's other personal name is *Rolihlahla* and yet the world calls him *Nelson*. He was given the name on entering school, as he reports in his autobiography:

> On the first day of school my teacher, Miss Mdingane, gave each of us an English name . . . Miss Mdingane told me that my new name was Nelson. Why she bestowed this particular name on me I have no idea. Perhaps, it had something to do with ... Lord Nelson, but that would only be a guess. (Mandela, 1994: 13)

---

[1] In Shaka's praise names this information is captured when the praise singer refers to him as *isiShaka kasishayeki* ('the disease cannot be cured').

That students are given school names different from those they have at home widens the gap between home and school. The student subsequently has an identity at school which is different from that at home. Thus the difference between the home and school is not limited to the fact that the language used at school is different from that used at home, but that the child carried with them different identities at home and school, rendering it diffi cult for the child to utilise what they have learnt at home and in school, and vice versa. This means that trying to make the language at school approximate that at home, however desirable it is, is not a panacea for the problems which children confront at school and does not overcome the home/school divide.

While some people seem to use a number of names interchangeably, others refect a shift towards a radical orientation in which they explicitly state their preference for the use of names with a clear African language etymology. For example, in South Africa, the Eastern Cape Premier, Arnold Stofile, changed his name to *Makhenkesi Stofile*. The South African Minister of Defense, Patrick Terror Lekota, changed his name to *Mosioua Lekota*, thus dropping the two English names. In Zimbabwe a famous literary scholar changed his name from *European* to *Tafadzwa*, a name drawn from chiShona. Since "naming practices provide an important window on the construction of ethnic identities" (Harrison, 2000: 11), in the above examples the change of name reflects self-identification as an affirmation of ethnic identity. Even though there is a tendency among public officials to shift towards the use of African names as the above examples illustrate, it is not clear how widely pervasive the phenomenon is among ordinary citizens.

Naming Practices and the Development of New Englishes
The literature originating in Africa on new Englishes in Africa is inspired by the work of Kachru (1985) and others (Arua, 2001; Dako, 2001; Gough, 1996; Igboanusi, 2003; Letsholo, 2000;

Magura, 1985). Most of these studies analyse ways in which new Englishes are used phonologically, semantically and pragmatically. They also investigate how English is adapted to local contexts. It therefore enhances our understanding of the status of Englishes in Africa.

However, there are three key problems that arise from research into New Englishes. First, the use of the nation state as the prism through which New Englishes are analysed is problematic. It overlooks massive migration across African states and the interaction amongst individuals originally from different countries. The concept of the nation state is not useful in language planning because it renders it unnecessarily difficult for interstate programmes to be developed even though a large number of African languages are deployed across borders (Makoni *et al.*, 2006).

The second problem is the lack of clarity regarding the criteria upon which the features that form the basis of the descriptions are based. Third, the exclusion of names as sources of data for analysing New Englishes (Dasgupta, 1993; Makoni & Meinhof, 2004) constitutes a shortcoming as English-like names are a common feature, particularly in Southern Africa. Even when the criteria for determining the linguistic features that characterise New Englishes are touched upon, the extent to which the use of New Englishes reflects the users' own appropriation of the language is not addressed. Further, there are no systematic studies that analyse the naming practices used by the speakers of New Englishes and the extent to which the names reflect their experience of English. The naming practices of the speakers of New Englishes provide important insights into how these speakers relate to English. This is indicative of the adoption of English in Zimbabwean language policy.

A Study of the Discursive Construction of Personal Names
Aims of the study

This paper investigates the discursive construction of personal names. We explore whether, historically, one pattern of naming is characterised by a shift from European names to names drawn from African languages. Naming a child is an important rite of passage in many African cultures (Lubisi, 2002). We hypothesise that if naming is so important so is the language used in the naming. Therefore an analysis of the language used in the naming enhances an understanding of the practice of language planning in African settings (Lubisi, 2002). This will, furthermore, enable us to explore whether there is any shift in the language of naming in Zimbabwe from African languages to English or from African languages to urban vernaculars and the implications this has on language planning.

In drawing a distinction between Western and African names, Herbert and Bogatsu (2001) state that:

> The criterion ... often employed in distinguishing African and Western names is that of name meaningfulness. It is well known that African names 'have meaning' and that speakers readily identify that meaning. Western names, on the other hand, are very largely devoid of meaning for modern speakers (e.g. Jonathan, Barbara).

Suzman (1994) cites the criterion of meaningfulness as a distinguishing factor between African names and their Western counterparts, which she describes as mere 'labels' (Suzman, 1994: 253). In view of the above, this article seeks to establish whether the names that are not in African languages are indeed 'English' names. It investigates whether there are modifications of naming under the impact of Anglicisation. The following are the research topics:

(1) The language used in personal names.
(2) The meaning of the name.

(3) The reasons or explanations offered by namers for selecting that particular name.
(4) The identity of the name-givers, that is whether the person had been named by the father or by the mother or some other person in the family or community.
(5) Attitudes of the name-bearers towards the names assigned to them.

Research methodology
Names were randomly selected from a graduation list of students who graduated from the University of Zimbabwe in 1983, and then compared with those who graduated in 1993 and in 2005. The students who graduated in 1983 were born in the early 1960s. Those who graduated in 1993 were born in the 1970s and the 2005, graduates in the 1980s. One of the limitations in the analysis of names from the graduation list is that the data did not provide insight into the 'real' meaning behind the names and the attitudes of the name-bearers to their names. In order to supplement these data, a much more systematic survey was carried out.

The survey was conducted with a total of 60 people[2] randomly selected from people from different regions in Zimbabwe born 1960–1990. A questionnaire was used to elicit data on naming. The survey was necessary to establish the meaning of the names and the attitudes of the name-holders towards their names. Participants were randomly selected from the different languages. The interviews were conducted mainly in the homes of the informants. The assistant researchers were drawn from the areas where the interviews took place and were known to the participants. As participants were drawn randomly, there were

---

[2] Although we analysed a total of 60 informants, we had more that 60 people who participated in the survey. We discarded some of the data in instances where the name-giver was dead, or those named could not remember when they were born and could only refer to the year when they were born as the 'year of the locust' when it was not clear what year this referred to.

differences in the sample in terms of the gender divide. There were more females in the sample than males (ratio 3 : 2), perhaps since the survey took place during working hours when most males were at work.

The information elicited included the background of name-holders (name/s, identity of name-giver/s, date and place of birth). Considering the fact that naming is a linguistic act that is linked to values and traditions, the questionnaires had specific questions to both name-holders and those that had assigned names to the informants to elicit their attitudes towards the names, and the language used in the names. The following questions were posed to the name-holders:

(1) What are the names that you are called by?
(2) Who gave you these/this name/s?
(3) Why do you think you were given these names and not any other names?
(4) Do you like your names and if so why is this so and if not why don't you like your names?
(5) Given the chance, would you change your name/s, and if so what would you want to be called and why?

The five questions above were posed because of an interest in ascertaining the range of names which the individuals had. The questions were also posed in order to ascertain the languages in which the names have their origin. There was also an interest in finding out the reactions of the named towards their names. An analysis of the attitudes of name-bearers towards their names, particularly the language of the names, sheds light on the local ideologies towards language, and is thus relevant to language planning. It is also possible that since ideologies about language are much more than attitudes towards language, an analysis of the local ideologies about language would further enhance understanding of the various ways in which the individuals reacted to Zimbabwean language policies.

In addition to administering the questionnaire to name-holders, a second questionnaire was administered to name-givers. Name-givers were asked to explain the reasons for assigning particular name/s and not others. They were also asked for the meaning behind the name. They were also asked for the general uses to which each name was put and their attitudes towards the names they had assigned. It is primarily this information that was used in investigating shifts in the language of naming (if any) towards English or urban vernaculars. This enables us to examine whether there is any justification in claims of endangerment of African languages in Zimbabwe. Theoretically, the analysis contributes towards scholarship in language policy in those issues in which the main argument for promoting 'indigenous' languages is to protect them from the 'bigger' languages such as English (Nettle & Romaine, 2000; Phillipson, 2003; Skutnabb-Kangas, 2000).

The following questions were posed to the name-givers.

(1) Why did you give xxx these names?
(2) What do these names mean?
(3) Are all the names used all the time?
(4) If not when is each name used and why?
(5) Would you consider changing these names and if so why?
(6) If you were to give xxx names again, what would these names be?

The questions were posed to enable the researchers to ascertain how those who do the naming respond to naming, and whether over time they might have wished to change the names they gave. Such questions enable us to explore the potential for language shift, and to ascertain its direction.

Data were elicited from a total of ten people within each age group. The rationale was to establish whether there was a change in naming practices as a result of the attainment of independence from white rule in 1980 (Ranger, 2003). It was reasoned that the 1960s group were born in the midst of the liberation struggle, whilst those born in the 1990s belonged to the post-white rule and may adopt different names. The following are the periods:

(1) 1960–1969
(2) 1970–1980
(3) 1990–1995

Analysis of results: Data from the graduation list
In analysing the data, the first question posed was asked in order to examine whether naming has changed over the three decades. The following is a summary of some of the striking names in the period under investigation.

1983 graduation list (1960–1969 category): *Nevermore, Analyn, Africa, Letwina, Macleod, Johnfisher, Exaverlo*;
1993 graduation list (1970–1979 category): *Courage, Paris, Goodwill, Clever, Gift, Blessed, Last*;
2005 graduation list (1980–1989 category): *Moreangels, Nomore, Goodlucky, Census, Polite, Handsome, Overt.*

What is clear from the graduation lists is that there is a continued use of non-Standard English over the three decades. The list of names compiled from the names of students who graduated in 1993 is not significantly different from the first list, i.e. the list of individuals who were born in the 1960s and graduated in 1983. Although most of the students who graduated in 2005 were born in the 1980s, most of them have names consistent with those found on the 1983 and 1993 list. Comparatively, the three lists suggest that there is a continuation of non-Standard English names within Zimbabwe. Thus, there has been no change in the language of naming that is used when assigning a name.

Notably, a majority of the names taken from the graduation list are not native English names. These names consist of lexical items which are drawn from English but which may not be frequently used as names from a native English speaker's perspective. For example, names such as *Lookon, Luckymore* (Neethling, 2005: 99) and *Sinfree* sound strange in the English-speaking world. From the viewpoint of a standard language ideology (Milroy & Milroy, 1985) the names are unusual because they deviate from conventional standard native English spelling. For example: *Exavier* (Xavier); *Funwell* (Fanuel); *Jerald* (Gerald); *Indirance* (Endurance); *Bigg* (Big); *Happinos* (Happiness).

Some of the spellings of the names reflect forms of writing conventions by second language users of English in which English names are inserted into a first language, that is the chi-Shona or Ndebele writing systems. The fact that these spellings are retained even in official documents reflects the extent to which New Englishes have permeated Zimbabwe. The spread of English does not seem to have endangered African languages as 'dystopic' theories (Jacquemet, 2005) of language spread focusing on English might lead us to believe. From the perspective of those who name their children using non-Standard English spelling, the spelling is not considered incorrect, just as *Umtali, Gatooma, Tjolotjo* and *Amatoli* are not incorrect from a European perspective on African languages. What these names reflect are efforts on the part of both Europeans and Africans to appropriate second languages (Fabian, 1986).

It is, however, striking that the non-Standard English spelling forms are retained even when the name-holders are formally educated and able to spell in a manner consistent with Standard English. The continued use of non-standard spelling forms as names by the educated reflects the limitations of standard language ideology in the discursive construction of naming (Milroy & Milroy, 1985).

In some cases the names reflect the namers' language learning experience of English as demonstrated by the use of contracted forms of fuller English idiomatic expressions that are used within Zimbabwean. For example: *Lordwin* (The Lord wins over the devil); *Shameon* (Shame on you); *Learnfirst* (Learn first before acting); *Eventhough* (God blessed me even though I was rejected); *Withus* (God is with us).

Most of the names in the above examples are derived from words combined in a manner inconsistent with Standard English word division, but provide important insights into how non-Standard English is acquired in African contexts. The resultant compounds are not the kind that one learns from a formal educational setting. These are names the namers acquired from their interaction with family members in informal settings. Perhaps the desire to speak English motivates them to pick expressions, which they give permanence by using as names for their children. And yet structurally, the construction processes involved in names like *Withus*, *Lordwin* and *Learnfirst* resemble the linguistic processes involved in the formation of such names as *Bonangani* ('How do you see?') (Mphande, 2006), *Isheanesu* ('The Lord is with us') and *Mukundindishe* ('The Lord wins') in African languages, suggesting that even though the names were English in form, the structure and model on which they are based is African. In terms of the rhetorical and phonological structure, these names are closer to African languages than Standard English. Non-Standard English provides Africans with opportunities to appropriate English because it blurs boundaries between English and African languages. The distinction between English and African languages is seen as a seamless continuum.

Some other English names are derived from translations from chiShona proverbs. For example, *Shout* and *Talkmore* are translated from chiShona proverbs: *mwana asingacheme anofira mumbereko* ('a child who does not cry will die on their mother's back') which means speak out loudly or shout so that you can get help. In some cases, Africans use African sounding names that reflect European Christian concepts. In fact, the use of names such as *Lordwin* ('The Lord wins over the devil'), *Isheanesu* ('The lord is with us'), *Thembinkosi* ('Believe in the Lord') or *Vusolwenkosi* ('The Lord's resurrection') reflects the language effects of Christianity (Pennycook & Makoni, 2005). In other words, the use of African names within a Christian purview reflects the extent to which Christianity is being articulated through African languages (Fabian, 1986; Mashiri, 2003). The converse applies equally as Africans' continued use of names drawn from non-Standard English is indicative of the degree to which Africans have also appropriated English for their own purposes. The promotion of English in terms of language policy has therefore resulted in the emergence of non-Standard English, which is increasingly becoming the target for most names.

Analysis of the results: Survey data
There is a total of 60 informants with at least 10 in each category and random samples of 10 people are chosen within each category. For the purposes of this article we confine ourselves to 43 informants born from 1960 to 1965, and those born from 1985 to 1990 (20 in the category of those born after 1980).

A total of 17 informants' names of people born between 1960 and 1964 were used; although 20 informants had taken part in the project, three were difficult to decipher hence these were discarded. The following are the five categories used in the classification the data.

(1) African language (AF): has one name only and the name is from an African language.
(2) African language + African language (AF + AF); has two names both of which are drawn from African languages.
(3) English + African Language (ENG + AF): has two names, one from English or a variety of English and the other from an African language.

(4) English (ENG): has one name only which is drawn from a variety of English.
(5) English + English (ENG + ENG): has two names both of which are drawn from varieties of English.

However, what needs to be pointed out is that due to the size of the sample, the survey is only indicative of a trend in patterns of naming and does not, in itself, provide conclusive findings.

Table 1 Summary of names of people born in the 1960s

Language/s	No. of informants	Percentages
AF	1	5.9%
AF + AF	2	11.8%
Sub-total	3	17.7%
ENG + AF	9	52.9%
ENG	4	23.5%
ENG + ENG	1	5.9%
Sub-total	5	29.4%
Total	17	100.0%

Table 2 Summary of names for those born 1980–1985

Language/s	No. of informants	Percentages
AF	7	30.4%
AF + AF	1	4.3%
Sub-total	8	34.7%
ENG + AF	6	26.2%
ENG	8	34.8%
ENG + ENG	1	4.3%
Sub-total	9	39.1%
Total	23	100.0%

For the 1960s group (see Table 1), a majority of the informants have names from both English and African languages

(52.9%). Only 29.4% have one or both personal names which are English. Some 17.7% have one or both names in African languages. There is clearly a trend among those born in the early 1960s is to have names from both English and an African language.

After analysing the naming pattern for those born in the 1960s we now turn to those born in the 1980s, to examine the extent to which the same pattern of using names drawn from both English and an African language continues into the 1980s.

In the data of those born in 1980–1985 there are 23 informants (see Table 2). In the 1960s the dominant naming pattern was to have two names, one English and another drawn from an African language. By the 1980s the dominant pattern, by contrast, is to have English names (39.1%), followed by African names (34.7%). Having both an English and an African language (26.2%) was down from 52.9% in the 1960s. The dominant naming pattern has, therefore, changed between 1960 and 1980, from having an English name plus an African name, to having either English name/s only or African name/s only. Of the 15 English names used, only three were Standard English, suggesting the pervasive nature of non-Standard English. This might be construed as one of the consequences of the promotion of English in language planning. Notably the use of African names has also risen significantly from 17.7% in the 1960s group to 34.7% suggesting, perhaps, that the promotion of indigenous African languages in post independent Zimbabwe has been partially successful.

While a number of studies have reported on the continued dominance of English in education, our study supports the continued use of a variety of non-Standard English but in a separate domain: naming practices. What is important to note is that the type of English in circulation is the non-standard variety, which linguistically approximates African languages structurally as well as through cultural patterns. This suggests that the vitality of African languages and cultures are retained through non-Standard English.

A total of 17 informants took part in the section of the study on name-givers (see Table 3). Fathers named a majority of the children born in the 1960s (65%). The rest are named either by mothers (18%), teachers (12%), or others such as doctors (1%). That their fathers gave the names is important from a gender perspective. It suggests that naming practices reflect the role which gender plays in shaping their children's identities. This is not surprising considering the fact that most ethnic groups in Zimbabwe are patriarchal except the Nambyaians.

Table 3 The identity of name-givers in the 1960s

Namers	No. of informants	Percentages
Fathers	11	65%
Mothers	3	18%
Teachers	2	12%
Others	1	5%
Total	17	100%

Table 4 The identity of name-givers in the 1980s

Namers	No. of informants	Percentages
Fathers	13	48%
Mothers	7	26%
Teachers	0	0%
Other	7	26%
Total	27	100%

Further analysis, however, needs to examine whether fathers are more likely to give a child an African name rather than an English name; or both are equally possible. Such an analysis would be illuminating because it would demonstrate whether there are gender-specific orientations towards English and non-Standard English. In other words, are women more English-inclined than men, and what variety of English would they opt for? For instance, Cook (2002) demonstrates gender differences in the use of language with males more likely to use Afrikaans while women are more likely to use English. We, however, do not have systematically collected data on whether there would be a difference between women and men in Zimbabwe in terms of language preferences between English and African languages. Such data would be useful for the burgeoning literature on language and gender in Africa.

Even in the 1980s the fathers were still the dominant name-givers (see Table 4), though they were down from 65% to 48%. Mothers as name givers had risen from 18% to 26%. At the same time the category of 'other' name-givers had risen from only 5% in the 1960s to 26%, making them equal with mothers as name-givers. It is difficult to give specific reasons for the significant increase in the category 'other'. However, during this period it seems single-parenting was on the increase and grandparents, uncles and siblings were prominent namers in this category. In some cases mothers left their children before assigning them a name, as shown in the case of Never below. Another difference that emerges is that while teachers did some naming (12%) in the 1960s, by the 1980s they were no longer visible as name-givers. It is possible that the ENG + AF category in the 1960s was enhanced by teachers, priests and government administrators. These groups of people assigned an English name leading to an individual having a school name and a home name, in which case the school name was, in most cases, English (see Mandela, 1994) and the home name in an African language.

Discussion

In order to analyse the language ideologies of the name-bearers, we collected some qualitative data on whether the name-bearers liked their names or the language of their names. The intention in analysing the attitudes of the namebearers was to explore the name-bearers' orientation towards the language their names derived from. The hypothesis was that if naming a child is so important then so is the language, or the variety of language, used in the naming process. An analysis of the language used in the naming will therefore enable us to further understand the nature of ideologies of language and the implication this has for language planning in African settings. The assumption is that people's personal liking of the language of their names is an important aspect in our understanding of how people may relate to language planning.

In analysing the name-bearers' orientation towards the language of their names, we found complex and varied responses. In some instances the name-bearers professed to like their names irrespective of whether the name was in Standard or non-Standard English, suggesting that the variety of language their name is in does not affect their attitudes towards their names. That the name-bearers are likely to endorse names from non-Standard English raises a number of issues. One possibility is that the name-bearers do not distinguish between Standard and non-Standard English.

The complexity of the responses to the individual names highlights the problematic nature of making generalisations about language ideologies even for people living in the same community and same historical period. The individuals may entertain ideologies of language influenced by individual experiences with the specific language. It is this element of individual experiences with language which is frequently overlooked in the analysis of ideologies of language when locally grounded perspectives (Canagarajah, 2005) on language are explored. Locally grounded perspectives of language, although contributing to a radical shift away from top-down perspectives, tend to overlook the fact that even people living within the same communities have different experiences of the same language and therefore by overlooking the diversity in the individuals' experiences they conjure an inaccurate image of a uniformity that does not exist.

The informants who had English names like their non-Standard English names, for example *Cornermore* and *Happymore*. Of the 26 informants with African names only, 20% did not like them particularly. Notably, those who did not like their names attributed this to the meaning and not the language the name was derived from, for example *Mabenzi* who did not like his name because, although his name means 'problem' in Tonga, in chiShona it means 'fools' or 'mad people', and everyone construes his name from a chiShona perspective. Interestingly, those who had two names considered themselves 'bi-cultural' and thought that their names were a significant marker of their identity as 'distinctively Zimbabwean'.

The empirical study shows that the period 1960–1990 involved an onomastic shift in Zimbabwe. It demonstrates that contrary to our expectations there is a radical shift away from the combined use of English and African language names to names in African languages only or English only. The combined use of ENG + AF fell by half, from 52.9% in 1960s to 26.2% in 1980s, that is there was a strong trend away from ENG + AF. Counterbalancing this trend there was a trend towards using more AF or AF + AF and ENG or ENG + ENG. The use of African-only names almost doubled from 17.7% in the1960s to 34.7% in the 1980s, while the use of English-only names also rose, though less markedly, from 29.4% in the 1960s to 39.1% in the 1980s. While the rise in the use of African-only names is more marked, they are still marginally below the use of English-only names. This pattern indicates that although the Zimbabwe national language policy promotes the use of African languages, there is still strong adherence to the use of English in naming. Africans continued using non-Standard English to articulate their culture. In the light of some theories of language change such as linguistic imperialism (Brutt-Griffler 2005; Canagarajah 2005; Swigart, 2000), one might be compelled to believe that the emergence of a new onomastic tradition is an imposition, and yet the evidence suggests that the emergence of such a tradition was not one imposed upon Africans, but one which Africans actively sought and maintained (Makoni, 1993).

The use of names from English reflects a complex attitude towards English in that when discussing language policy issues one is typically referring to Standard English, while in discussions about names reference is made to non-Standard Zimbabwean English. The use of English names also reflects a racialised orientation towards language. For example, Mike (born December 1984) claims he was given an English name because:

> *Ngazalwa ngibomvu, ngimuhle. Ubaba wami wathi ngifanana lekhiwa. Ubaba nguye owanginika ibizo leli ngoba efi sa ukuthi ngondliwe ngamakhiwa.* [I was born light in complexion and handsome, and my father likened me to a white man. My father gave me an English name because he wished that I be adopted and raised by whites.]

This should not be construed to mean that when parents feel that their children are light in complexion they are always given English names. In other cases, for example, light complexioned children are given names using African language words that are typically used to refer to whites such as *Khiwa* (Ndebele 'European' or 'white person').

English or European sounding names are drawn from various sources. In some instances, the names come from the Bible and other literature which the name-givers had encountered. For example, Miriam (born 1984) suggests that she was given that name from the Bible because her mother admired the biblical Miriam. The ideologies towards English are complex because they also entail the use of words as names which the name-givers do not understand. This suggests that comprehensibility is not an important criterion in naming. For example, *Never* (born 1984) explains why he was given such a name by stating that:

> *Mina ibizo elithi Never ngaliphiwa ngumalume. Umalume wayengazi lokuthi litshoni. Wayeswele ibizo wase dobha nje ibizo elafi ka masinya enqgondweni yakhe. Umama wangitshiya ngisanda kuzalwa. Wasuka engakanginiki lebizo.*
> [My uncle who did not know the meaning of the word 'never' named me. He just settled for that name after failing to come up with any name because my mother had left me before giving me a name.]

The use of names from English which the name-givers did not understand suggests that there was a considerable aesthetic element in naming involving the sounds of words. It is this element of aesthetics which is frequently not considered in discussions about naming in spite of its significance in language planning. Naming children while drawing on a language which one does not understand leads to the use of names that are inappropriate. For example, among the Tonga researchers in this study encountered names such as *Lizadi* ('lizard'), M*i*sisi ('Mrs') and *Anasi* ('anus'). The name-givers had heard the words used and thought they would be nice as names for their children although they did not know what they meant.

In some cases the continued use of English names has less to do with linguistic aesthetics and thus does not reflect a form of linguistic consciousness. It is a continuation of an African naming tradition. For example, Joseph (born 1964) claims he was named after his maternal uncle and explains this as follows:

> *Ngathiwa ngumfowabo kababa. Kithi sethiwa ngebizo likababa omncane.*[My father's brother (uncle) named

me. It is a family trend to pass one's name to a nephew. I too have already passed this name to my nephew.]

In other cases the names reflect more mundane matters such as attempts tonavigate the complexities of educational systems in Zimbabwe. Zimbabwean education requires that before writing the national examinations for qualifying for high school, one needs to have a birth certificate. Often one has to go through a lot of bureaucratic processes to obtain one. In such cases, siblings who have birth certificates often lend them to those who do not. The process of lending a birth certificate means that the individual subsequently assumes the name of the person named on the certificate. The name on the birth certificate is typically an English and African language one in the 1960s. English names are associated with official documents. For example, in some cases the child adopts the name of a sibling in order to get permission to write primary school leaving examinations as is the case of Vuso Andrew Doctor (born 1962) who explains this as follows:

> *Uvuso umele uVusolwenkosi okutsho ukuvuka kwenkosi njengebhayibhilini. Eish, ummh, angazi ukuthi uAndrew utshoni. Ibizo lami lami lokuzalwa ngu Effort. Ibizo elithi Doctor ngaliphiwa nges'khathi ngisesibhedlela. Ngatsha ngisemncane. Ngahlala esibhedlela isikhathi eside kakhulu onesi baze bathi yimi udokotela. Lelibizo laliyi nickname kodwa ngacina sengilisebenzisa sengisiya esikolo. Ibizo elithi Effort abantu bacina sebelikhohlwa. Ngaqala eprimary ngingu Doctor manje kwasekufuneka ibirth certifi cate. Mina ngangingelayo.* My mother then gave me my brother's birth certificate *ngasengisiba yimi uVuso Andrew.*
> [Vuso is short form of Vusolwenkosi meaning the Lord's resurrection like in the Bible. I don't know the meaning of Andrew. A medical practitioner assigned me the name

Doctor. Initially my name was Effort. I then fell into a fire at an early age getting serious burns. Owing to my long stay in hospital I was given a nickname Doctor. The nickname then stuck and slowly the name Effort was forgotten. I started primary school as Doctor but when I needed a birth certificate I was given my brother's name Vuso Andrew. These became my official names.]

The adoption of a sibling's name is not a cause for identity confusion because the sibling did not go as far as the end of primary school, and in any case his home name is different. By taking another individual's name Vuso is assuming another individual's identity in school contexts.

Directions for Future Research
This article has sought to address a number of questions. It explores whether there is indeed a language shift manifested in the naming patterns by specifically focusing on personal names in Zimbabwe over three historical periods. The survey looked at two historical periods while the graduation list provided a glimpse of the 1990s. The results suggest that there is a continued use of non-Standard English over the three historical periods although African languages significantly emerge as languages of naming in the 1980s. In other words there is indeed a form of language shift in the area of naming. The trend in using English names is to use non-Standard English names with a non-Standard variety of English that seems to closely approximate African languages as the use of names such as *Lookon* and *Lordwin* closely approximates African languages both syntactically and morphologically (see page 20 for an analysis of how these names approximate African languages). The use of non-Standard English names is construed as a continuing process in the maintenance of tradition, particularly in those families where the name was used in previous generations. In such a case non-Standard English was used to retain African tradition, and Afri-

can languages and culture are not under threat. This challenges what Jacquemet (2005) refers to as a 'dystopic' vision in which the spread of English is 'indelibly linked to Americanization and homogenisation of world culture and to media imperialism' (Nettle & Romaine, 2000; Pennycook, 2007; see Phillipson, 1992, 2003, for an elaboration of such a position).

In spite of the fact that the spread of non-Standard English is not threatening African cultures (if anything it is enhancing it by facilitating change) as reflected in the continued use of a tradition of using names from previous generations, it is bizarre to name a child using a language one has limited control of. Even if English is not dominating African languages and poses no significant threat to African cultures, a serious discussion of the issue is complicated by a number of conceptual issues: the notion of domination has not been adequately conceptually analysed (see, however, Janks (2000) postulating that domination, access and diversity may be useful in further clarification of the concept). If the concept of domination is not framed rigorously, it becomes a non-testable and possibly un-testable hypothesis. It is important for the hypothesis to be testable if it is to be meaningful in Zimbabwe.

In an African context, it might be worth reiterating that the notion of domination is a metaphor and languages do not dominate people, people dominate each other. Paradoxically, even though the metaphor of languages dominating people is meant to be a clarion call to political action, framing the discussion in such an apolitical manner renders it more difficult rather than easier for political intervention to take place, exactly in those contexts in which active social intervention is warranted. Furthermore, the discussions about the spread of English need to go beyond what Pennycook (2007) refers to as the 'homogemy' and 'heterogemy' debates. It is necessary to conceptualise research into naming which takes into account the transcultural and translocal cultural flows arising in part as a consequence of globalisation and migration in how naming practices occur. In turn, this suggests that language planning in Africa has to be founded on an analysis of transitional and transnational networks. An analysis of naming and its impact on language planning has to be designed as part of a comprehensive identity package, which has implications for "how you talk or how you walk, ... how you do yo thang, how you let it hang – how you let it swang" (Alim, 2004: 61). State-centric approaches, which have been the norm in African sociolinguistics, blind us to the diversities within nation states and the similarities across different states.

By and large, future research has to analyse ways in which migrants may adopt new names to assimilate into their new environments or as responses to xenophobia, and racism directed at, for example, Black Zimbabweans in South Africa (Sisulu *et al.*, 2007). If research into naming is to retain a state-centric/nation perspective it needs to work with a more vigorous analytical template in which the state/nation is conceptualised broadly enough to incorporate aspects that deal with its diaspora.

References

Abdulaziz, M.H. and Osinde, K. (1997) "Sheng and English: Development of mixed codes among the urban youth in Kenya" *International Journal of the Sociology of Language* 125, 43–63.

Afful, J.B.A. (2005) "Non-kinship address terms in Akan: A sociolinguistic study of language use in Ghana" *Journal of Multilingual and Multicultural Development* 27 (4), 275–288.

Akinnaso, F.N. (1980) "The sociolinguistic basis of Yoruba personal names" *Anthropological Linguistics* 22 (7), 275–304.

Alexander, N. (1995) "Multilingualism for empowerment" In K. Heugh, A. Siergrühn and P. Plüddeman (eds) *Multingual Education for South Africa* (pp. 37–41). Johannesburg:

Heinemann.

Alford, R.D. (1988) *Naming and Identity: A Cross-Cultural Study of Personal Naming Practices*. New Haven, CT: Human Relations Area File Press.

Alia, V. (1984) "Women, names and power" *Women and Language* VIII (1/2), 34–36.

Alim, H.S. (2004) *You Know my Steez: An Ethnographic and Sociolinguistic Study of Styleshifting in a Black American Speech Community*. Durham, NC: American Dialect Society and Duke University Press.

Arua, A. (2001) "Aspects of Swazi English accent" In E. Ridge, S. Makoni and S.G. Ridge (eds) *Freedom and Discipline: Essays in Applied Linguistics from Southern Africa* (pp. 129–138). New Delhi: Bahri.

Bakhtin, M. (1934/1981) *The Dialogic Imagination: Four Essays*. M. Holquist (ed.) Austin: University of Texas Press.

Bangeni, G.N. and Coetser, A. (2000) "Xhosa first names, societal values and power relations" *Nomina Africana* 14 (2), 19–42.

Batibo, H.M. (2005) *Language Decline and Death in Africa: Causes, Consequences and challenges*. Clevedon: Multilingual Matters.

Bauman, R. and Briggs, C.L. (2003) *Voices of Modernity: Language Ideologies and the Politics of Inequality*. Cambridge: Cambridge University Press.

Blommaert, J. (2005). *Discourse: A Critical Introduction*. Cambridge: Cambridge University Press.

Brutt-Griffler, J. (2003) "World English: A study of its development. *Language Policy* 2 (3), 295–297.

Brutt-Griffl er, J. (2005) "'Who do you think you are, where do you think you are?' Language policy and the political economy of English in South Africa" In C. Gnutzmann and F. Intemann (eds) *The Globalization of English and the English Language Classroom* (pp. 25–37). Tubingen: Gunter Narr Verlag.

Buhlungu, S., Daniel, J., Southall, R. and Lutchman, J. (2006) *State of the Nation: South Africa 2005–2006*. Pretoria: Human Sciences Research Council.

Canagarajah, A.S. (2005) "Introduction" In A.S. Canagarajah (ed.) *Reclaiming the Local in Language Policy and Practice* (pp. xii–xxx). Mahwah, NJ: Lawrence Erlbaum.

Childs, G.T. (1997) "The status of Isicamtho, a Nguni based urban variety of Soweto" In A. Spears and D. Winford (eds) *The Structure and Status of Pidgins and Creoles* (pp. 341–370). Amsterdam and Philadelphia, PA: John Benjamins.

Chimhundu, H. (1993) "The status of African languages in Zimbabwe" *Southern Africa Political and Economic Monthly (SAPEM)* (October) (pp. 57–59). Literary Studies Series: Harare.

Chitando, E. (1998) "What's in a name: Naming practices among African Christians in Zimbabwe" In K. Fiedler, P. Gundani and H. Mijoga (eds) *Theology Cooked in an African Pot* (pp. 106–119). Zomba: Association of Theological Institutions in Southern and Central Africa (ATISCA).

Cook, S. (2002) "Urban language in a rural setting: the case of Phokeng, South Africa" In G. Gmelch and W.P. Zenner (eds) *Urban Life: Readings in the Anthropology of the City* (pp. 106–114). Prospect Heights, IL.: Waveland Press.

Cooper, R.L. (1989) *Language Planning and Social Change*. New York: Cambridge University Press.

Dako, K. (2001) "Ghanaianisms: Towards a semantic and a formal classification. *English World Wide* 22 (2), 23–53.

Dasgupta, P. (1993) *The Otherness of English: India's Auntie Tongue Syndrome*. New Delhi: Sage Publications.

de Klerk, V. and Bosch, B. (1995) "Naming in two cultures:

English and Xhosa practices" *Nomina Africana* 9(1), 8–87.

Errington, J. (2007) *Linguistics in the Colonial World: A Study of Language, Meaning and Power*. Malden: Blackwell Publishers.

Fabian, J. (1986) *Language and Colonial Power: The Appropriation of Swahili in the Former Belgian Congo, 1880–1938*. Cambridge: Cambridge University Press.

Ferguson, G. (2006) *Language Planning and Education*. Edinburgh: Edinburgh University Press.

Fishman, J. (1990) "What is reversing language shift and how can it succeed?" *Journal of Multilingual and Multicultural Development* 11, 5–36.

Fishman, J. (2004) "Ethnicity and supra-ethnicity in corpus planning: The hidden status agenda in corpus planning" *Nations and Nationalism* 10 (1–2), 79–94.

Foucault, M. (1977) "A preface to transgression" In his *Language, Countermemory, Practice* (D.F. Bouchard (ed.)) (pp. 15–52). Ithaca, NY: Cornell University Press.

Githiora, C. (2002) "Sheng: Peer language, Swahili dialect or emerging Creole?" *Journal of African Cultural Studies* 1 5 (2), 159–181.

Gough, D. (1996) "Black English in South Africa" In V. de Klerk (ed.) *English Around the World: Focus on South Africa* (pp. 53–78). Amsterdam and Philadelphia: John Benjamins.

Guma, M. (2001) "The cultural meaning of names among Basotho of South Africa: A historical and linguistic analysis. *Nordic Journal of African Studies* 10 (3), 265–279.

Hachipola, S.J. (1998) *A Survey of the Minority Languages of Zimbabwe*. Michigan: Michigan University Press.

Harrison, K.D. (2000) "Naming practices and ethnic identity in

Tuva" In Proceedings of CLS 35: The panels. On WWW at http://www.swarthmore.edu/SocSci/dharris2/Harrison-CLS(corrected).pdf. Accessed 7.6.07.

Haugen, E. (1971) "The ecology of language" *Linguistic Reporter*, supplement 25, 13 (1), 19–26.

Herbert, B. and Bogatsu, S. (2001) *Changes in Northern Sotho and Tswana Personal Naming Patterns*. Berkeley: University of California Press.

Igboanusi, H. (2003) "Semantic dislocation in Nigerian English" In P. Lucko, L. Peter Lothar and H-G. Wolf (eds) *Studies in African Varieties of English* (pp. 69–83). Peter Lang.

Irvine, J. and Gal, S. (2001) "Language ideology and linguistic differentiation" In P.V Kroskrity (ed.) *Regimes of Language Ideologies, Politics and Identities* (pp. 35–85). Santa Fe: School of American Research Press.

Jacquemet, M. (2005) "Transidiomatic practices: language and power in the age of globalization" *Language and Communication* (25), 257–277.

Janks, H. (2000) Domination, access, diversity and design: a synthesis for critical literacy education. *Educational Review* 52 (2), 175–186.

Jeater, D. (2006) *Law, Language & Science: The Invention of the 'Native Mind' in Southern Rhodesia*. Heinemann: Portsmouth, USA.

Joseph, J. (2004) *Language and Identity: National, Ethnic, Religious*. Basingstoke: Palgrave Macmillan.

Joseph, J. (2006) *Language and Politics*. Edinburgh: Edinburgh University Press.

Kachru, B.B. (1985) "Standards, codification and sociolinguistics. In R. Quirk and H.G. Widdowson (eds) *English in the World*: *Teaching and Learning the Language and Literatures* (pp. 11–30). Cambridge: Cambridge University Press.

Kamwangamalu, N. (1998) "Identities of English and

codeswitching in post apartheid South Africa" *Multilingua* 17 (2/3), 277–296.

Khubchandani, L.M. (1983) "Demographic imperatives in language planning" On WWW at http://www.linguapax.org/congres/plenaries/kutchandani.html. Accessed 19.12.06.

Koopman, A. (1989) "The aetiology of Zulu personal names" *Nomina Africana* 3 (2), 31–46.

Lawson, E.D. and Laimute, B. (1996) "Latvian Naming Patterns, 1880–1991" In *Proceedings of the XIXth International Congress of Onomastic Sciences*, Aberdeen, 4–11 August, 3, 244–249.

Le Page, R.B. and Tabouret-Keller, A. (1985) *Acts of Identity: Creole Based Approaches to Language and Ethnicity.* Cambridge: Cambridge University Press.

Letsholo, R. (2000) "English in Botswana: A sociolinguistic description" In S. Makoni and N. Kamwangamalu (eds) *Language and Institutions in Africa* (pp. 161–179). Cape Town: Centre for the Advanced Studies of African Societies.

Lubisi, P.M. (2002) "A glance into African personal names" *Nomina Africana* 16 (1&2), 118–124.

Magura, B. (1985) "Southern African Black English. Attitudes of parents to their children's use of English in Botswana. *World Englishes* 4 (2), 251–256.

Makoni, S. (1993) "Multiple forces on New Englishes" *UNISWA Research Journal* 17, 23–32.

Makoni, S., Brutt-Griffler, J. and Mashiri, P. (2007) "The use of urban vernaculars in Zimbabwe" *Language in Society* 36 (1), 1–36.

Makoni, S., Dube, B. and Mashiri, P. (2006) "Zimbabwe colonial and post colonial language policy and planning practices" *Current Issues in Language Planning* 7 (4), 377–414.

Makoni, S. and Mashiri, P. (2007) "Critical historiography:

Does language planning in Africa need a theory of language as part of its theoretical apparatus?" In S. Makoni and A. Pennycook (eds) *Disinventing and Reconstituting Languages*. Clevedon: Multilingual Matters. *(Bilingual Education and Bilingualism series)*.

Makoni, S. and Meinhoff, U. (2004) "Western perspectives on applied linguistics" *AILA Review* 17, 77–105.

Makoni, S. and Pennycook, A. (eds) (2007) *Disinventing and Reconstituting Languages*. Clevedon: Multilingual Matters. *(Bilingual Education and Bilingualism series)*.

Makoni, S., Smitherman, G., Ball, A.F. and Spears, A.K. (ed.) (2003) Introduction. *Black Linguistics: Language, Society, and Politics in Africa and the Americas* (pp. 1–19). London: Routledge.

Mandela, N.R. (1994) *A Long Walk to Freedom: The Autobiography*. Randburg, South Africa: Macdonald Purnell Press.

Mashiri, P. (2003) "The semantic and morphological aspects of Shona Christian personal names. *Malawi Journal of Linguistics* 3, 1–14.

Mathangwane, J.T. and Gardner, S.F. (1998) "Language attitudes as portrayed by the use of English and African names in Botswana. *Nomina Africana* 12 (2), 74–87.

Mazrui, A.A. and Mazrui, A.M. (1998) *The Power of Babel: Language and Governance in the African Experience*. Chicago: University of Chicago Press.

Milroy, J. and Milroy, L. (1985) *Authority in Language: Investigating Language Prescription and Standardisation*. London: Routledge and Keagan Paul.

Mkanganwi, K. (1992) "Language planning in Southern Africa" In N.T. Crawhall (ed.) *Democratically Speaking: International Perspectives on Language Planning* (pp. 6–11). South Africa: National Language Project.

Moyo, T. (1996) "Personal names and naming practices in Northern Malawi" *Nomina Africana* 10 (1–2), 47–57.

Mphande, L. (2006) "Naming and linguistic Africanisms in African American culture" In J. Mugane, J.P. Hutchison and D.A. Worman (eds) *Selected Proceedings of the 35th Annual Conference on African Linguistics* (pp. 104–113). Somerville, MA: Cascadilla Proceedings Project.

Mufwene, S. (2002) "Colonisation, globalisation and the future of languages in the twentyfirst century" *International Journal on Multicultural Societies* 4 (2), 162–193.

Mumpande, I. (2006) *Silent Voices: Indigenous Languages in Zimbabwe: A Report.* Harare: Weaver Press.

Neethling, B. (2005) *Naming Among the Xhosa of South Africa.* Lewiston: Edwin Mellen Press.

Neethling, S.J. (2003) "Perceptions around the English name of Xhosa speakers. *Nomina Africana* 17 (2), 45–65.

Nettle, D. and Romaine, S. (2000) *Vanishing Voices: The Extinction of the World's Languages.* Oxford: Oxford University Press.

Pennycook, A. (2004) "Language policy and the ecological turn" *Language Policy* 3, 213–239.

Pennycook, A. (2007) *Global Englishes and Transcultural Flows.* London: Routledge Press.

Pennycook, A. and Makoni, S. (2005) "The modern mission: The language effects of Christianity" *Journal of Language Identity and Education* 4 (2), 137–157.

Phillipson, R. (1992) *Linguistic Imperialism.* Oxford: Oxford University Press.

Phillipson, R. (2003) *English Only Europe? Challenging Language Policy.* London: Routledge.

Pongweni, A.J.C. (1983) *What's in a Name? A Study of Shona Nomenclature.* Harare: Mambo Press.

Raftopolous, B. (2006) "The Zimbabwean crisis and the challenges for the Left. *Journal of Southern African Studies* 32 (2), 203–219.

Ramanathan, V. (2005) *The English-Vernacular Divide: Post*

Colonial Language Politics and Practice. Clevedon: UK: Multilingual Matters.

Rampton, B. (1997) "Second language research in late modernity: A response to Firth and Wagner" *Modern Language Journal* 81 (3), 329–333.

Ranger, T. (1985) *Peasant Consciousness and Guerilla War in Zimbabwe: A Comparative Study*. Oxford: James Currey.

Ranger, T. (1989) "The invention of tradition in colonial Africa" In E. Hobsbawm and T. Ranger (eds) *The Invention of Tradition* (pp. 211–262). Cambridge: Cambridge University Press.

Ranger, T. (ed.) (2003) *Evangelical Christianity and Democracy in Africa*. Oxford: Oxford University Press.

Rapoo, C.K. (2002) "Naming practices and gender bias in the Setswana language" *Journal of Women and Language* 25 (1), 41–43.

Roy-Campbell, Z.M. and Gwete, W.B. (1997) *Language Policy and Planning (ECS207)*. University of Zimbabwe: Centre for Distance Education.

Saarelma-Maunumaa, M.M. (1996) "The influence of Westernization on Ovambo personal names in Namibia" *Nomina Africana* 10 (1–2), 274–282.

Sisulu, E., Moyo, B. and Tshuma, T. (2007) "The Zimbabwean community in South Africa" In S. Buhlungu, J. Daniel and J. Lutchman (eds) *State of the Nation South Africa 2007* (pp. 552–575). Cape Town: HSRC Press.

Skutnabb-Kangas, T. (2000) *Linguistic Genocide in Education or Worldwide Diversity and Human Rights?* Mahwah, NJ: Lawrence Erlbaum.

Spitulnik, D. (1988) "The language of the city: Town Bemba as urban hybridity" *Journal of Linguistic Anthropology* 8 (2), 30–59.

Summers, C. (2002) *Colonial Lessons: Africans' Education in Southern Rhodesia, 1918–1940*. Portsmouth: Heinemann.

Suzman, S. (1994) "Names as pointers: Zulu personal naming practices" *Language in Society* 23, 253–272.

Swigart, L. (2000) "The limits of legitimacy: Language ideology and shift in contemporary Senegal" *Journal of Linguistic Anthropology* 10 (1), 90–130.

Viriri, A. (2003) "Language planning in Zimbabwe. The conservation and management of indigenous languages as intangible heritage" On WWW at http://www.international.icomos.org/victoriafalls2003/papers.htm. Accessed 6.2.07.

Woolard, K. and Schieffelin, B. (1994) "Language Ideology" *Annual Review of Anthropology* 23, 55–82.

VII

Language Planning, Language Ideology and Entextualization: War Naming Practices
(with Busi Makoni and Charles Pfukwa)

Abstract
This article examines the relationship between language and war by investigating naming practices through three prisms: language planning, language ideology and entextualization. The article focuses on names assigned to combatants during the War of Liberation for Zimbabwe's independence. In African cultures, names often address a kaleidoscope of issues which may include the collective history and life experiences of the individual name bearer and the people surrounding him or her. In most African contexts changes in an individual's personal circumstances are marked by a name change, which suggests that names are variable and are not immutable. Entering the guerilla movement in Zimbabwe was a significant transformation which, in accordance with African cultural practices, required a new name to be assigned to signify the entry into a new phase of life. The names assigned reflect a "discourse" about the hopes and aspirations of the combatants. However, it appears that the underlying principles of naming in war are not significantly different from those during peacetime. In addition, war naming practices have implications for language planning from below, language ideologies and entextualization.

Introduction
This study investigates the dynamics and politics of names assigned to guerilla fighters during the liberation struggle for Zimbabwe's independence. There is a very impressive body of literature on personal naming practices. One of the main topics of this research is the etymology and social significance and meanings of the names in their respective communities (Akinasso 1980; Kimenyi 1978; Mathangwane and Gardner 2002). Our article differs from this tradition in that it uses sociolinguistic theoretical frameworks for interpretive insight in investigating naming practices during the Chimurenga War. War names refer to the names given to the fighters themselves, or the labeling of those against whom the combatants are fighting. The Chimurenga War took place in the past, and therefore the linguistic analysis of naming is a form of a "linguistic turn" of historiography in that the analysis is situated at the intersection of linguistic analysis and history.

Specifically the article addresses the following questions:

(i) What do naming practices look like when viewed through the prisms of language ideology and language planning, and conversely what do language planning and language ideology look like when viewed through naming practices during war?
(ii) What is the sociolinguistic significance of discourse processes such as entextualization on naming practices during war?
(iii) Are there any significant gender differences in the names assigned to the guerillas?

Since in most African communities "every level of personal development has a name-giving ritual, in which the new name symbolizes the achievement of a new state of social being" (Coplan 1994:47), joining the combatants in a liberation war requires a rite of passage in which a new name is vital for marking this change. However, unlike other name changes in rite of passage situations, in the case studied here, the name change affected both the first name and the surname. In ordinary rites of passage name changes, it is very seldom that the surname is changed. Yet in wartime, at least in the case of the Chimurenga War, the change of name represents the construction of a new identity for the guerilla, in which both first and surname are changed.

In the Chimurenga War, given names were deeply embedded in a politics of resistance and depict futuristic endeavors in an imagined independent state. As such, the war names or names assigned by and to individuals during the war of liberation were pseudonyms (Finnegan 2003) or *noms de guerre* which discursively constructed an "us" and "them" dichotomy wherein "the former is imbued with morally good qualities and the latter constitutes the evil, even inhuman enemy" (Brinkman 2004:2). The new names initiated, legitimated, and changed the identity of the individual during the liberation war. In fact, the war names were seldom used again after the end of the liberation war.

By and large, this article is a continuation of our earlier work (Makoni et al. 2007) in which we analyzed names in a context where the individuals were not engaged in the liberation war, during the period 1960–1990. In this article, we analyze the names of Zimbabwe's war veterans (then referred to as guerilla fighters or *Vakomana* ("boys" in Shona)). These are names they either were given or gave themselves not only to disguise their identities, but also at the same time to construct a new identity; possibly in preparation for the new independent state. We chose the Chimurenga War because it was the most significant nationalist war in the history of Zimbabwe.

War is both a physical act of violence and a social process with discourse practices that have a substantial impact on corpus planning. In wartime, language undergoes rapid changes as new words are added to the language or old words acquire new meanings associated with war experiences (Brinkman 2004). New words are introduced into the language as part of "code-language." This furtive language is often used "to prevent the enemy from knowing about war strategies and plans" (Brinkman 2004:3). Language change also occurs in part because of the deployment of old words/terms to new contexts and the creation of new linguistic configurations made up of multiple languages. The process of creating new words or expressions, as well as modifying old ones, or selecting among alternative forms, is a part of corpus planning. In most cases, corpus planning aims to develop the resources of a language so that it becomes an appropriate medium for communicating new concepts which cannot be communicated using the existing repertoire of words in the language.

Corpus planning, like any other form of language planning, is typically a top-down activity. Yet war naming practices create opportunities for corpus planning from below, as the act of naming is an instance of ground-level practices. From an applied linguistic perspective, naming practices during wartime are indicative of processes of corpus planning from below. Thus, studying war names not only provides insight into language planning from below, but also offers significant insight into "an encompassing social and political history" (Ferme 2001:177).

The article views war names from the quintessential triad of discourse-identityideology. War names discursively construct a particular identity and reflect specific ideologies through language use. The paper therefore is conceptualized not only as a contribution to onomastics but also to language planning and ideologies of language (Blommaert, 2005; Makoni and Pennycook, 2006; Woolard and Schieffelin, 1994). Ideologies of language are viewed as contextual sets of beliefs about languages, as cultural and political systems of ideas about social and linguistic relationships (Pennycook, 2007). The manner in "which languages are constructed is never about language only, but also about how individuals are thought about in society and definitions about" (Makoni et al. 2007:6) "languages are always definitions about human beings in the world" (Woolard and Schieffelin, 1994: 55). Ideologies of language are examined through the discursive construction of war names.

In African contexts, names, by their very nature, are "discoursed" or "languaged" (Maturana 1988; Mignolo 2001). Names indicate "the collective history and life experiences" (Mphande 2006) not only of the individual but also of the people surrounding the individual. The term "languaged" encapsulates active engagement, support, appropriation and subversion. To this end, "names of all kinds are social documents, which fix a person's position in the social structure and define his relations to other members of society" (Koopman 1992:1). This phenomenon of using names as discourse elements is also evident in the naming of dogs (Tatira 2004). Dog names "are used to comment on human social relationships" (ibid.:85), especially those things that cannot be expressed on a face-to-face basis. Names are therefore a vital communicative resource and provide a "languaging" opportunity. In wartime, "enemy-construction" (Brinkman 2004) is articulated through the use of names. For instance, the name *Bhidliza Mabhunu* (Destroy Boers/whites) is in its own right an internal or in-group discourse about the outgroup, as it expresses a wish by the in-group. The names are therefore situated within putative discourses which provide an opportunity to analyze processes of entextualization (Blommaert 2005; Bucholtz 2009).

Even though the names analyzed here are from a specific period, the use of names may transcend a particular historical period. For example, *Chimurenga* was the name of the legendary Shona ancestor Murenga Sororenzou (whom mythology describes as an extremely big man with a head the size of an elephant (*nzou*). Murenga was famous for the songs he composed which were sources of inspiration to his war colleagues. "Chimurenga" was subsequently used to refer to any battle against tyranny of any sort, including, ironically, opposition to institutional politics in independent Zimbabwe articulated through a type of protest music referred to as *Chimurenga*. *Chimurenga* has also been used as a metaphor for nationalistic history. It has been actively mobilized in the construction of a national memory, history, and common tradition.

The origins of the name *Chimurenga* can be traced as far back as the battles between the Portuguese and the Munhumutapa Empire in the seventeenth century. It was used again in the 1830s resistance by the Shona against Ndebele raids, and later in the conflict between the British and the Ndebele and Shona. More recently, it has been used by the Zimbabwean government to legitimate its land acquisition from Zimbabwean whites. The semantic and teleological history of a word like *Chimurenga* shows the complicated, constantly shifting, and at times conflicting nature of the concept. It also demonstrates how it has been effectively and astutely used to create continuity in the "nationalistic historiography" (Ranger 2004) of Zimbabwe. The meaning of the word *Chimurenga* shows the complex relationship between the construction of national imagination, entextualization, naming and history. Naming in war encapsulates the tension within post-colonial Africa as it tries to imagine its past by creating what it imagines to be "authentic" preceding epochs through retrospective naming while framing the rendition of that history along the linear Western model of history.

Background: Zimbabwean social and political war context
The naming practices and the attendant names analyzed fall within a very specific political context during Zimbabwe's War of Liberation in the 1970s. In the late nineteenth century, Zimbabwe was colonized by the British South African Company, an occupation which came to an end when Ian Smith unilaterally declared independence (UDI) from Britain in 1965. After the UDI, it became apparent to most African nationalists that the government of Ian Smith would not voluntarily concede power. As a result, the nationalists became militant and the military

conflict reached its apogee in the 1970s. The two major political parties during the nationalistic period were the Zimbabwe African National Union (ZANU) led by Robert Mugabe, and the Zimbabwe African People's Union (ZAPU) led by Joshua Nkomo. Robert Mugabe's military wing was based in Mozambique, while the main base of Joshua Nkomo's party was in Zambia. A political solution was found in 1979 and was mediated by the British government at Lancaster House in London. The focus of this article is on the naming practices of Robert Mugabe's war combatants, members of the Zimbabwe African National Liberation army (ZANLA) forces. Restricting the analysis to one period and one ethnic group, i.e., the Shona controls the contexts as tightly as possible.

Robert Mugabe's war combatants were predominantly but not exclusively Shona, while Joshua Nkomo's combatants were drawn mainly from the Ndebele and Kalanga ethnicities in south-western Zimbabwe. Notably, the adoption of new names is a characteristic feature of most guerilla movements. Although a new name might be used for security reasons, there is a sense in which the use of war names is an act of defiance against the existing government which, from the viewpoint of the guerillas, is an illegitimate government that has to be deposed. By not using state-registered names, the guerillas are essentially building "a society outside state control" (Brinkman 2004:8). Nonetheless, high profile leaders of the guerilla movements continued to use their registered names. It is possible that the top leadership felt the need to maintain their actual names for purposes of international recognition (Brinkman 2004). In addition, the Chimurenga War had both male and female fighters, yet there has not been any study that investigates whether female combatants were named in the same way as their male counterparts. In this article, an attempt is made at filling this gap.

Data collection
The names analyzed were drawn from a corpus of about 1875 names of war combatants. Analyzing the names of a clearly defined group, such as war combatants during a specific period (the 1970s), enables us to investigate the nature of prevailing language ideologies during that epoch and the *de-facto* language planning policies therein. More importantly, the corpus was composed of the names of guerillas that died in the war, from a list published in 1983 by the Zimbabwean Ministry of Information. In the data corpus, the meaning of each name is given wherever possible. The meanings of the names were interpreted by one of the co-authors who is not only a linguist and a native speaker of Shona, but also a former combatant in the Chimurenga War. His experiences and involvement in the War rendered it possible to acquire an insider or *emic* (Pike 1944) perspective of the war and the meanings of the names. Even though the interpretation of the entries was made by a linguist-cum-scholar-cum-war combatant, we cannot claim that his interpretations necessarily and identically correspond to the intended meanings of the name-bearers or name-givers. An exact match between the meanings of the names is also rendered difficult because the meaning interpreted by the person named might be different from the meaning intended by the name-giver. Even in instances when the name-bearers named themselves, it is difficult to know the intended meaning as the combatants were deceased.

Data analysis
In analyzing the names, we (a) explored the languages used in the names, and (b) whether the same language was used for both first and surname, i.e. whether first names were predominantly in English and surnames in Shona. In the case of the names whose etymology appeared to be English, we explored whether the name may be found in localized English usage, if not, we then examined the nature of the linguistic processes on which the name was based (e.g. nominalization, compounding). Wher-

ever possible we tried to establish the source of the name; i.e., whether it had been drawn from popular culture or fiction as part of entexualization.

In this sample, we found that the first name came either from English or from Shona, but the surname was always in Shona. Thus, a name could be a combination of the two languages in that the first name is in English and the surname in Shona. This practice in naming is not unique to wartime in Zimbabwe. Evidence presented in Makoni et al. (2007) shows that while names in Zimbabwe are drawn from English and African languages, very rarely do Africans have surnames drawn from the English lexicon. In the corpus, there were only 5% or 95 cases in which both the first name and surname were in English.

There were also 188 (about 10 %) in which both the first name and surname were in an African language such as *Teurai Ropa* (Spill blood), *Bvuma Zvipere* (Agree and its over). Ideologically, this suggests that while bilingual practices of Shona and English are widespread, the exclusive use of African languages is feasible, and the use of English-only names is limited. These examples show the degree to which English had spread in African communities as well as the extent to which it had been appropriated as one of the local languages even amongst war combatants. This reflects a paradoxically polemical issue. On the one hand, nationalist freedom fighters associated English with colonialism and viewed it as a tool of oppression to be denounced at all costs. Yet, on the other hand, in wartime, they embraced the use of the language in their camps because in that context the "out-group" was not the colonialists but rather the African comrades who were from different ethnic groups (Mazrui 1975). Using a language of any other ethnic group would have been potentially hegemonic. The use of English by combatants who were all non-native speakers of English invoked some "imagined" collective identity and thus avoiding any possible form of ethnic "othering."

In names such as *Admire Chimurenga* "liberation war," *Strongman Hondo* "war," *Liberty Makata* "uphill," and *Talkmore Tichatonga* "We shall rule," the English lexical items are not used as first names in English-speaking communities. There are other names based on English language lexical items which seem to have been formed through a process of nominalization. Names such as *Toasted, Worry* and *Stubborn* are examples of the process of nominalization. The proper nouns were derived from verbs (toast), transitive verb (worry) and adjective (stubborn). In some situations, the process of nominalization produced names which were inconsistent with localized English spelling but were an attempt at approximating Shona phonological structure. For example, *Wonderous* "wondrous," *Winai* "win," and *Sayizi* "size" show an approximation of Shona phonology. There is, however, some difference between *Wonderous, Winai,* and *Sayizi. Wonderous* is made up of morphemes which may be encountered in English (-ous) as a bound morpheme in words such as "riotous" and "righteous." English-like names such as *Winai, Sayizi,* and *Seriyasi* "serious" have the CVC Shona syllabic structure. These names are examples of Africanized spellings of English words. The spellings are based on Shona phonetics reflecting the varying degrees to which both languages are combined in practice in multilingual contexts. Names such as Talkmore, Youngman, Saymore, Stepmore, Trymore, Edmore, etc. reflect a novel form of compounding not found in native-speaker varieties of English. Clearly, some of the names reflect a combination of processes, for example, nominalization and the conversion of English words into Shona phonology. There are also names such as David, Peter and Maxwell which are used as first names in both war and peacetime (see Makoni et al. (2007) for peacetime). Names such as Peter, David and John are also found in English-speaking contexts as first names or surnames.[1]

---

[1] These are in fact highly unusual in this form as surnames. Surnames of British origin when they contain a personal name are usually based on a patro-

However, what is worth noting is that in the corpus of Chimurenga War names these names are used as first names only. The surnames are all in Shona. The use of English or English-like naming practices in war suggests that English is treated as a "local" language (Higgins 2009) in a manner analogous to the ways in which indigenous languages are framed.

Words such as "strongman" or "talkmore" are also commonly used as first names in peacetime (see Makoni *et al* 2007). Names such as *Sinfree, Learnmore* and *Lovemore* are very common in Zimbabwe, reflecting that this form of compounding in name formation is as much a feature of naming practices in peacetime as it is in war. Perhaps this convention for forming names is a cultural practice that found its way into wartime practice. On the whole, the principles underlying naming practices in war are not substantially different from those in peacetime. Thus, naming practices in war and peace are instances of comparable principles under dissimilar circumstances.

Examples such as *Youngman Zvichaita* "young man it will happen," *Stepmore Chamboko* "increase or step up the beating," *Addmore Mauto* "increase the number of soldiers," *Trymore Magorira* "try harder guerillas," *Trymore Shungu* "be more determined," *Newman Hondo* "a new person for the war," *Liberty Makatu* "liberty is an uphill struggle," *Talkmore Tichatonga* "with more talking we will rule," *Winai Nyika* "win the country," *Wonderous Udzai* "wonderful to tell" and *Siriyasi Tichatonga* "we are serious we shall rule" are all examples of bilingual naming practices. This is interesting because, in colonial language policies, it was not the Africans who were expected to be bilingual. White settlers were to be bilingual in English and an African language (Makoni et al. 2007). This suggests that language planning may, in fact, produce unintended outcomes.

The examples cited above are all in non-standard English with the surname drawn from Shona. Yet the war surnames do

---

nymic, indicated by the suffix "son" or just "s"; e.g. from the Christian name Peter, the surnames are Peterson or Peters, but not normally just "Peter."

not resemble any known surnames used during peacetime. The surnames are striking in that they reflect war situations or aspirations. They are, therefore, interesting from an "interpersonal" and "ideational" perspective. From an interpersonal perspective, the names sound as if the name-bearers were engaged in a conversation interpersonally directed in some cases at the individual, but in other cases at the targeted oppressor regime. *Hondo* "war," *Tichatonga* "we shall rule," *Nyika* "the country" are all "discoursing" about war. The discursive aspect of war names is also evident in instances where both names are in Shona. Names such as *Bvuma Zvipere* "give in and it will be over," *Bvuma Titonge* "give in so that we can rule," *Batanai Muhondo* "be united in war" and *Bvrurai Mabhunu* "kill all whites" reflect the aspirations and hopes of war combatants.

This raises the question of whether war has dissimilar effects on naming practices than peace. The answer is "probably not," because at least in the Zimbabwean case, the two social activities, war and peace, are governed by similar naming principles. The difference between war names and those used in peacetime is the propositions of the names and not the underlying principles of name-assignment. In both war and peace, the names chosen are dialogic and reflect the prevailing context. The practice of using names which are sensitive to context and individual experiences is widespread and common in both war and peace. The differences, however, lie in the nature and type of discourses of the names. For example, war names such as *Mabhunu Muchapera* "all whites shall be killed," *Teurai Ropa* "blood shall be spilt" are encountered in the war corpus and not in civilian usage, which suggests differences in topical issues between war and peace. Similarly, names such as *Runyaradzo* "peace," *Tanatswa* "we are happy" and *Rugare* "we are comfortable" are common in civilian names but are not found in war names. War names are therefore suggestive of a future-oriented sense of agency characterized by a desire to bring to fruition a specific and desirable outcome. War names are therefore "a hidden transcript" (Brinkman 2004:12) through which guerillas express their true feelings about the government they were fighting. The surnames appear to be a dialogue wherein the guerilla fighters are venting their feelings "against the colonial state" (Brinkman 2004:10).

There are also names in the data corpus that are drawn from literature in African languages. Names such as *Chaminuka*, from the 1963 novel *Feso* "the rising white spear" by Mutsvairo, reflect processes of entextualization as the name is associated with a legendary hero who led the defense of the Rozwi empire against invaders. The novel is an allegory of the conflict between Zimbabweans and the British. The use of such a name in war naming practices reflects an astute understanding of the past in nationalistic circles (Kahari 1982).

Names of female combatants
Most female names reflect a similar pattern to those of male combatants. All surnames are in Shona whereas the first names are a mix of Shona and English. There are "conventional" English first names such as *Susan, Violet, Martha,* and *Lucia*, all of which can be found in civilian naming practices (see Makoni et al. 2007). However, another set of names are either verbs or nouns that are rarely used as proper nouns, for example, *Resistance* and *No Rest and Fix*. There is a small set of names about 2% whose origins are from Afrikaans, a language associated with South Africa and particularly the apartheid regime. For example, in the name *Pfutseki Mabhunu* "f_ _ _ off you whites," the first name is a Shona rendition of the Afrikaans curse word *voetsek*. Pfutseki has a more offensive sense than the Afrikaans "*voetsek*." By and large, however, there were no significant differences between male and female war naming practices.

Discussion
In this article, we set out to establish a connection between language and war by analyzing names assigned to war combatants

during Zimbabwe's Chimurenga war. In analyzing the names, the focus was on the potential implications of war naming practices on language planning, language ideology, and entextualization. Even though naming is a potential source of language planning, it has only recently been viewed as a resource for framing language planning, a position which seems to be changing gradually (see the 2007 special issue of the *Journal of Current Issues in Language Planning*). The creation of new words, or the acquisition of new meanings for old words, is all part of the process of corpus planning. The difference, however, in war naming practices is that this form of language planning is from the bottom up. Similarly, the use of localized varieties of English in naming raises the question of the relationship between language ideologies in naming practices and the nature of language planning involved. Typically, in language planning, the variety of language being promoted and developed is a standard and not a localized one. War names challenge this aspect of language planning and at the same time provide concrete examples of bottom-up language planning.

From the perspective of a normative standard of language ideology, names such as *Addmore* and *Trymore* may be analyzed as a combination of independent morphemes; while perhaps from an *emic* view of the war combatants, the names constitute a chunk, or a fused lect (Auer 1999). The frequency of their occurrence means the process of this form of compounding is quite common. When a multilingual approach is adopted which treats the two names as a single proposition, their meanings become easily apparent: some of the names and surnames seem to be a description of a prevailing state of affairs. *Newman Hondo* "the new individual to the war," and *Trymore Magorira*, (Try harder liberation fighters) wherein the guerillas are urged to try harder. It is relatively easy to conceive of a state of affairs in which a newlyrecruited guerila may describe himself as a new individual to the war, or in which a third person calls upon the guerillas to try harder to achieve their goals. The names describe a prevailing state of affairs or a desired one. The striking aspect is that the description entails drawing upon linguistic resources. The linguistic resources come from two different languages, reflecting the type of participants' bilingualism. The retention of the mixed forms as names even in writing gives them some degree of permanence or institutionalization. They can no longer be treated as fleeting and idiosyncratic even though they might be perceived as such by outsiders. A multilingual interpretation of the names means combining the meanings of the two in order to make "ideational" sense. For example, the first name *Winai* makes nationalistic sense in light of the surname *Nyika*, because the two combined mean "win the country," which was the intended outcome of the struggle. A comparable analysis can be made of *Siriyasi Tichatonga* "we are serious we shall rule."

The fact that most of the names are made up of localized varieties of English and Shona words implies that English and Shona are strongly integrated into the Zimbabwean milieu and this influence is also evident during wartime. Given the fact that one of the main objectives of colonial and Rhodesian language policy was to reduce the availability of English to African language speakers, their wide prevalence as names indicates that English, or a variety of English, has permeated this African society more widely than one might have expected.

The use of non-standard names is suggestive of the localization of English. The use of Africanized English names blurs the distinctions between English and African languages. Localization is a powerful ideology which is not restricted to language but applies to other aspects of Zimbabwean culture such as Christianity. For instance, Christianity in Africa introduced drums to go with church hymns. The drums reenact a template that exists in African societies in praise hymns. English has been localized to the same extent that Christianity in Africa has.

By and large, the war on independence in Zimbabwe had two main dimensions; both guns in the field and discourses in contexts emerging from the names given to the guerillas. War discourses and the languaging of the war were constantly evolving and dynamic. Some of the war discourses were to become part of everyday Zimbabwean discourses after the war. For the discourses to circulate, they had to be reified and extracted from one context and embedded in another context or (re)entextualized (Bucholtz 2009; Sarangi 2009). Karigoga is an instance of entextualization (i.e. extracting discourse from its original context and then re-inserting it into a new context). An excellent example of entextualization is *Bvuma*, a popular name during the war, meaning "concede." This name was to become the title of a popular song by one of Zimbabwe's top musicians, Oliver Mutukudzi. If the target of the critique in Oliver Mutukudzi's song *Bvuma* is now Robert Mugabe, it is indeed ironic that when the name was introduced before being entextualized, it named the aspirations of Robert Mugabe who led combatants to dislodge Ian Smith. Some other examples of entextualization are the use of words originating from other languages with which the combatants had been in contact. The process of entextualization is also apparent in the use of names derived from Zimbabwean African literature thus providing the literature with a certain degree of nationalistic legitimacy. The entextualization of discourses from African literature is ironic because literature in African languages was initially produced under the tight auspices of a government controlled institution which censored most of it.

Conclusion

Even though naming is an instance of everyday linguistic practices, an analysis of naming practices is invaluable because it provides insight into the interplay between language ideologies and language planning. Language planning and language ideologies provide analytical frameworks within which naming may occur. In this regard, sociology, constrains the type of naming practices which are "authenticable" (Heller 2008) and popular to communities in times of war. Names in wartime are discoursed as much as those used in peacetime. After all, any name is paradigmatically possible, but names that violate sociological norms may not be acceptable. For example, a name praising racist behavior or white supremacy would violate the expected norms and philosophical convictions of a liberation movement.

In this article we have argued that war naming practices are based on exactly the same principles as those on which names in peace are generally based. War names, like other names in peacetime, are texts that provide a dialogue in which the namers/named are engaged with society at large. In wartime, the discourse that emerges from the names constructs the enemy as the "evil other" who must be wiped out. Furthermore, war naming practices give insight into language planning and language ideology. Entextualization also plays a significant role in war naming practices. The use of names drawn from other languages suggests the need to stress the degree to which heterogeneity, multiplicity, and variability are constitutive of linguistic practice (Nicolai 2008). These sociolinguistic processes are of course significantly facilitated in part through the contacts between war combatants and their host communities.

References

Akinasso, Niyi, F. (1980). "On the differences between spoken and written language" *Language and Speech* 25: 97-125.

Auer, Peter (1999). "From code-switching via language mixing to fused lects: toward a dynamic typology of bilingual speech." *International Journal of Bilingualism* 3: 309–332.

Blommaert, Jan (2005). *Discourse: A Critical Introduction.* Cambridge: Cambridge University Press.

Brinkman, Inge (2004). "Language, Names, and War: The Case of Angola." *African Studies Review* 47(3): 143–163.

Bucholtz, Mary (2009). "Captured on tape: professional hearing and competing entextualizations in the criminal justice system." *Text & Talk — An Interdisciplinary Journal of Language, Discourse & Communication Studies* 29: 503–524.

Chakaipa, Patrick (1963). *Karikoga Gumiremiseve*. Longman. Salisbury: Rhodesia

Chidzero Bernard (1957). *Nzvengamutsvairo*. Salisbury, Zimbabwe: Longman.

Coplan, David B. (1994). *In the Time of Cannibals: The Word Music of South Africa's Basotho Migrants*. Johannesburg: Witwatersrand University Press.

Ferme, Mariane C. (2001). *The Underneath of Things: Violence, History, and the Everyday in Sierra Leone*. Berkeley CA: University of California Press.

Finnegan, Ruth (2003). "Anonymity and pseudonyms." *Anthropology Today* 19(2): 22–23.

Heller, Monica, ed. (2008). *Bilingualism: A Social Approach*. Basingstoke: Palgrave Macmillan.

Higgins, Christina (2009). *English as a Local Language: Postcolonial Identities and Multilingual Practices*. Clevedon United Kingdom: Multilingual Matters.

Kahari, George (1982). *The Rise of the Shona Novel: A Study in Development 1890–1984*. Gweru: Mambo Press.

Kimenyi, Alexandre (1978). "Aspects of naming in Kinyarwanda." *Anthropological Linguistics* 20(6): 258–271.

Koopman, Adrian (1992). "The socio-cultural aspects of Zulu ox- and dog-names." *Nomina African Journal* 6: 1–13.

Makoni, Busi, Sinfree Makoni & Pedzisai Mashiri (2007). "Naming practices and language planning in Zimbabwe." *Current Issues in Language Planning* 8(3): 1–31.

Makoni, Sinfree & Alastair Pennycook (2006). *Disinventing and Reconstituting Languages*. Clevedon, United Kingdom: Multilingual Matters.

Mathangwane, Joyce. T. & Sheena Gardner (2002). "Language

attributes as portrayed by the use of English names in Botswana." *Nomina Africana Journal* 16(1 & 2): 74–87.

Maturana, Humberto R. (1988). "Ontology of observing: the biological foundations of self-consciousness and the physical domain of existence." *Conference Workbook: Texts in Cybernetics*. American Society for Cybernetics Conference, Felton, CA.

Mazrui, Ali A. 1975. *The Political Sociology of the English Language: An African Perspective*. Mouton Publishers: The Hague and Paris.

Mignolo, Walter. 2001. "Coloniality of power and the subaltern." *The Latin American Subaltern Studies Reader*. Ed. Ileana Rodríguez. Durham NC: Duke University Press, 224–244.

Mphande, Lupenga. 2006. "Naming and linguistic Africanisms in African American culture." *Selected proceedings of the 35th Annual Conference on African Linguistics*. Eds. John Mugane, John Hutchison and Dee A. Worman. Somerville, MA: Cascadilla Proceedings Project.

Mutsvairo, Solomon (1963). *Feso*. Salisbury, Zimbabwe: Longman.

Nicolai, Robert (2008). "How languages change and how they adapt: some challenges for the future." *Journal of Language Contact-THEMA*, 312–330.

Pennycook, Alastair (2007). *Global Englishes and Transcultural Flows*. London: Routledge.

Pike, Kenneth L. (1944). "Analysis of a Mixteco text." *International Journal of American Linguistics* 10:113–138.

Ranger, Terence (2004). "Nationalist historiography, patriotic history and the history of the nation: the struggle over the past." *Journal of Southern African Studies* 30(2): 215–234.

Sarangi, Srikant (2009). "Editorial: Entextualizing the

institutional." *Text & Talk — An Interdisciplinary Journal of Language, Discourse and Communication Studies* 29: 481–484.

Tatira, Liveson (2004). "Beyond the dog's name: a silent dialogue among the Shona people." *Journal of Folklore Research* 41: 85–98.

Woolard, Kathryn & Bambi Schieffelin (1994). "Language ideology." *Annual Review of Anthropology* 23: 55–82.

VIII

Language Planning from below: The case of the Tonga in Zimbabwe
(with Busi Makoni and Nicholus Nyika)

Abstract
Arguments for bottom-up approaches in language planning are currently in vogue. Rarely, however, are such arguments supported by evidence demonstrating how such bottom-up planning leading to successful implementation can be achieved. This article presents evidence based on archival documentation in the form of annual reports and manuscripts written by administrators that document how, through community empowerment, the Tonga, a minority (a term which the Tonga do not use) language group from Zimbabwe, successfully lobbied for the promotion and development of Tonga as the language of instruction in all Tonga-speaking areas. But the success of the promotion is constrained by the nature of the framework within which language, heritage and micro-nationalism form the basis of the promotion exercise.

Introduction
Language planning projects in Africa are characterised by top-down and authoritarian approaches typical of nation-building projects in most polities around the world. Ekkehard states that

"status planning ... is most often initiated from the top (government) rather than from below (speech communities) at grassroots level" (2000: 335). In recent years, there have been strong suggestions that top-down approaches to language planning generally fail and that bottom-up approaches may be more successful. However, there has been limited evidence that convincingly demonstrates that the latter necessarily lead to successful acquisition planning. The main purpose of this article is therefore to broaden the scope of research in language planning by analysing language-in-education policy and planning for Tonga, a minority language in Zimbabwe, by considering realities on the ground. Specifically, the article examines how different language activists lobbied for the promotion and development of Tonga to counter the perceived hegemonising effects of other indigenous African languages such as Shona and Ndebele.

A relatively large amount of sociolinguistic literature on Zimbabwe focuses largely on Shona, Ndebele and English, their characteristics, evolution and status (Hachipola, 1998; Ndhlovu, 2007; Thondhlana, 2002). This article departs from this approach by examining one of the less commonly studied languages, Tonga. We use data drawn from multiple sources such as archival documentation, annual reports and academic manuscripts written by administrators directly involved in language promotion through community empowerment, i.e. from the bottom (Conyers & Cumanzala, 2004). The theoretical basis of the article is a combination of language ideologies and 'Discourses of authority' consistent with Gee's discourse formulation (Gee, 1996).

This paper explores the complementary and sometimes conflicting and shifting discursive positions of different stakeholders in the promotion and preservation of Tonga and what promotion and preservation means to them. The stakeholders include Tonga researcher/activists, chiefs, and funders of language associations. In this article, we argue that multiple discursive positions have a direct bearing on communities and might engender new social formations.

Our focus is on the Tonga situated in Zimbabwe, although there are three groups of Tonga speakers situated on the Zambian, Zimbabwean and Mozambican sides of the political boundaries. In Mozambique, the Tonga-speaking communities are found in the Inhambane province which is located in the south-east of Mozambique (Gerdes, 2003). The variety of Tonga spoken in the Inhambane province is also spoken in some parts of the Limpopo province in South Africa. Specifically, the Tonga spoken in Giyani and Malamulele areas bears a striking resemblance to the Tonga spoken in Mozambique. Some researchers have gone further and argued that the Tonga spoken in Inhambane is identical to the one spoken in South Africa (Matsinhe, 2006). It has been further suggested that due to the proximity of the South Africa–Mozambique border post to Malamulele and Giyani, the Tonga found in South Africa might have emigrated from Mozambique. The Tonga spoken in South Africa is often referred to as XiTsonga and uses the same orthography used in the Inhambane Tonga.

On the other hand, the Tonga in Zambia and Zimbabwe may speak the same language but they have experienced different historical trajectories even though both were directly affected by the construction of the Kariba dam in 1957. Those in Zambia were assimilated into Zambian national politics, whereas the Tonga in Zimbabwe were resettled and left economically impoverished and marginalised by the forced resettlement process. The relocation had long-term effects on the Tonga in that it disrupted their social, economic and agricultural habits (Colson, 1971; Cumanzala, 2002; Scudder, 1962; Tremmel, 1994). Even though the Tonga people were the ones most directly affected by the construction of the Kariba dam, they were not consulted in the planning of the dam, nor did they have a say with regard to where they were to be resettled. Some of the Tonga people were placed in geographical areas where they were a minority. Families were split and those settled in Zimbabwe subsequently lost contact with those in Zambia and the lack of contact resulted in the development of linguistically diverse forms between the Tonga spoken in Zambia and Zimbabwe. Even within Zimbabwe itself, the Tonga people were scattered right across the country. In fact, as Hachipola (1998) points out, a number of Tonga people are found in the Kariba district (or Zambezi Valley), the Midlands districts of Gokwe and in the Matabeleland North districts, specifically Hwange and Binga (Figure 1) and yet Binga, located in a remote village in Matebeleland north on the south eastern part of Lake Kariba, is one of the most isolated of Zimbabwe's 57 districts, furthest from regional and national centres. It is thus interesting to note that changes in some key aspects of Zimbabwean national language policy could, in part, be driven and shaped by the efforts of an impoverished indigenous group most distant from centres of power.

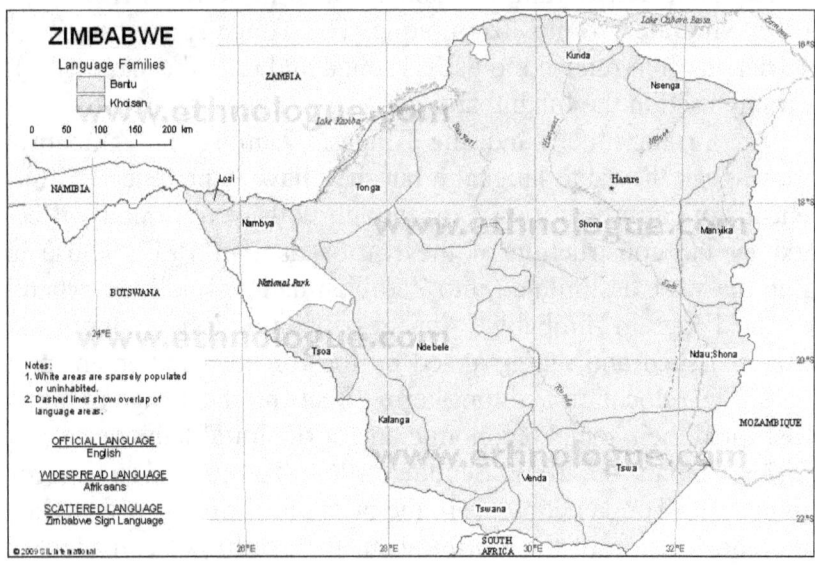

Figure 1 Map of Zimbabwe showing location of the Tonga
Source: Ethnologue (2008).

However, the forced relocation of the Tonga in order to make way for the construction of the Kariba dam had two conflicting consequences: some were submerged in the host communities, losing their language over a number of generations; others, as a result, ferociously held on to their heritage which was historicised in order to give it more legitimacy. It appears that one of the lessons which the Tonga might have learnt from the construction of the Kariba dam was the need to be actively engaged with national government in all aspects which directly affect their lives, including language. Perhaps because of this history, the Tonga played a substantial role in shaping the development of language polices related to the role of minority languages in the Zimbabwean educational milieu. Robbins's observation about the Urapim in Papua New Guinea is also apt for the Tonga when he writes "different kinds of futures require different kinds of linguistic possibilities" (2001: 903).

The official recognition of minority languages such as Tonga in the discourse of language planning and as media of instruction has been fraught with problems. Very few teachers have been trained to teach in these languages and teacher deployment does not take into consideration the issue of language. For example, Ndebele-speaking teachers who are deployed in a predominantly Nambya or Tonga community to teach Grade 1 are not likely to be proficient enough to teach in these languages. The interaction in classes is therefore likely to involve teachers using Ndebele or English as a medium of instruction, while the students may use Nambya and Tonga as languages of learning. Codeswitching as a strategy here may not be readily feasible because the teachers and students do not have a language in common, so there is no common code to switch into. Communication between teachers and students is facilitated by the strategic role played by some students as brokers, mediators between teachers and students and within the peer group itself. In such polyglossic contexts, partial understanding and active brokerage demonstrate the ability of speakers to exercise agency within severe constraints as they position themselves in multiple and shifting ways.

In Zimbabwe, the relationship between minority languages and Shona, Ndebele and English is complicated and has been changing historically and indeed varies from one locality to another. In some places, speakers of minority languages form the majority of the population. For example, in Hwange and other mining areas, ciNyanja is the dominant language and yet surprisingly it is not used as a language of instruction, presumably because of a shortage of native speakers of the language who are trained as teachers. The prestige languages in the Hwange area are Ndebele and English. These are far from being the languages of the majority of the people living in this area. How the relationships between minority languages and dominant languages evolve is apparent in the shift in the status of some minority languages. For example, while in pre-independent Zimbabwe (prior to 1980) languages such as Tonga were looked down upon, the situation is increasingly complicated with the radical assertion of the Tongan sense of linguistic and cultural pride, to the extent that to find employment in the Binga area competence in Tonga is a prerequisite. For the development of insights into such complicated relationships, sensitivity to locality, site and historical context is required.

In order to contextualise the discussion on Tonga language planning, we begin this article with a brief historical overview of Zimbabwe and its language situation.

Zimbabwe: A Brief Historical Note

The history of contemporary Zimbabwe can be traced back to the 1890s when the British South African Company occupied most of current Zimbabwe after defeating the Ndebele and Shona in the 1896 wars (see Makoni et al. (2006) for a detailed description of the pre- and post-colonial history of Zimbabwe). In 1923 Southern Rhodesia, as it was then referred to, was annexed by the British Government after voting against inclusion as a South African province. In 1965, at a time when most African countries were securing their independence from Britain, the Rhodesian Front, a party led by Ian Douglas Smith, issued a Unilateral Declaration of Independence (UDI). However, UDI was not recognised by the international community. It is interesting to note that while the present-day Zimbabwe is experiencing international isolation, this is not a new phenomenon as its previous colonial government experienced exactly the same fate.

Nonetheless, the declaration of independence from Britain provoked in part an armed revolution which ended when Robert Mugabe's party, the Zimbabwe African National Union Patriotic Front (ZANU PF) won power in the 1980 elections. Mugabe's party still retains considerable influence in the running of Zimbabwe in spite of the fierce opposition from the Movement of Democratic Change.

Zimbabwe's language policy can be categorised into three phases. In the colonial era, circa 1890–1923, the main agenda of the colonial regime was to create White colonial officials who were proficient in Shona and Ndebele. The focus during this phase was not the imposition of English on local populations. Instead, the focus was on developing and learning African languages by white Rhodesians. The unintended consequence of this is that the initial grammar books on indigenous African languages were often a product of 'mishearings of whites' (Makoni, 1998) or what, in psycholinguistics approaches to language acquisition, would be referred to as interlanguages.

From 1923 until 1980, the language policy changed drastically. Ndebele, Shona and English were recognised as official languages. English was the main language of trade and commerce whilst Ndebele and Shona were used in the first phases of education before switching to English after the fourth grade. In the third phase, the main principles of the pre-1980 language policies were retained, in that English still maintained its status as the dominant language of business. The difference, however, was the increasing pressure from 'minority' language groups who vociferously demanded the recognition of their languages as languages of instruction in schools and business in their own locale. This paper can be read as an analysis of the efforts of the minority language groups in developing their languages and the discourses of framing languages which ensued during the advocacy campaigns initiated by the different stakeholders.

Historical Background to the Tonga and the Spread of the Tonga Language

According to Ndhlovu (2004), there are about 200,000 (or 4%) Zimbabweans who are presumably ethnically affiliated to Tonga out of a Zimbabwean population currently estimated to be about 12 million. Most of the Tonga-speaking people live in the northwestern parts of Zimbabwe, namely Gokwe and Binga, although they are also found in other areas such as Hwange. As already stated, Tonga is spoken not only in Zimbabwe and Zambia but also in some parts of Mozambique and South Africa. The fact that the 'same' ethnic groups might be found in different nation-states 'disarticulates' (Mignolo, 1996) the relationship between place and language founded on a philosophical relationship between language and space which is largely a product of nineteenth century colonialism and expansion. In fact, because of the many cross-border languages, transnational language policies (Gadelli, 2007) are emerging as reflected in collaborative initiatives between Venda and Sotho linguistic communities in South Africa and Zimbabwe, and the Kalanga in Zimbabwe and Botswana (Nyati-Ramahobo, 2002). To some extent, 'migratory movements [whether voluntary or forced] are disarticulating the idea of national' (Mignolo, 1996: 191) languages that are confined to specific geographical places or boundaries. Consequently, the widely pervasive character of cross-border languages poses a serious challenge and at the same time creates opportunities to re-orient epistemology in language research, an argument forcefully articulated by Mignolo when he writes:

> The challenges presented to language and literary scholarship by transnational and transimperial languaging processes are epistemologically and pedagogically serious, for they impinge on the very conception of the humanities as a site of research and teaching ... Transnational languaging processes demand a theory and philosophy of human symbolic production predicated on languaging and transnational and transimperial categories, on a new philology, and on a pluritopic heremeneutics. ... (Mignolo, 1996: 183)

Zimbabwe has three national languages which enjoy significant prominence under the present Education Act. Among these, English, Zimbabwe's official language, plays a central role, especially in education. Although it remains steadfastly the official language of trade and industry, mass media, parliament and education, Shona and Ndebele (see Figure 1 for the spread of languages in Zimbabwe) are central in government structures such as the senate, state media and as languages of instruction in lower primary education (Thondhlana, 2002).

The term Tonga means independent or grumblers (Lancaster, 1974). The Tonga defined themselves in opposition to the groups who were vassals to senior Shona chiefs. They have been known by various names: Goba, Nyai and Chikunda. The use of these alternative terms is complicated because the Tonga who are the subject of this study have at times distinguished themselves from the communities which they would refer to as Goba (refugees of low and at times slave status), Nyai and Chikunda (Lancaster, 1974). The Tonga, Nyai and Chikunda, even when defining themselves as distinct groups and using different ethnic labels, have long constituted a 'single social and cultural field, intermarrying, living together, crossing rivers, and moving freely across the rivers and ... throughout the area' (Lancaster, 1974: 711). All things being equal, the Tonga can be defined in terms of shifting political fortunes in Shona-speaking worlds.

The Tonga played a major role in ferrying combatants during the Ndebele and Kalolo wars in the 1840s. In the late nineteenth century, they paid tribute to both the Ndebele and Lozi. A substantial number of Tonga were killed in 1893, when they were hit by smallpox which they presumably caught from their encounters with the Zambians. The Tonga did not have a centralised authority. Instead, they had senior elders who acted as arbitrators in situations of conflict. It is precisely for this reason that the Tonga have often been described as a 'stateless society', 'amorphous' and 'characteristically unorganized' (Colson, 1951: 94–102). Nevertheless, the fact that the Tonga did not traditionally have chiefs is critically important because, to some extent, this compromised individuals who were subsequently imposed as chiefs in a bid by British colonialism to establish uniform governance across different ethnicities. On the one hand, because of the histories of chiefs as imposed by outsiders, it compromised their campaigns for the expanded use of Tonga. On the other hand, because Binga has the largest number of chiefs in any Zimbabwean district, language planning activists were therefore assured of a substantial number of persons who would amplify their activities. The fact that the Tonga are a mixed group is clearly important in terms of how they projected and might have reacted to language promotion campaigns. The Tonga people were therefore using a language campaign to partially contribute towards the establishment of an 'imagined' (Anderson, 1984) homogeneous community which is inconsistent with the realities of history (Conyers & Cumanzala, 2004).

Shift from a Minority to an Indigenous Language
The notion 'minority' is objectionable to some Zimbabwean minority language groups, for different reasons. During the colonial period, the term was used to refer to settlers who were

politically and economically dominant, even though they were a minority in terms of numbers. After independence in 1980, whites were still referred to as a minority although this time they were a minority both in terms of numbers *and* political power. To the general populace, the use of the word *minority* conjures images of abuse of power during the colonial period. From the perspective of the Tonga, the use of the term *minority* to refer to a group which is numerically small is derogatory and politically restricting. Their preference is for the term *indigenous*. For the Tonga the term *minority* metaphorically signals their exclusion from the Zimbabwean state, thereby limiting their access to state resources. In this regard, promoting Tonga when it is framed as a 'minority' language has the opposite effect to the general assumption that it will enhance the status of the language and their opportunities for inclusion into the Zimbabwean state. Being a minority enhances the status of the community in that more and more state resources will be made available to the community as part of the promotion and development exercise. And yet, from the viewpoint of the Tonga, it consolidates their exclusion since the state is imagined as consisting of Shona or Ndebele. To some extent, the view of the Tonga is echoed in the definition of the term by Kubik:

> ... a minority is anything smaller than something else. A minority language therefore, is spoken by a community that is smaller in numbers in relation to one or more other language communities in the same area, territory or country, and whose members feel that their language and culture is [sic] threatened, oppressed or otherwise denied expected roles within the larger communities. (1989: 2)

For the Tonga, the objection is on the basis that in spite of their position on the margin of the political and economic spectrum, they feel that they are ideologically central to their own lives.[1] Their view is that the term *minority* is inappropriate because it creates the impression that the Tonga are of secondary importance to their own lives. Zimbabweans strongly define themselves in terms of place, particularly where their umbilical cords are buried, as forcefully articulated by one of the Tonga researchers/activists:

> ... the very government that we fought to install turned around and labelled us a minority group. We are very bitter about this dehumanization, disparagement in the land of our ancestors. (Mumpande, 2006: 14)

Accordingly, the term does not encapsulate how the Tonga people perceive themselves socio-psychologically. For the Tonga, being referred to as a *minority* is disempowering, and in order to assert their own sense of self-pride they insist on their language being classified as indigenous. It seems, as Kymlicka and Patten point out, for the Tonga:

> ... debates over the status of a regional language are also debates over nationhood. For the minority language group, recognition of its language is seen as a symbol of recognition of its nationhood. For the minority group, official multilingualism is desired in part because it is a symbol of, and a step towards acceptance that it is a multination state, a partnership of two or more nations within a single state. (2003: 5)

For the Tonga, one of the major objectives of language planning is to create latitude and scope for their voices to be heard. Thus they prefer the term *indigenous*. For them the term *indigenous*

---

[1] Note that the Tonga are not the only minority language group that has lobbied aggressively for the promotion of their language. A similar approach is reported in Nyati-Ramahobo (2002) about the Wayeyi in Botswana.

creates opportunities to claim a legitimate status within Zimbabwe. However, the concept *minority* is also theoretically and practically problematic because it essentialises language and ethnicity including the relationship between the two. It treats language and ethnicities as natural, 'timeless, authentic' (Makoni et al., 2007: 26) and 'stable depositories of cultures' (Fabian, 1986: 5) and not culturally and historically contingent (Joseph, 2006). The idea of languages as timeless or static draws in part from ecological discourses in which diversity is inherently to be applauded (Fabian, 1986; Hornberger, 2003; Nettle & Romaine, 2000). Ironically, treating minority languages and ethnicities as natural renders it relatively more difficult for language planning activists to create contexts in which change may occur. Yet for advocates of minority languages, change is one of the critical objectives of language planning (Makoni et al., 2007).

The Tonga, therefore, do not regard themselves as minorities but as citizens of Zimbabwe. Citizenship in Zimbabwe in part revolves around the notion of indigeneity or *vana vevhu* (Shona for 'children of the soil') and *abantu bohlanga* (Ndebele for 'people from the reeds'). From the perspective of the Tonga elite, minorities are neither children of the soil nor people from the reeds. The issue of the recasting of the term *minority* to *indigenous* is not only a semantic one, but one clearly linked to issues about linguistic citizenship. Citizenship has a number of different dimensions, and language is one of them. Linguistic citizenship in such a context captures more powerfully the processes under way than language rights (cf. Trudell, this volume). By insisting that they are *indigenous*, the Tonga are forcefully articulating a case for linguistic citizenship (Stroud, 2000; Stroud & Heugh, 2004), although on the surface the quest for the promotion of Tonga might appear to be one of linguistic rights. The Tonga might have felt that they were precluded from exercising their linguistic citizenship if they were regarded as minorities because their language was merely *in* the State and not a language *of* the State, i.e. a denial of legitimate nationhood.

In an argument which supports linguistic citizenship (Stroud, 2000), the Tonga link the official recognition of Tonga to Zimbabwean national citizenship. As a result, the researcher/activists and traditional authorities feel that if Tonga is not recognised as an indigenous language but rather as a minority language, this is tantamount to depriving the Tonga people of their national citizenship. However, because of the serious debates about who is a *bona fide* citizen of Zimbabwe, the extent to which linguistic citizenship may contribute to national Zimbabwean citizenship is contentious. To some extent, the preference for the term *indigenous* over *minority* by Tonga elites demonstrates the degree to which *emic* Tonga discourses are incommensurable with scholarly ones. In this case, scholarly discourses are clearly *etic* in nature in that these are typically derived from western epistemology and thus inadvertently reinforce western epistemologies (Makoni & Meinhof, 2004).

In order to align *emic* with *etic* discourses and taking cognisance of the objection of the Tonga to the term *minority*, we will opt for the notion *indigenous* instead. However, this is not to suggest that using the word *indigenous* is not problematic. The term *indigenous* creates an image of a sharp distinction between indigenous and exogenous languages, with the former requiring protection. The negative connotations of the term arise in that its use is associated with being 'primitive' and having low prestige.

Although the Tonga prefer the term *indigenous*, there are conceptual challenges in that it is inadvertently still caught up in a monoglot ideology that reinforces the notion of a 'stable language regime' (Kroskrity, 2000) in which 'invented' (Ranger, 1989) languages including the Tonga are easily named, are autonomous and 'hermetically sealed' (Makoni, 1999: 144) mother tongues. Even though the Tonga people were challenging official Zimbabwean language policy positions, they were indirectly reinforcing the nation-state rather than a micro-nation (Coluzzi, 2006) perspective. It seems that the preference for the term *indigenous* by the Tonga is part of a discourse of proto-ethnic nationalism or micro-nationalism. In this regard, proto-ethnic nationalism challenges the narratives that frame Zimbabwe as a predominantly Shona/Ndebele state and constructs it as more diverse. The diversity does not, however, challenge the political and epistemological power of Shona/Ndebele elites in how Zimbabwe as a state is perceived.

Paradoxically, although the advocates of recognition of minorities such as the Tonga are themselves bilingual, their strategies are monolingual in orientation. Since Tonga, like any language, as Bakhtin (1983) reminds us, is 'heteroglossic', the advocacy is therefore not only promoting particular languages but defining them in such narrow and specific ways that restrict the range of discursive possibilities, which is also limiting in terms of the semiotic process of 'iconization' (Irvine & Gal, 2000).

Tonga Language in Education
The Tonga traditionally believed in educating youth for life and did not draw distinctions between education and building moral responsibilities. Girls and boys were kept strictly apart and learned modes of speaking deemed appropriate to their age and sex. Although the use of Tonga as a medium of education might be seen as authenticating Tonga traditional lives, its use in formal education affected the pragmatics of Tonga and some modes of Tonga cultural organisation and living. As a medium of instruction it was also not accompanied by the teaching of geometrical-mathematical knowledge of the Tonga embedded in the famous Tonga bag weaving (Gerdes, 2003). The curriculum did not fully capture Tonga "counting, numeration systems, calculation, games, algebraic algorithms in divination, and geometrical explanations" (Gerdes, 1998: 1). Furthermore, the idea of Tonga as a medium is a metaphor which might be partly mis-

leading. It conjures up an idea of a teacher with fully formed ideas which are expressed via language, with students' roles being to decode the messages, a philosophical position drawing in part on Reddy's (1979) 'conduit metaphor' and the assumption that speakers can always mean what they say and are able to say what they mean. In fact, this is an ideological position underpinning a lot of research into pragmatics (Austin, 1975; Searle, 1969).

The Zimbabwean educational system is examination-driven. In such a context, the fact that Tonga, although taught and used as a medium of instruction, is not examined means, according to the students' and perhaps from the government's perspective, it is not important enough to be examined. In an intellectual climate in which some scholars are extremely critical of language tests, it is encouraging that for the Tonga, and perhaps other minority people, being examined in Tonga, or other minority languages, enhances rather than detracts from its educational validity in the eyes of the students. In fact, this echoes an argument by McGroarty et al. (1995) who, with reference to Navajo communities, state that:

> For indigenous languages, often disparaged or at least neglected by the dominant society, tests can be powerful pieces of evidence that a hitherto 'invisible' language does indeed exist in terms that an educational bureaucracy can understand and, consequently, must acknowledge. (1995: 324)

During the colonial era, Tonga was taught as a language, and language teaching materials from Zambia were used in Zimbabwe,[2] or what was then referred to as Rhodesia. The teaching of

---

[2] This was in spite of the fact that the varieties of Tonga spoken in the two countries were somewhat different. However, this practice is not unique in Southern Africa as Zulu learning materials were used for teaching Ndebele in Zimbabwe and siSwati in Swaziland.

Tonga was suspended at the UDI by Ian Smith, the leader of the White Rhodesian settlers, in 1965. This led to economic sanctions being imposed on Southern Rhodesia by the United Nations. The sanctions included the banning of the export of Tonga books to Southern Rhodesia. As a result, it became difficult to obtain Tonga books, and the colonial government introduced Ndebele in schools, effectively replacing the Tonga language. In response to this development, Tonga chiefs protested against the imposition of the Ndebele language as they considered the Ndebele language and culture to be foreign.[3]

Although there has been an extensive and extremely strong narrative on the history of Zimbabwe dominated by the Shona/Ndebele and White settlers, this excluded the contributions of other ethnic groups in the nationalist project. Urban legend has it that because of the geographical location of the Tonga in Northern Zimbabwe, the Tonga communities encountered a lot of liberation fighters who promised them that their language would be introduced as a language of instruction after Zimbabwe attained independence. Unfortunately, this promise was not kept by the Zimbabwean government, which led the Tonga to actively lobby the government.

Theoretical Framework: Language Planning from Below
Our theoretical framework is a combination of Cobarrubias (1983) and 'Discourses of authority' (Gee, 1996: 127) which has also been used by Trudell and Reeder (2006). Cobarrubias proposes four different categories which form the basis of language planning ideologies: internationalisation, linguistic assimilation, linguistic pluralism and vernacularisation. Internationalisation refers to the official granting of status to a language like English within important institutions in the country, education, justice, health systems, etc. Of course, the idea of an 'international language' is in itself an ideological and discursive approach to lang-

---

[3] Ironically, the Ndebele and Shona regarded written versions of their languages as foreign to them.

uage (Pennycook, 2007). Linguistic assimilation is defined as the integration into communities of all people irrespective of their race, linguistic origin and linguistic competence. Linguistic pluralism is the converse to linguistic assimilation in that it accepts diversity and recognises multiple languages. Vernacularisation is the development and promotion of 'indigenous' languages. In fact, vernacularisation is a form of status planning.

Status planning is closely related to corpus planning in that "the form and structure of a language must keep pace with its functional distribution" (Hult, 2004: 182). Indirectly, both status and corpus planning relate to acquisition planning because "the functional uses of a language, as well as the forms of language through which those functions take place, are inseparable from the users of a language and how they came to acquire the 'new' forms and functions of that language" (Hult, 2004: 182). Acquisition planning, which is sometimes referred to as language-in-education, is largely an attempt "to alter the language capacity of a community" (Spolsky, 1997: 100). It is precisely for this reason that language-in-education is viewed as "a key implementation procedure for language policy and planning" (Kaplan & Baldauf, 1997: 122). Although the conventional wisdom in African sociolinguistics is that corpus planning is a consequence of changes in status planning, the converse is also plausible.

On the other hand, the term Discourses of authority (upper case initial letter adopted from Gee, 1996) means a way of being an act of social existence and the practice of living in multiple worlds. In the case of Tonga, a typology of Discourses of authority is critically important because there are many stakeholders involved in the promotion of the Tonga language: elite researchers/activists; traditional authorities including chiefs and sponsoring institutions of the language committees (LCs). Each stakeholder articulates a specific type of Discourse and each Discourse is construed as a source of authority. The competing

Discourses may reflect "diverse and multiple ways in which realities are framed" (Gee, 1996: 174).

In line with Trudell and Reeder (2006), the following taxonomy will be used.

1. Academic discourses hold the authority of the linguistic ideal, theories of learning and technical arguments. The researchers and other intellectuals involved in the promotion of Tonga fall into this category. The authority of academic discourses draws upon a Western conceptualisation of scholarly research and what constitutes legitimate knowledge.
2. Institutional discourses are descriptions and rationales provided by powerful institutions that fund language promotion activities. In the case of Tonga, this would be institutions such as the Catholic Commission for Justice and Peace (CCJP) and Silveira House which funded language promotion.
3. Ideological and historical discourses are traditional authorities regarded by others who define themselves or are perceived by others as custodians of cultural and social behaviours. In the case of Tonga, these would be the heads of traditional institutions. Their authority capitalises on constructed historical precedent and tradition.

In our theoretical framework, the conceptual validity of the different language ideologies underpinning 'minority' language research as described by Cobarrubias is examined. Regarding Discourses of authority, we analyse the extent to which they are applicable to Tonga contexts, and we also try to establish the extent to which these different types of discourses converge or are in conflict. We also attempt extrapolating the reasons for the convergence or divergence. The convergence and/or conflict shed insight into issues about 'minority' languages and language planning as understood by minority language activists.

Description of the Study and Research Methods
The primary data for this paper consist of an analysis of archival records relating to lobbying and language promotion activities with primary reference to the Tonga. The archival analysis includes documentation from LCs, one of the main sources of language promotion of minority languages in Africa. The archival data include the analysis of annual reports of all the organisations that were involved in language promotion activities undertaken in each fiscal year, identifying who the sponsors were and what their role in the promotion activities was. In analysing the documentation made available to us, we examined the role of the different organisations/stakeholders involved in the promotion of Tonga. The archival data were meant to provide information on specific Discourses of Authority. Theoretically the archival data are used as a means to critically review some of the concepts underlying the promotion of Tonga such as heritage, preservation, and endangerment. The Cobarrubias framework is used as a template in an attempt to understand the activities and aims of the different stakeholder groups in terms of language planning.

Results and Discussion: Archival Data on the Formation and Operations of LCs
The Tonga Language and Cultural Association (TOLACO)[4] was formed in 1976 in response to perceptions by Tonga-speaking communities who felt that Tongan language and culture were threatened, not by English but by indigenous languages, in this case Ndebele and Shona. TOLACO was formed to rectify what the Tonga felt was their economic, political and linguistic marginalisation and the endangerment of Tonga culture and lang-

---

[4] This is not unique to Zimbabwe. Language activities have, in part, been driven by associations in other parts of Africa. For instance, in Botswana, the Kamanakao Association advocated for the promotion and development of Sjiyeyi. Other associations in Cameroon have also lobbied for the promotion of various languages in that country.

uage. TOLACO was financially supported by the CCJP. However, it is possible to assume that the financial support of TOLACO may have compromised its independence and thus also its effectiveness in being a voice of the ordinary Tonga person.

Tonga chiefs and headmen[5] were at the forefront of resisting the use of Ndebele in schools in Binga as they viewed this as an imposition of the Ndebele language and culture on the Tonga. One of the Tonga chiefs lamented the loss of social cohesion amongst the Tonga, especially among the younger generation when he said:

> The youth of today are more Shona or Ndebele than being Tonga or Kalanga. A lot of misunderstanding is going on between the old and new generations. Our ancestors are crying because our children no longer speak our languages. They even shun their own tribe and culture ... as they do not want to be identified as Tonga. (Mumpande, 2006: 37)

The District Commissioner responded to the mounting pressure by challenging the Tonga to produce their own literature and learning materials. In response to the challenge, the community formed a group of writers (as part of TOLACO) which produced manuscripts for use in schools. Some of these Tonga scripts were published in 1978–79 but the process was short-lived as the liberation struggle escalated and led to the attainment of independence in 1980. Following independence, all TOLACO's pre-independence activities were suspended. The expectation

---

[5] Note that most African societies had centralised forms of government. The chiefs and headman were community leaders for each ethnic group. The chiefs delegated some of their responsibilities to headmen and the chiefs reported to kings. Headmen are often considered as community elders who, because of their experience and wisdom, are involved in the day-to-day community disputes and provide leadership to their respective local communities.

was that the new democratic government would be more responsive to the needs of the former marginalised language groups. However, TOLACO's hopes were shattered as the language policy of Zimbabwe, which became a source of controversy for the Tonga, was based on Section 62 of the 1987 Education Act:

1. Subject to this section, the three main languages of Zimbabwe namely Shona, Ndebele and English shall be taught in all primary schools from the first grade as follows:
   a) Shona and English in all areas where the mother tongue of the majority of the residents is Shona or
   b) Ndebele and English in all areas where the mother tongue of the majority of residents is Ndebele.
2. Prior to the fourth grade, either of the languages referred to in paragraph a) or b) of subsection (1) may be used as the medium of instruction, depending upon which language is commonly spoken and better understood by the pupils.
3. From the fourth grade, English shall be the medium of instruction, provided that Shona and Ndebele shall be taught as subjects on an equal time allocation basis as the English language.
4. In all areas where minority languages exist, the Minister may authorise the teaching of such languages in primary schools in addition to those specified in subsection (1) and (3)

(Government of Zimbabwe, 1987).

The Tonga, Venda, Sotho, Kalanga, Shangani and Nambya languages were categorised as 'minority' languages and could only be taught as subjects up to Grade 3 in those areas in which they were predominantly spoken. After that the children were required to learn English and either Shona or Ndebele as subjects. According to the Act, English only became the medium of instruction from Grade 4.

Early challenges to the lack of adequate attention to 'minority' languages were pursued by a loose coalition of individuals from such language groups as Venda, Tonga and Kalanga who formed what was called the VETOKA Publishing Company. The aims of this company were to produce literature in all the languages that Section 62 of the Education Act had identified as minority languages. There was a great reluctance by publishing houses to produce materials in these languages. VETOKA collapsed for financial reasons and because of conflicts between the Tonga and Nambya (Annual Report: January-December 2001) mainly among the researchers/activists. The loss of some of VETOKA's senior members led to its rapid collapse, showing the extent to which the success of these language movements was dependent upon individual social activists.

In 1996, TOLACO, which had been disbanded in 1980, was revived. Its broad aim was the preservation of Tonga language and culture in all Tonga speaking areas.[6] Its primary task was to dispel and eradicate, among other things, pejorative perceptions of the Tonga people. According to Manyena:

> [TOLACO] aims at eradicating, among other things, the myths spread long back about the Tonga people being uncivilized, incapable of doing what other ethnic groups can do, and that the Tonga live in trees and have two toes, and other lies that have been spread about the Tonga people. Because of such untrue stories about the Tonga people, they have never been taken seriously in Zimbabwe. They have been underrated, overlooked and

---

[6] The definition of who constitutes TOLACO, the aims and objectives of the organisation and their strategies are contained in a document entitled 'A report on the 29–30 July 2000 TOLACO Workshop'. That there were all sorts of myths about the Tonga was corroborated by Mr Mumpande in an interview at his office in Bulawayo in July 2004.

undermined in many respects. It is therefore the aim of TOLACO to correct all the myths and present a clear picture of the Tonga people to the country and the world at large. (2000: 10).[7]

A key concern of TOLACO was that the Tonga language was not taught in schools to any significant level. This was viewed as a form of discrimination. Following protracted advocacy and lobbying initiatives aimed at the Ministry of Education and the Parliamentary Portfolio Committee on Education, TOLACO decided to incorporate other language groups defined as minorities by the Zimbabwean Constitution so that a concerted effort could be made from a broader base. The rationale was to influence the government to amend its language policy in a way that promoted the recognition and development of what it called 'minority' languages.

The initiatives that followed led to the formation of the Zimbabwe Indigenous Language Peoples' Association (ZILPA). ZILPA consisted of six LCs representing six 'minority' language groups: Tonga Language Committee, Kalanga Language Committee, Sotho Language Committee, Nambya Language Committee, Shangani Language Committee, Venda Language Committee. The main task for ZILPA was to forcefully push forward the agenda initiated by TOLACO and thereby challenge the provisions of Section 62 of the Education Act of 1987. As TOLACO had argued, it was on the basis of the Act that they were discriminated against. ZILPA then drafted what it termed an acceptable alternative to Section 62 of the 1987 Education Act:

Interpretation of terms
In this Section:

---

[7] Mr S.B. Manyena in 'A report on the 29–30 July 2000 TOLACO held at Binga Roman Catholic Hall on the teaching of Tonga language in Binga, Hwange, Gokwe North, and Nyaminyami' (2000: 10).

i) **Indigenous language** means the following languages: Kalanga, Ndebele, Shona, Tonga, Sotho, Venda, Shangani and Nambya
ii) **Area(s)** means district(s)

1. Subject to this Section, the indigenous languages of Zimbabwe including English and Sign language shall be treated equally, taught and examined from the first grade to university provided that, in each area or part of the area, the predominant indigenous language and English shall be taught.
2. The medium of instruction in any area or part of the area shall depend upon which indigenous language is more commonly spoken and understood by the majority of the pupils and shall be used in addition to the English language.
3. All indigenous languages shall be taught as subjects on an equal time allocation basis as the English language.
4. Subsection 4 of Section 62 of the Education 2 is to be deleted.

(Minutes of ZILPA meeting, 7 April 2001).

It is important to note that the names of the 'minority' languages are written in the ZILPA Constitution using an orthography which these language groups prefer and not the more widespread Shona and Ndebele version in Zimbabwe. This can be interpreted as an act of affirmation and a form of resistance to the hegemony of Shona and Ndebele. Thus, Kalanga is written as TjiKalanga, Tonga as ChiTonga, Venda as TshiVenda, Nambya as ChiNambya, Shangane as ChiChangana and Sotho as SeSotho. Furthermore, the Constitution of ZILPA provides insights into the aspirations of the language groups in terms of the Government's ascription of language status, as well as their desires regarding language use in the various domains. Foremost among the objectives of ZILPA is the promotion and development of the 'minority' languages for use in teaching and learning in schools, colleges and universities. They also want their languages recognised as official languages, as well as having them used in the media (radio and television):

> **Section 4: Objectives**
> The objectives of the association are to operate on a non-profit basis and to:
> 4.1 Promote the teaching of TjiKalanga, ChiTonga, TshiVenda, ChiNambya, ChiChangana, and SeSotho in schools, Colleges and Universities;
> 4.2 Lobby the Government of Zimbabwe to recognise and permit the use of TjiKalanga, ChiTonga, TshiVenda, ChiNambya, ChiChangana, and SeSotho as official languages;
> 4.3 Assist and encourage the writing and production of literature in TjiKalanga, ChiTonga, TshiVenda, ChiNambya, ChiChangana, and SeSotho languages for use in schools, colleges and universities;
> 4.4 Promote the use of TjiKalanga, ChiTonga, TshiVenda, ChiNambya, ChiChangana, and SeSotho languages on national radio and television;
> 4.5 Network with organisations with similar objectives in Africa and beyond;
> 4.6 Solicit for and receive donations;
> 4.7 Do all things necessary to further these objectives and for the general and cultural well being of the association's beneficiaries
> (ZILPA, n.d.).

Viewed from Cobarrubias's (1983) theoretical framework, ZILPA was resisting any form of linguistic assimilation within their individual ethnic groups. At the national level, the aggressive promotion of the so-called minority languages was a quest for linguistic pluralism. The conflict, insofar as the quest for linguistic pluralism is concerned, is evident at the level of micronationalism. Here the Tonga are, in fact, not in support of linguistic pluralism, especially in Tongaspeaking communities. Instead, the activities of ZILPA are all geared towards exclusive vernacularisation.

It is interesting to note the bi-directional relationship between corpus and status planning evident in the ZILPA Constitution. The proposed changes of Tonga, Kalanga, etc., demonstrate how changes in orthography were being used as an instrument to bring about and reflect changes in the status of these languages. Resistance by the Tonga, Kalanga and Nambya and other groups to using Shona and Ndebele orthography is indicative of the degree to which, as in many other contexts in sub-Saharan Africa, orthography is both a technical matter and at the same time an important index of identity. Success in the development, revision and implementation of orthography thus requires active participation by a wide range of groups and diverse communities if it is to succeed (Bird, 2000).

Traditional Institutions: The Role of Community Leaders in the Promotion of Tonga

The role of chiefs among the Tonga, as in many other communities in Zimbabwe, has been a source of controversy. The controversy arises because in some cases they are viewed as custodians of tradition, central to local governance, while in other cases as puppets of both colonial and postcolonial governments, and more recently compromising the land rights of the Tonga by facilitating the acquisition of land by Shona and Ndebele migrants (Dzingirai, 2003). Resentment against the chiefs and migrants was accentuated by the fact that the migrants not only belonged to different ethnic groups, but were as a rule more educated than an average Tonga. Because some people were suspicious of the Tonga chiefs, the effectiveness of their language promotion activities was somewhat compromised because they could not be viewed as *bona fide* critics of government in any area including language policy.

In spite of the fact that the relationship between chiefs and local Binga citizens was ambivalent, which compromised their 'authenticity'[8] (Coupland, 2003; Heller, 2006), they proved to be important allies in the struggle for the promotion of language. Their involvement in the Tongan case took place after being recruited to take part in the project for the promotion of language and cultural rights of their people. Two advocacy officers of the Binga Justice and Peace Project (BJPP) convinced them of the value of the engagement in such a project. The objective of the meetings with the chiefs and officers of the BJPP was to raise the chiefs' awareness over the educational problems affecting school students because they were being taught in a language other than their own.

The awareness campaigns targeting chiefs also brought to the forefront issues that threatened their full cooperation. First, the advocacy officers realised that some chiefs were reluctant to participate in the promotion and preservation of Tonga because they were not remunerated for their involvement. Secondly, in a context characterised by acute political tension, some chiefs were apprehensive of taking part in language promotion activities and enterprises aimed at preserving their own heritage because they felt that the government would link advocacy with oppositional political activism (Conyers & Cumanzala, 2004). Strategically, TOLACO and BJPP ran workshops to provide them with opportunities to discuss the advantages of preserving their languages and heritage and to raise their awareness to the potential adverse effects of the Shona and Ndebele dominance. Another strategy which was proposed was to strongly recommend to School Development Committees that if

---

[8] 'Authenticity' in this context means originally from within the communities and not externally imposed. Note that chieftainship has been extremely controversial among the Tonga because some chiefs were imposed by colonial governments and the postindependent Zimbabwean government.

schools were not being responsive to introducing local languages, the local communities would withdraw their children from those schools.

According to Mumpande (2006) government officials listened to ZILPA because of the involvement of the chiefs. ZILPA also functioned at community levels by engaging school principals. When a school principal was reluctant to introduce Tonga, the traditional authorities forced the principal to transfer to another region. The use of the role of chiefs and headmen conferred on language advocacy a mixed sense of 'authenticity' because of their controversial role. It is this discursive regime of authenticity which underpinned the language-in-education policies from the perspective of the traditional leaders. The chiefs took over the schools and expelled headmasters who were regarded as being against implementing the Tonga language policy. This shows the extent to which the language-in-education policy was rapidly becoming one of the strategies that traditional chiefs used to assert authority and achieve control over the social and political structures in Binga. The role of the chiefs effectively changed the discourse from one of being about language to one of restoration of cultural heritage.

Externally Funded Institutions: The Role of Silveira House
Silveira House is a leadership training and development centre founded in 1964 during a period of heightened political tension in Zimbabwe. It is owned and operated by the Society of Jesus, more popularly known as the Jesuits.[9] To some extent, Silveira House played an important role in the struggle to liberate the country from colonialism. A number of current leaders of the country, including the president, Robert Mugabe, have gone through Silveira House either as fugitives from Rhodesian forces, as trainees or as trainers. Silveira House was, therefore,

---

[9] Information on the history, structure and activities of Silveira House is based on a document titled 'Silveira House Civic Education and Advocacy Programme August 1999–August 2001' by Sr Janice McLaughlin.

actively involved in the struggle for the liberation of Zimbabwe from colonialism. With the advent of political independence in 1980, Silveira House's role changed to focus on reconstruction and development. Attention, therefore, was given to skills training programmes and employment creation, as well as to community development.

In the period after 1999, Silveira House's focus shifted to respond to a new scenario characterised by an economic and political crisis, as well as perceived unaccountability and human rights abuses perpetrated by the political leadership. Silveira House shifted its focus to work on enhancing citizen participation in economic and political decision-making through advocacy training. This entailed raising consciousness and demanding accountability from local authorities and politicians including members of parliament, chiefs and headmen. The Civics Department introduced a Civic Education and Advocacy Program.

The involvement of Silveira House in the struggle to develop and promote 'minority' languages is traced back to the launch in 1994 of a book by Fr Mike Tremmel, a Catholic priest based in the Binga District. According to Mumpande (2006), Fr Tremmel wrote a book, *The People of the Great River*, which told the story of the Tonga people, their lives and experiences until the time when they were displaced from the Zambezi Valley following the construction of the Kariba Dam in 1957. Mumpande (2006) explains that the ceremony to launch the book brought together members of the Catholic Commission for Justice and Peace in Zimbabwe (CCJP(Z)) in the Binga District, Silveira House officials, the Tonga chiefs, the Tonga headmen and many other members of the Tonga-speaking community.

In an attempt to make the language promotion activities as inclusive as possible, a children's unit that also manages the needs of women was formed. It operated through schools and women's groups. Silveira House provided all the financial and material resources to make the promotion and development of Tonga a realisable dream. However, the Tonga language promotion activities were constrained by the funding agency and, at a conceptual level, by how the issues of language promotion were framed.

Discussion

In the theoretical framework, we proposed a taxonomy which tries to capture and describe the discourses of the administrators/ researchers/activists, traditional chiefs and funding agencies. We subject to critical scrutiny the discourses that emerge from the different groups, first by examining the implications of Cobarrubias's theoretical framework for the Tonga language promotion activities. Secondly, we examine the Discourses of authority that emerge from the different stakeholder groups and what their implications are for language planning from below.

From the perspective of Cobbarubias's theoretical framework, the campaigns did not entail a systematically developed project for developing Tonga students' proficiency in English. In fact, English did not seem to be at stake at any one point, in which case the issue of internationalisation did not arise in the Tonga language promotion discourses by all the different stakeholders. In the Tonga universe, it was not English that was posing a threat to the survival of the Tonga language. For this reason, the promotion of Tonga falls under the category of vernacularisation as the campaigns focused on Shona and Ndebele dominance. The Tonga were drawing attention to perceived Shona and Ndebele hegemony. The promotion of Tonga was in part also driven by political considerations since the ruling party, the ZANU was, from a Tonga perspective, viewed as a predominantly Shona party with a smattering of Ndebele who were included in the 1985 Unity Accord signed as part of the political compromise which brought peace to southern Zimbabwe. National discourses that recognised Shona and Ndebele were construed as discriminating politically and economically against the Tonga. It seems that from the viewpoint of the Tonga "inequalities in access to a privileged language were a major source of other social inequalities" (Kymlicka, 2001: 216). In this regard, from the Tonga perspective, "social equality could only be achieved by equality in the learning and use of language" (Kymlicka, 2001: 216). To the Tonga, it appears that the continued use and designation of Shona and Ndebele as indigenous languages and Tonga as a minority language would have "placed an irrevocable obstacle in the way of true equality" (Kymlicka 2001: 216).

Academic arguments in support of the promotion of Tonga were conceptually inspired by discourses about language endangerment and linguistic human rights especially "group differentiated rights" (May, 2008). Tonga elites argued that with the continued use of Shona and Ndebele in their schools, their language would in all probability be faced with extinction. The validity of the argument on the probable 'death' of the Tonga language was based on well-established but contested literature on language death and endangerment (Batibo, 2005; Nettle & Romaine, 2000). In spite of the fact that there was limited empirical evidence to support the idea that Tonga was nearing extinction, the discourse continued to be amplified in the advocacy campaigns by Tonga elites. Since real possibilities of Tonga dying were remote, the only rationale for explaining the discourses of endangerment is that the promotion of Tonga framed on the basis of language loss was more of an emotional discourse about political and economic exclusion (Heller, 2007) than the impending 'death' of the Tonga language. In addition, the large presence of Shona and Ndebele migrants in predominantly Tonga-speaking environments made this imagined fear real in the minds of Tonga language activists. At another level, discourses about the extinction of Tonga were part of broader African "apocalyptic discourses" (Ridge, 2001: 15) which have emerged at various points in Africa's unfolding historical trajectory. Fears of the extinction of African cultures go back a long way in African historiography.

It is therefore possible that discourses by chiefs as representatives of traditional institutions were not only ideological but also historical in orientation. They adopted a specific orientation towards the past and the future based on constructing a myth of the continuity of Tonga cultural patterns which were being disrupted by the teaching of Shona and Ndebele. The discourses of continuity which sought to exclude Shona and Ndebele from Tonga classrooms and treated other languages as threats are interesting because the Tonga have always been immersed in a predominantly Shona/Ndebele-speaking universe. The discourses of the loss of culture and language articulated by chiefs are comparable to those articulated by researchers/activists in which languages were conceptualised as "stable depositories of culture" (Fabian, 1986: 5). Both types of discourses emphasised the danger of the loss of Tonga as a language and of Tonga cultural practices. For chiefs, the loss of Tonga cultures and ways of life were prompted by the expanded use of Ndebele and Shona, although most of them were multilingual with some proficiency in both languages. Even if the language loss was empirically verifiable, it could also be argued that the loss of Tonga might have been a positive thing for the Tonga youth who live in a rapidly changing context in which conventional Tonga might be of limited value.

Although the discourses of the chiefs and researchers are comparable, they are driven by different philosophical underpinnings. The chiefs were using a traditional theory that "naturalizes culture, projecting it into an ideal space in which order and harmony ... reign" (Quijano, 1999: 99). The researchers, on the other hand, were using a critical theory that "emphasizes the political and social" (Quijano, 1999: 109) aspects of culture. The two stakeholders were driven by common discursive practices that were in turn underpinned by different philosophical positions which also reflect the conflictive nature of the meaning of culture and heritage.

The success of the Tonga in raising awareness of the status of their language was in part a result of an astute interpretation and use of Freire's (1972) *Pedagogy of the Oppressed*. Central to Freire's work is the claim "that oppressed people must be aware" (Conyers & Cumanzala, 2004: 385) of their oppression and can organise to challenge it. The case of the Tonga which we have described can be seen as one of the few cases that unequivocally demonstrates "how democratic governance may be fostered from initiatives from below" (Hyden, 2000: 29) when institutions and academics and traditional authorities collaborate, although there is still the possibility that the oppressive nature of the regime might limit the degree to which they can operate (Conyers & Cumanzala, 2004).

For the language activists, the status of the Tonga language has a strong bearing on the status of the Tonga people as an ethno-cultural group. Tonga language activists and traditional leaders view the Tonga language as an important constitutive factor of their individual and at times their collective identities (May, 2008). Thus, Tonga culture, ethnicity and language are treated as if they were natural in spite of the fact that there is a relatively large amount of literature in African studies that highlights "the socially and historically constructed nature of ideas about Africa, ethnicity, customary law, and other social processes, much work on African languages [still] remains rooted in an essentialist/primordial paradigm" (Makoni et al., 2007: 26). As a result, indigenous African languages may mean different things to different people depending upon the activities which they are engaged in: rural, backward, combative and politically courageous (see also Harris, 2006; Rampton, 2006).

Although the traditional leaders, researcher/activists and indeed the funding agencies advocate a promotion of African heritage which is typically projected as static, unchanging and stable, the notion of Tonga as heritage is an extremely complicated one. Smith (2006: 11) argues that heritage is a "politically situated cultural practice". As such, while not necessarily immutable, it is a set of practices that are negotiated, at times jointly constructed and therefore appealing to a mythical past. The preservation of heritage using schools as a site is founded on efforts to align the values of the students with those of the larger community. In this regard, Tonga heritage is conceivably possible when, as Bourdieu felicitously articulates, "heritage can be passed when the heritage has taken over the inheritor" (Bourdieu, 2000: 152) or when the inheritor has been 'appropriated' by the heritage. If heritage is fluid or changeable and not rigidly bound, the challenge for the Tonga chiefs is that the variety of Tonga they were promoting might have been viewed by the other Tonga as not representative of their heritage.

Even though the Tonga have been vociferous and extremely assertive in aggressively demanding some partnership in influencing the direction of key language developments within Binga, the process was closely tied to issues about identity as shown by changing the spelling of names. Changes in the spelling of names, though, was much more than an orthographical technical matter for the Tonga (as for many other societies in Africa) but an important index of identity. One critical way in which Tonga heritage was retained was through a reviving of rituals which they deemed traditional and presented as if they were always performed in the past. Tonga efforts to revive their own heritage by evoking the past was, however, partially undermined by their 'telescopic' view because according to Colson (2007: 351) many Tonga people could only provide accounts of the events during their own life time, although a minority could also provide brief accounts of the social histories of their villages' notions of history. In most traditional African communities what constitutes the past is often subject to debate and more often than not, the past is not history because "[m]any 'traditional' societies foster a non-formal and loosely institutionalized view of the past which is extremely difficult to capture" (Hofmeyr, 1994: 4).

While language activists strategically essentialised the relationship between ethnicity and language, in which individuals who spoke Tonga as a language were viewed as essentially Tonga ethnically, the implied relationship between ethnicity and language has been disputed by historians. The notion of every Tonga speaker being a Tonga ethnically cannot be supported historically because Tonga communities were always extremely heterogeneous. Given the impact from different countries such as Angola, Mozambique and Malawi (Colson, 2007), a homogeneous Tonga community is therefore a myth. The notion of a monolithic Tonga (indeed like the notion of indigenous languages) is a post-colonial and post-independent Zimbabwean consequence rather than an accurate reflection of the ecological systems in pre-colonial Africa. It is indisputable that social ideology was emphasised as competition for national resources became acute, thus attenuating differences within heterogeneous communities (Colson, 2007). As she rightly points out, the evidence that the Tonga are a post-colonial phenomenon in a social/linguistic ideology of a monolithic identity can be supported by the fact that those who may regard themselves as Tonga (or are regarded as Tonga today) may not necessarily have done so half a century ago.

The promotion of Tonga in post-independence Zimbabwe should be seen as part of a slow and unfolding historical process of language standardisation which reduces linguistic differences. The reduction of linguistic differences and the ideology of linguistic homogenisation were initially effected through "schools, frequent encounters at government and other centres, and most recently by radio broadcasts" (Colson, 2007: 347). Linguistic differences were therefore more pronounced in the early 19th century. Ironically, the process of preserving Tonga is a continuation of language standardisation which, in turn, has nothing to do with heritage. Language activists, by promoting a specific variety of Tonga, are 'inventing' a more homogeneous variety that never existed before. Similarly, for the chiefs to promote a specific variety of Tonga as part of heritage is also a form of inventing heritage or constructing a mythical past. In fact, the emerging homogeneity runs contrary to what Matthews characterises as:

... rather than a sharp ethnic divide ... an unbroken and logical continuum of social forms ... between the patrilineal and matrilineal extremes of 'plateau Shona' and 'plateau Tonga' respectively which passes through a stage, coinciding with the Zambezi valley, of bilingualism, bilateral descent, and lack of cattle (Matthews, 1978, 120–121 in Vickery, 2007: 9)

Concluding Reflections
Conceptually, the promotion of Tonga and other languages is predicated on a philosophical assumption of the existence of a 'hermetically sealed' (Makoni, 1999: 144) entity named Tonga which is an ongoing invention of a complex interplay between colonial and post-colonial standardisation. The promotion of Tonga, and indeed language planning generally, is faced with a serious challenge if we adopt a post-modernist/colonial position which challenges the very existence of languages (including heritage and culture) and opt for a social constructionist position in which languages are historically contingent (Joseph, 2006) and are embedded in social contexts which cannot be separated from other semiotic systems (Pennycook, 2007; Reagan, 2005). If languages are not objects and are embedded in social contexts, then it becomes extremely difficult to argue that the promotion of Tonga is a realistic enterprise.

Even if we accept a modernist position (which is what we have largely adopted) for the sake of argument that languages exist as objects out there and that Tonga can be distinguished from Nambya, Shona, etc., we still require a broader view of Tonga which is not only linguistic but also includes what the users of Tonga believe and the value they attach to language. It is these beliefs and their meta-discourses about Tonga which to a large extent may have motivated the researcher/activists and traditional chiefs when they were advocating for the promotion of Tonga as an indigenous language.

Although the Tonga succeeded in getting Tonga reclassified as indigenous, like Shona and Ndebele, in terms of language planning theory it is still conceptually different from Shona and Ndebele in that Tonga as indigenous is part of micro-nationalism while Shona and Ndebele are central to macro-nationalism (Coluzzi, 2006), which is a key aspect of 'governmentality' (Foucault, 1991).

The idea of language rights/linguistic citizenship as constitutive components of micro-nationalism is potentially problematic, if we adopt an African perspective in which language and culture are inextricably linked to each other as these are founded on a conceptual duality between language and rights, language and culture and language and politics. Discourses about rights may resonate differently in African communities from those of academic and other Tonga promotion activists. In some Tonga communities, advocacy of language rights/linguistic citizenship can be interpreted as parts of cultural practices because language is embedded in culture. Consequently, the promotion of language rights/linguistic citizenship is a contemporary legitimation and authentication of a specific view of culture on the basis of a reconstructed and 'invented' and imagined past which is spoken or written about in contemporary linguistic idiom. Representations of the past are therefore inevitably constrained by linguistic idioms and may vary depending on the nature of the linguistic idiom used. This is particularly relevant in contexts such as that of the Tonga in which the past described through Tonga might be different from that rendered in Shona, Ndebele or English. The challenge for language planning, especially when taking the case of Tonga into account, is that if languages do not exist as objects and "[t]here is, really, no such thing as heritage" (Smith, 2006: 11), ethnicities are constructed and that if ethnic identities emerge from "interaction between cultures" (Adejunmobi, 1999: 583), then the quest for a homogenous Tonga cultural heritage is like going down the proverbial garden path.

References

Adejunmobi, M. (1999) "Routes: language and the identity of African literature" *Journal of African Studies* 32 (4), 581–596.

Anderson, B. (1984) *Imagined Communities: Reflections on the Origins and Spread of Nationalism*. London: Verso.

Austin, J.L. (1975) *How to Do Things with Words*. Cambridge: Cambridge University Press.

Bakhtin, M.M. (1983) *The Dialogic Imagination*. Austin: University of Texas Press, (C. Emerson & M. Holquist, Trans).

Batibo, H.M. (2005) *Language Decline in Africa: Causes, Consequences and Challenges*. Clevedon: Multilingual Matters.

Bird, S. (2000) "Orthography and identity in Cameroon" *Written Language and Literacy* 4 (2), 131–162.

Bourdieu, P. (2000) *Pascalian Meditations*. Cambridge: Polity Press.

Cobarrubias, J. (1983) "Ethical issues in status planning" In J. Cobarrubais and J.A. Fishman (eds) *Progress in Language Planning* (pp. 41–86)). Berlin: Mouton.

Colson, E. (1951) "The Plateau Tonga of Northern Rhodesia" In E. Colson and M. Gluckman (eds) *Seven Tribes of British Central Africa* (pp. 85–120). Manchester: Manchester University Press.

Colson, E. (1971) *The Social Consequences of Resettlement: The Impact of the Kariba Resettlement on the Gwenbe Tonga*. Manchester: Manchester University Press.

Colson, E. (2007) "Biases, place, time and stance" In C. Lancaster and K. Vickery (eds) *The Tonga-Speaking Peoples of Zambia and Zimbabwe* (pp. 307–345). New York/Toronto: University Press of America.

Coluzzi, P. (2006) "Minority language planning and micro-nationalism in Italy: The cases of Lombardy and Friuli" *Journal of Multilingual and Multicultural Development* 27 (6), 457–471.

ZILPA (n.d.) *Constitution of the Zimbabwe Indigenous Languages Promotion Association.*

Conyers, D. and Cumanzala, F. (2004) "Community empowerment and democracy in Zimbabwe: A case study from Binga District" *Social Policy and Administration* 38 (4), 383–398.

Coupland, N. (2003) "Linguistic authenticities" Essay written for the Stanford University Conference on 'The Authentic Speaker', October 2002. *Journal of Sociolinguistics* 7 (3), 417–431.

Cumanzala, F. (2002) *Community Participation as a Methodology in the Promotion of Human Rights and Human Development: The Case of Binga Human Rights and Development Programme in Zimbabwe.* Masters thesis, The Hague. Institute of Social Studies.

Dzingirai, V. (2003) "The new scramble for the countryside" *Development and Change* 34 (2), 243–254.

Ekkehard, W.H. (2000) "Language and society" In B. Heine and D. Nurse (eds) *African Languages: An Introduction* (pp. 298–347). Cambridge: Cambridge University Press.

Ethnologue (2008) Map of languages of Zimbabwe.

Fabian, J. (1986) *Language and Colonial Power: The Appropriation of Swahili in the Former Belgian Congo 1880–1938.* Cambridge: Cambridge University Press.

Foucault, M. (1991) "Governmentality" In G. Burchell, C. Gordon and P. Miller (eds) *The Foucault Effect: Studies in Governmentality* (pp. 81–104). London: Harvester Wheatsheaf.

Freire, P. (1972) *Pedagogy of the Oppressed.* New York: Continuum Publishers.

Gadelli, K. (2007) *Language Planning: Theory and Practice.*

New York: Languages Division Education Sector, UNESCO.

Gee, J.P. (ed.) (1996) *Social Linguistics and Literacies: Ideology in Discourses*. London: Taylor & Francis.

Gerdes, P. (1998) *Women, Art and Geometry in Southern Africa*. Lawrenceville, NJ: Africa World Press.

Gerdes, P. (2003) "Exploring plaited plane patterns among the Tonga in Inhambane (Mozambique)" *Symmetry: Culture and Science* 12 (1–2), 115–126.

Government of Zimbabwe (1987) *Education Act*. Harare: Government Printers. (Chapter 25, Section 4).

Hachipola, H. (1998) *A Survey of the Minority Languages of Zimbabwe,* University of Zimbabwe Research Report.

Harris, Roxy. (2006) *New Ethnicities and Language*. Basingtoke: Palgrave Macmillan.

Heller, M. (2006) *Linguistic Minorities and Modernity*. Toronto: Continuum Publishers.

Heller, M. (ed.) (2007) *Bilingualism: A Social Approach*. New York: Palgrave Macmillan.

Hofmeyr, I. (1994) *'We Spend Our Years as a Tale That is Told': Oral Historical Narrative in a South African Chiefdom*. Johannesburg: Witwatersrand University Press.

Hornberger, N. (2003) "Continua of biliteracy" in N. Hornberger (ed.), *Continua of Biliteracy: An Ecological Framework for Educational Policy, Research and Practice in Multilingual Settings* (pp. 3–34). Clevedon: Multilingual Matters.

Hult, F.M. (2004) Planning for multilingualism and minority language rights in Sweden" *Language Policy* 3(2), 181–201.

Hyden, G. (2000) "Introduction" In G. Hyden, D. Olowu and H.W.O. Okoth (eds) *African Perspectives on Governance* (pp. 1–30). Trenton, NJ: Africa World Press.

Irvine, J. and Gal, S. (2000) "Language ideology and linguistic differentiation" In P.V. Kroskrity (ed.) *Regimes of Language: Ideologies, Polities and Identities* (pp. 35–84). Santa Fe, NM: School of American Research Press.

Joseph, J.E. (2006) *Language and Politics*. Edinburgh: Edinburgh University Press.

Kaplan, R.B. and Baldauf, R.B. Jr. (1997) *Language Planning: From Practice to Theory*. Clevedon: Multilingual Matters. Kroskrity, P.V. (ed.) (2000) *Regimes of Language: Ideologies, Polities and Identities*. Santa Fe: School of American Research Advanced Seminar Series, School of American Research Press.

Kubik, G. (1989) "Minority languages and cultures in Central Africa: Situation analysis and research priorities" Lecture, Department of African Languages and Literature, University of Zimbabwe.

Kymlicka, W. (2001) *Politics in the Vernacular: Nationalism, Multiculturalism and Citizenship*. Oxford: Oxford University Press.

Kymlicka, W. and Patten, A. (2003) *Language Rights and Political Theory*. Oxford: Oxford University Press.

Lancaster, C.S. (1974) "Ethnic identity, history, and 'tribe' in the Middle Zambezi Valley" *American Ethnologist* 1 (4), 707–730.

Makoni, S. (1998) "In the beginning was the missionaries' word" In K. Prah (ed.) *Between Distinction and Extinction: The Harmonization and Standardization of African Languages* (pp. 157–164). Johannesburg: Witwatersrand University Press.

Makoni, S. (1999) "Shifting discourses in language studies in South Africa" In K. Prah (ed.) *Knowledge in Black and White Cape Town* (pp. 130–156). Cape Town: Centre for Advanced Studies of African Society.

Makoni, S. and Meinhof, U.H. (2004) "Western perspectives in applied linguistics in Africa" In S.M. Gass & S. Makoni (eds). Special Issue on World Applied Linguistics, *AILA Review* 17 (1), 77–104.

Makoni, S., Dube, B. and Mashiri, P. (2006) "Zimbabwe colonial and postcolonial language policy and planning practices" *Current Issues in Language Planning* 7 (3), 377–414.

Makoni, S., Mashiri, P. and Brutt-Griffler, J. (2007) "The use of 'indigenous' and urban vernaculars in Zimbabwe" *Language in Society* 36 (1), 25–51.

Manyena, S.B. (2000) *Catholic Commission for Justice and Peace in Zimbabwe: Binga Justice and Peace Project. A report on the 29–30 July 2000 TOLACO Workshop held at Binga Roman Catholic Hall on the teaching of Tonga language in Binga, Hwange, Gokwe North and Nyaminyami.* [Binga: Catholic Commission for Justice and Peace in Zimbabwe]

Matsinhe, S.F. (2006) "XiTsonga and Tonga: A rose in another name" Paper presented at the African Day Conference of the Commission for the Promotion and Protection of Cultural, Religious and linguistic Community Rights., May 24–25, Cape Town, South Africa.

Matthews, T. (1978) "Notes on the precolonial history of the Tonga, with emphasis on the Upper River Gwembe and Victoria Falls areas" In C. Lancaster and K.P. Vickery (eds) (2007) *The Tonga Speaking Peoples of Zambia and Zimbabwe: Essays in Honor of Elizabeth Colson* (pp. 13–25). New York: University Press of America.

May, S. (2008) "Language, education, pluralism and citizenship" In S. May and N. Hornberger (eds) *Language Policy and Political Issues in Education: Encyclopaedia of Language and Education* (2nd edn, Vol. 1, pp. 15–29). New York: Springer.

McGroarty, M., Beck, A. and Butler, F. (1995) "Policy issues in assessing indigenous languages: A Navajo case" *Applied Linguistics* 16 (2), 323–343.

Mignolo, W. (1996) 'Linguistic maps, literary geographies, and cultural landscapes: Languages and languaging' *Modern Language Quarterly* 57 (2), 181–197.

Mumpande, I. (2006) S*ilent Voices: Indigenous Languages in Zimbabwe*. Avondale: Weaver Press.

Ndhlovu, F. (2004) "Is there anything minor about minority languages? Another look at the politics of language in Zimbabwe" Paper presented at the Fourth International Conference on Preserving African Languages organized by the University of Maryland Eastern Shore, November 4–7 2004.

Ndhlovu, F. (2007) 'The role of discourse in identity formation and the manufacture of ethnic minorities in Zimbabwe' *Journal of Multicultural Discourses* 2 (2), 131–147.

Nettle, D. and Romaine, S. (2000) *Vanishing Voices*. Oxford: Oxford University Press.

Nyati-Ramahobo, L. (2002) "From a phone call to the high court: Wayeyi visibility and the Kamanakao Association's campaign and cultural rights in Botswana" *Journal of Southern African Studies* 28 (4), 685–709.

Pennycook, A. (2007) "Postmodernism in language policy" In T. Ricento (ed.) *An Introduction to Language Policy* (pp. 55–77). Malden and Oxford: Blackwell Publishers.

Quijano, A. (1999) "Colonialidad del poder, cultura y conocimiento en América Latina" In S. Castro Gómez, O. Guardiola Rivera and C. Millan de Benavides (eds) *Pensar (en) los intersticios.* (pp. 89–115). Santa Fe de Bogotá: CEJA.

Rampton, B. (2006) *Language in Later Modernity: Interaction in an Urban School.* Cambridge: Cambridge University Press.

Ranger, T. (1989) *Democracy and Traditional Political*

Structures in Zimbabwe, 1890–1999. Harare: University of Zimbabwe Publishers.

Reagan, T. (2005) *Critical Questions, Critical Perspectives: Language and the Second Language Educator*. Greenwich, CT: Information Age Publishing Inc.

Reddy, M.J. (1979) "The conduit metaphor: A case of frame conflict in our language about language" In A. Ortony (ed.) *Metaphor and Thought* (pp. 284–297). Cambridge: Cambridge University Press.

Ridge, S. (2001) "Discourse constraints on language policy in South Africa" E. Ridge, S.G. Ridge and S. Makoni (eds) *Freedom and Discipline: Essays in Applied Linguistics from Southern Africa* (pp. 15–30). New Delhi: Bahri Publishers.

Robbins, J. (2001) "God is nothing but talk: Modernity, language, and prayer in a Papua New Guinea Society" *American Anthropologist* 103 (4), 901–912.

Scudder, T. (1962) *The Ecology of the Gwembe Tonga. (Vol. 11). Kariba Studies*. Manchester: Manchester University Press.

Searle, J. (1969) *Speech Acts: An Essay in the Philosophy of Language*. Cambridge: Cambridge University Press.

Smith, L. (2006) *The Uses of Heritage*. London: Routledge.

Spolsky, B. (1997) "Multilingualism in Israel" *Annual Review of Applied Linguistics* 17, 138–150.

Stroud, C. (2000) "Language and democracy: The notion of linguistic citizenship and mother tongue programs" In K. Legere and S. Fchat (eds) *Talking Freedom: Language and Democratization in the SADC Region* (pp. 67–74). Windhoek: Gamsberg Macmillan.

Stroud, C. and Heugh, K. (2004) "Linguistic human rights and linguistic citizenship" In D. Patrick and J. Freeland (eds) *Language Rights and Language Survival: A Sociolinguistic Exploration* (pp. 35–53). Manchester: St Jerome.

Thondhlana, J. (2002) "Using indigenous languages for teaching and learning in Zimbabwe" In B. Burnaby and J. Reyhner (eds) *Indigenous Languages Across the Community* (pp. 31–39). Flagstaff, Arizona: Northern Arizona University.

Tremmel, M. (1994) *The People of the Great River*. Gweru: Mambo Press. (Silveira House Series, No. 9)

Trudell, B. and Reeder, J. (2006) "Discourses of authority and stakeholder perspective: Processes of language development in Benin" Paper presented at the Conference on Languages and Education in Africa. University of Oslo, 19-22 June 2006.

Vickery, K. (2007) "Introduction: Elisabeth Colson and Tonga scholarship" In C. Lancaster and K. Vickery (eds) *The Tonga-speaking Peoples of Zambia and Zimbabwe* (pp. 1–18). Lanham: University Press of America.

IX

Zimbabwe colonial and post colonial language policy and planning practices.
(with Busi Makoni and Pedzisai Mashiri)

Abstract

This monograph focuses on the development of colonial and post-colonial language policies and practices in Zimbabwe, attributing changes to evolving philosophies and politics in colonial and post-colonial Zimbabwe. In colonial Zimbabwe, we argue that the language policies had as one of their key objectives the development of a bilingual white colonial ruling class proficient in both English and at least one African language. Contrary to what some scholars might think, we will show that what was being imposed during the colonial era was not English on Africans but European variants of African languages on Europeans. The monograph also describes how, through linguistic description, Europeans appropriated African languages as a prelude to the imposition of European variants of African languages on Africans under the guise of the promotion of indigenous language. Despite the power and influence of the colonial regime, we demonstrate how Africans still retained a strong sense of agency during the colonial period which enabled them to select, albeit within restricted limits, the nature and type of education they received, the languages through which they were taught, and indeed even the materials which were used in teaching them languages, particularly English.

INTRODUCTION

The main objective of this monograph is to analyse the nature of the language policies and practices in colonial and post-colonial Zimbabwe. It traces the historical changes in the nature of the Zimbabwean language policies, and examines how Zimbabwean politics was shaped by language policies, as well as by the impact these language policies had on colonial and post-colonial Zimbabwean politics. The monograph also examines the role of Christianity in the codification and promotion of African languages, and it ends by examining the nature of the language-in-education policies in contemporary Zimbabwe. Although the monograph focuses on Zimbabwe, there is a bias towards Shona because of the limited amount of published academic material on other languages, particularly on Ndebele. In the following section, the nature of the terminology used to refer to Zimbabwe is analysed, illustrating the complexity of the terms used and showing how, in some cases, the African and the English terms had different referents.

A note on terminology

The name Zimbabwe has a number of variants: *dzimbabwe; dzimbahwe*. *Dzimbahwe* is a generic term for stone dwellings (pl. *madzimbabwe*). The etymology and the origins of the term are, however, open to dispute. One conventional view involves interpreting the term as a contracted form as illustrated in the following phrases: *dzimba* (large house) *mabwe* (stones) or *dzimba woye* (venerated house). At times *dzimbahwe* is also translated as either a walled grave or a royal court.

In English the term *Zimbabwe* refers to a series of famous stone structures of which the Great Zimbabwe is only one, albeit the most famous. In 1980 Zimbabwe became the official name of the country, and in a political context replaced the name *Rhodesia*.

Like all other scholars working on Africa, we are faced with a problem of how to refer to the areas we are studying. In this monograph we follow Burke (1996) in using the names which have been in use since Zimbabwe attained its independence in 1980. The names therefore apply retrospectively to Zimbabwe, Harare and Masvingo, rather than to Southern Rhodesia, Salisbury and Fort Victoria. Using Zimbabwe retrospectively simplifies the presentation; otherwise it would be more accurate to talk about Southern Rhodesia (1890s–1969), Rhodesia (1970–1978), Zimbabwe Rhodesia (1979) and Zimbabwe (1980–). Although the names of towns and cities have been changed, the cities still retain their colonial names in official records, and at the Deeds Office most of the records still retain colonial names. For example, a notice in the *Herald Daily Newspaper* of 16 July 2004, for compulsory land acquisition in line with the Land Acquisition Act (Chapter 20: 10) refers to a "... piece of land situated in the district of Salisbury" (*Herald Daily Newspaper*, July 2004 (p. 11).

The fact that the term Salisbury is still used in contemporary property documents, even though it was changed to Harare in 1981, reflects the discrepancy in the naming practices between private and official documents, and the way in which post-colonial language policies have not rendered private naming practices commensurate with those in the public domain.

GEOGRAPHIC LOCATION

Having described the emergence of the name Zimbabwe, it is necessary to turn now to an analysis of the geographical location of Zimbabwe. Zimbabwe is a landlocked country with an area of 390,757 square kilometres (150,698 sq. mi.) (roughly comparable in size to Germany, Iraq or Japan), situated in the southern part of Africa between the Victoria Falls and the Kariba Dam to the north, and the Limpopo River to the south. It is surrounded by South Africa to the south, Botswana to the west, Zambia to the north, and Mozambique to the east.

The map in Figure 1 shows the distribution of the various languages spoken in Zimbabwe. The map shows that chi-

Shona and isiNdebele are the main languages of Zimbabwe. The minority languages are confined to specific geographic areas. The map does not show instances in which African languages are spoken as additional languages. For example, most isiNdebele first language speakers living in areas in which chiShona is a dominant language are likely to have acquired chiShona as a third language with English as a second language, and vice versa; i.e. that chiShona speakers living in areas in which isiNdebele is the dominant language will probably have acquired isiNdebele as a third language with English as a second language. The dominant status of isiNdebele, chiShona and English are reinforced educationally by a language-in-education policy which uses these languages as media of instruction from the first grade even in contexts in which they are not the first languages of the school children.

In terms of population distribution, the 2002 national census estimates the Zimbabwean population at 11,631,657 and its language distribution is estimated at Shona 71%, Ndebele 16%, other African languages 11%, Asian languages 1% and European languages 1%.

PRE-COLONIAL ZIMBABWE

Beach suggests that the term *Zimbabwe* is problematic; hence he adopts the term the *Zimbabwean plateau* to describe the land that lies in the south-eastern region of Africa, between the Zambezi and the Limpopo rivers. The Shona (although this term was not used by the people who now call themselves by that name until the last century) were the most numerous and important people in that plateau from at least the 10th to the mid-19th centuries CE (Beach, 1994: 1). The Great Zimbabwe, about 27 km from the modern town of Masvingo, was the capital of a state created by the Shona between the 12th and 16th centuries (Sinamayi, 1998: 93). The site, a great monument and tourist resort in modern Zimbabwe, played an important role in the development of nationalism and a sense of unity among Zimbabweans.

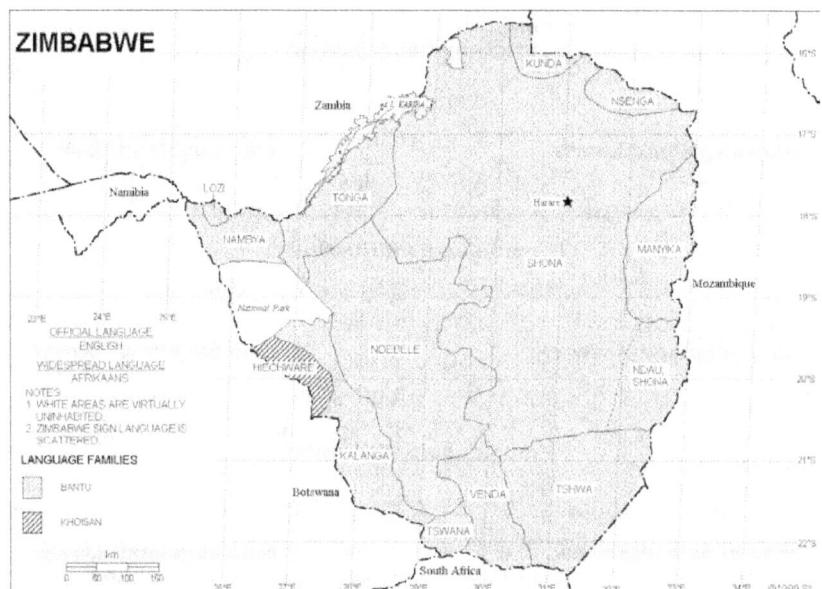

Figure 1 Distribution of languages spoken in Zimbabwe

Zimbabweans were generally great architects, as demonstrated by the spectacle in the Great Zimbabwe monuments. Modern researchers regard the site as a purely Bantu creation, although the early archaeological investigators ascribed it to Phoenicians, Persians and Arabs. Shona oral tradition abounds with stories of building some edifices, towers and so on, by the Rozvi-Karanga. Great Zimbabwe sites were built all over the country as district headquarters. Hence, "these sites functioned as major centres expressing a southern Zimbabwean culture that gradually dominated the local population" (Pikirayi, 1998: 85). At the territorial level, these sites were viewed either as provincial centers or courts of the state, based at Great Zimbabwe (Garlake, 1973) or as semi-autonomous political units largely supported by a transhuman, livestock economy (Pikirayi, 1998: 85).

However, the Shona were not the only inhabitants. By the 1830s migrations of Nguni speakers (among others) from the south – the Ndebele and the Gaza – had taken place. "By 1889 there was a large island of Nguni speech within the sea of Shona" (Beach, 1994: 113), suggesting that multilingualism has a long historical tradition traceable in some cases even to colonial Zimbabwe. Although the predominant form of multilingualism comprises only African languages, most studies into multilingualism nevertheless focus on a type of multilingualism consisting of an African language and either French or English. Epistemologically, presenting a type of multilingualism made up of an African language and English as the dominant object of analysis has had the unintended effect of making it look like the norm. Firstly, scholarship that focuses on African languages and English bilingualism ideologically exaggerates the importance and widespread nature of either English or French. Secondly, since only a minority of Africans are bilingual in an African language and either English or French, such an orientation in scholarship does not capture the experiences of a majority of Africans who historically, and even in contemporary Africa, are still bilingual only in African languages (see Makoni & Meinhof, 2004; Wolf 2002, 2003).

Except for the Ndebele and the Gaza, all Nguni groups that passed through the Zimbabwean plateau stayed very briefly and had less impact on the local people than is often portrayed in colonial school history books. The Ndebele and Gaza established themselves around the edges as well as inside the old Shona boundaries, with the former settling more permanently in one place at Bulawayo than the latter whose capital shifted constantly between the eastern highlands and the Limpopo valley (Beach, 1984). Beach says:

> The Gaza affected their subjects in many different ways, including introducing traces of Nguni into their languages, but in the end they left no significant Nguni-speaking population, but instead adopted their subjects' tongues. The people of the much more compact Ndebele state were unique among the Nguni ... in that their language

survived colonial rule and has flourished up to the present. (1994: 112)

Beach's claims are rather on the all or nothing side. Yet, in reality the Ndebele and Gaza culture and language were as much affected by local cultures and languages as they affected them (Mazarire, 2003: 2). The relations between the Ndebele and their neighbours were not always antagonistic as the missionaries and colonialists have generally portrayed them. Even in contexts in which the two were engaged in military conflict, the Ndebele were not necessarily always victorious. The Ndebele economy did not rely predominantly on raiding, but rather it was in fact based on a sound agricultural structure with a strong herding component (Cobbing, 1976).

Linguistically, Ndebele occupy the south-western part of the country, an area representing a long-established culture and dialectical zone, into and out of which many different groups have passed. As Mazarire (2003) observes, the case of the Ndebele language is fairly straightforward and can easily be explained in terms of Zuluisation of the Ndebele both by Ndebele aristocrats and the colonial officials. To quote Mazarire at length:

> Ndebele rulers attached a lot of importance to language and Lobengula like Mzilikazi[1] before him is said to have required his subjects to speak 'Zulu' – the language of the conquerors; it was this language which was later transformed into the Ndebele of today. The Zulu language and culture was imagined as an identity for the Ndebele although the Ndebele aristocracy may never have perceived of themselves as such. This Zuluness was aspired for as a political culture despite the fact that the Khumalo clan from who[m] they descended was not itself Zulu. The language however was promoted in its

---

[1] Mzilikazi was an army general who defected from the Zulu king Shaka and fled to Zimbabwe. Lobengula was his son.

original form but gradually began to acquire an identity of its own quite distinct from Zulu as it was adopted by people both within the immediate and far off radius of the central state. (2003: 7)

The language also became important as a symbol of class superiority associated with the *mzansi*, a language through which all the dramas of superiority were re-enacted and communicated – e.g. praise poetry and nostalgic musical recitals (Vail & White, 1989). That Mzilikazi demanded that the conquered peoples learn Zulu, the language of the conquerors, is significant historically because other militarily victorious people such as the British demanded, not that the Africans should learn English but that the British should learn African languages in order to enhance their control over the Africans. The social policies adopted by the militarily successful regimes thus varied considerably. It is therefore crucial to take cognisance of the historical contexts and the relationships between the victorious and the defeated and not necessarily assume that military victory is always accompanied by the imposition of the language of the victor as one might be inclined to infer from discussions of linguistic imperialism. Furthermore, the tendency by the social and militarily powerful to learn the languages of those whom they have defeated may account for the reported discomfort some African communities may have when powerful communities learn to speak their languages. The communities may feel that the bilingualism of the powerful which includes proficiency in their language(s), as socially and politically conquered peoples, does not necessarily serve their interests.

Although bilingualism is often seen as conferring specific cognitive and linguistic advantages to bilingual individuals (Baker, 2001), in some social and historical contexts politically powerful people may utilise their bilingualism against the interests of the less powerful as the history of colonial encounters in Africa demonstrates. This concept has implications on how some language planning discourses that promote bilingualism are received particularly by members of less powerful communities. For example, white farmers in southern Africa are typically bilingual but they use that bilingualism to exploit the farm workers. Superficially, when they use an African language it might look like the farmer is identifying with the farm workers and yet the farmers are using the language expertise to enhance their exploitation of the workers. Research into language planning in Africa has to focus not only on the political and academic elite who can articulate their ideas but examine the complex and at times contradictory ways in which subaltern classes respond and assimilate such ideas (Hill, 2002; Ranger, 2003).

Language planning policies, particularly in Africa, encourage a view of African languages in purely linguistic and structural terms. Such a view may be a product of positivist approaches to linguistic description of African languages. "The fundamental belief underpinning such linguistic description is the belief that languages are natural and not historically contingent, and that they are countable, discrete and bounded" (Makoni & Trudell, 2006). A lot of African language planning scholarship including the Ethnologue falls into this type of discourse of enumeration.

The idea of African languages described in purely linguistic terms has been challenged in linguistic theory (Harris, 1998, 2006; Yngve, 1996, 2004) but is also in sharp conflict with local views of language in African contexts. A view of African languages in purely linguistic terms, referring to what the Shona or Ndebele speak, is a recent creation reinforced by literacy. For example, the Shona used terms that did not differentiate between language and culture – i.e. *chivanhu* or *isintu* in Ndebele (being human) referred to both language and culture interchangeably (Makoni, 2003). Other terms used interchangeably with *chivanhu* (even today) in Shona are *chiKaranga* and *chizezuru* which refer to both language and culture. It is important for scholarship in African languages to consider seriously the possibilities and consequences for language planning if African languages are inherently hybrid (Canagarajah, 2006).

Not only was the distinction between language and culture not always available in Zimbabwean language history, but the language-dialect distinction did not exist in pre-colonial Zimbabwe. The notion was a product of the work of religious denominations working in different geographical areas. Thus, the different dialects came to be associated with different denominations.

More than 50 years later, Ranger (1985) adopted Doke's views and championed a constructivist perspective, evident in his 'Invention of Tradition' thesis that has influenced many contemporary studies on Africa. According to Ranger, tribalism as it prevails, particularly as expressed in the inter-ethnic relations between the Shona and Ndebele, did not exist in pre-colonial Zimbabwe (Mazarire, 2004: 2). People never thought of themselves as Shona or Ndebele since they could not equate this to a tribal or ethnic identity. Ethnicity to Ranger, therefore, derived from the establishment of dialect boundaries and the missionaries' production of maps showing distinct 'Manyika', 'Zezuru', and 'Karanga' territories. The creation of the dialect boundaries resulted from the turning of the spoken language into text. The Anglicans and the American Methodists produced 'chiManyika', while the Dutch Reformed Church produced 'chiKaranga' and the Jesuits 'chizezuru' (Ranger, 1985: 6).

A Zimbabwean linguist and lexicographer, Herbert Chimhundu, took up Doke's (Ranger's) views from an orthographic point of view. Chimhundu (1992) demonstrated convincingly how different church denominations developed the written versions of chiShona. However, it is important to point out that the missionaries' creation of ethnic identities in Zimbabwe which Ranger and Chimhundu present as straightforward was in fact a complex process – since the Africans themselves did not easily accept the invented traditions and linguistic enclaves – and was not always completely state driven (Mazarire, 2004).

For the inhabitants of the Zimbabwean plateau, the spirit world was very close and real. They believed in an all-powerful omniscient creator of all things, referred to as *Mwari* (God) and worshipped by the Mwari cult. The Shona, for example, refer to Mwari by several names; e.g. '*Nyadenga*' (the supreme one of the sky), '*Musiki*' (the creator), '*Musikavanhu*' (the creator of people), and 'Dzivaguru' (the big pool). Similarly, the Ndebele believed in an all-powerful omniscient supreme being who created all things. The Ndebele believe in the existence of *umvelinqangi* (the creator) or *unkulunkulu* (the supreme one). *Mwari* or *umvelinqangi* was considered to be too remote to affect people's daily lives. Thus, people relied upon the spirits of their ancestors for protection and guidance. They believed that only after death is the spirit of man competent to be in close touch with *Mwari* or *umvelinqangi*, and from this belief, a spirit hierarchy has been developed.

Apart from the physical features and the vegetation of the area, the most important factor in the existence of early people was the great variety of birds, animals and fish, some of which provided them with necessary food, others with sport, together forming the basis on which they constructed their identity. Many Shona speakers derive their surnames, initially given as nicknames, from those of some animals and birds, and the Ndebele use their totems or totemic or clan praise names as surnames. Linguistically, the first names of people born before Zimbabwe attained its independence in 1980 were predominantly English or were drawn from varieties of non-standard English; this practice changed to a more or less exclusive use of Shona and Ndebele first names after 1980. The shift in the use of African names as markers of identity were, however, not necessarily accompanied by a strong support for the expanded use of African languages in education.

LANGUAGE POLICIES AND PRACTICES IN COLONIAL ZIMBABWE

In this section of this monograph, language policies which existed in colonial Zimbabwe as well as practices over the *longue durée* (beginning in the 15th century after the collapse of the Great Zimbabwe State and extending until 1930, when chiShona was officially 'invented' by the South African linguist, Clement Doke, a Professor of Linguistics at the Witwatersrand University) will be analysed (Chimhundu, 1992; Dwyer, 2002). In this analysis, the origins of ethno-linguistic categories will be examined. It is important to look at ethnic labels as these play a role in language planning both in pre- and post-colonial Zimbabwe. The impact of Christianity on African languages is also examined, and the point that, whilst at this stage, Christianity seemed to promote a policy in favour of African languages is stressed. The promotion of indigenous languages facilitated the promotion of Christianity. In terms of language policy and planning, the promotion of indigenous languages was designed to facilitate the spread of Christianity. The use of indigenous languages unfortunately created a certain amount of indeterminacy in the ways in which Africans reacted to Christian concepts.

There was no total agreement among the missionaries on the ways in which Christian notions such as *God*, *Sin* or *Holy Spirit* might be translated. This lack of agreement reinforced the impression that these same Christian concepts had different meanings between languages, but could also have different meanings even within the same language. For example in chiShona God could be *Wedenga* (sky – excluding the God of the caves), or at times *Yahweh* (Jeater & Hove, undated; Pennycook & Makoni, 2005).

In this section, African responses to colonial education are examined, since they subsequently helped in shaping language policies during the colonial period. This analysis of colonial language policy and practices will draw, in part, on archival recordings and historical writings. Because this analysis relies so heavily on archival recordings to reconstruct the colonial language policies and language practices, it is not possible to paint a comprehensive picture of colonial language policies and language practices, particularly amongst African language speakers. As the archival records were written largely by Europeans, relating their experiences in Africa, the records reveal more about European language practices, their interactions amongst themselves and with Africans, and their philosophical beliefs, than about the language practices of Africans amongst themselves. When writing about 'colonial society' it is necessary to admit that the result is oversimplified. Bear in mind that there was no single colonial entity.

> In fact white society had many fissures (as also did black). These fissures provided some, if limited, space for Africans to define and push for rights. There were 'ethnic' tensions between Britons of 'Imperial stock' and English-speaking 'colonials', and between both and Afrikaners. (Bhebhe & Ranger, 2001: xxvii)

Because of the heterogeneity within colonial society and indeed even within the African societies, it is important to avoid unduly essentialising either the position that the colonial society adopted on language or the effects of the policy on Africans. In reality colonial policies were not fully formed and can best be described as works in progress. The effects of the policies also varied considerably depending on the social status, gender, and degree of formal education of the Africans.

Research into Zimbabwean language policies relies heavily on the use of ethno-linguistic categories; in the following section, an analysis of their contested origins and complexities is provided because they may have been blurred in the discourses of language policies.

Historical origins of ethno-linguistic categories

As already stated, the term *Shona* is highly ambiguous. The term was first used by the Nguni-speaking Ndebele to refer to the Rozwi peoples they encountered in the 1830s. The use of the term by the Ndebele was abusive in nature, although in contemporary Zimbabwe the term no longer carries any connotation of abuse. On the contrary, the term that has become abusive is *maSwina* (those whose skills are limited to cleaning chicken intestines). The origins of the term *Shona* remain unclear because, although it is widely attributed to the Ndebele, Andrew Smith had recorded the name Shona in 1835 – "three years before the Ndebele settled in the country". There were a number of alternative terms that were used to describe the Shona. The British used the term *chiSwina* to refer to the Shona (Variants: ...*svina* pl., *amaswina*, or *maswina*). The term *chiSwina* remained the name used to refer to Shona speakers until 1940. *chiSwina* was pejorative because it literally meant 'dirty people', but it also carries with it a connotation of being highly unskilled and incapable of learning any new and productive skills. *chiSwina*, from the noun *tsvina* (dirt), was the "white man's corruption of a Matebele term of contempt" (Hyatt, 1969: 91). It appears as if the use of the pejorative term *chiSwina* was drawn from the Ndebele, a notion that was further consolidated by a European perspective of African society because Europeans were seeing the Shona through Ndebele eyes.

On the other hand, the Shona referred to Ndebele speakers as *Madzviti*, 'small stinging ants' (Burke, 1996: 25), or people who fought all the time, irrespective of whether or not they had been provoked. While it is unclear why the Shona referred to the Ndebele as *Madzviti*, it is possible that the use of this term was largely influenced by the history of the origins of the Ndebele as a breakaway group that fought its way from KwaZulu Natal in South Africa overwhelming all the ethnic tribal groups they encountered along the way.

The Shona defined themselves in terms of the land or space they inhabited rather than in terms of the language they spoke. Space is of crucial significance in the Shona's self-construction of identity as it is viewed as a form of symbolic capital (Caftanzoglou, 2001). The Shona call themselves *vana vevhu* (or *wevhu*) (children of the soil), while the ancestors are referred to as *varidzi vepasi* (owners of the soil). On the other hand, although the Ndebele did not define themselves in terms of land, land played a significant role in their lives. The Ndebele define themselves as *abakamthwakazi* (people of Khoi San origins). Interestingly, like the Shona, the Ndebele refer to their ancestors as *abaphansi* (those from the soil). Conventionally, a child's umbilicial cord, for both the Shona and Ndebele, is also buried in the ancestral land (Lan, 1985 in Seirlis, 2004: 409).

The importance of land/space to the self-construction of the Shona is apparent in the distinction they draw between home as an ancestral place of origin (*musha*) and house as a physical structure (*imba*, plural *dzimba*). 'This distinction turns the tables to remind whites of their own transcience and foreignness. If blacks had their *dzimba* in white space (the city), then whites had theirs in black space – the country at large' (Seirlis, 2004: 409).

The tendency to classify people according to space was reinforced by racial categorisation and colonisation. Classification of people in terms of land had complex effects on how people were to be categorised as indigenous or nonindigenous. For example, the city was construed as white space; consequently, blacks in urban areas were regarded in Zimbabwe as "temporarily displaced tribesmen" (Epstein, 1992: 63).

If Europeans 'legitimated' some terms for Africans, Africans also had terms for whites: the terms *vasinamabvi* in Shona or *abangelamadolo* in Ndebele were used to refer to whites and meant 'those without knees' occasioned by the custom of wearing long pants – metaphorically, the veiling of white bodies was construed as part of a tendency to conceal white intentions and desires. Although the terms *vasinamabvi / abangelamadolo* were initially used to refer to whites, they subsequently were used to refer to any person who was perceived as lazy.

That some of the terms used to refer to African ethnic groups were initially pejorative is not unusual. For example, a Nguni-speaking group (Xhosa to be exact) originating from South Africa, also resident in Zimbabwe, is now officially called *Mfengu* which is a term that was initially used as a nickname meaning 'beggars'. It is important to stress the presence of Xhosa speaking Zimbabweans because the general tendency to focus on an analysis of language policies in terms of states and dominant groups has led to obscuring from view ethnic groups that may live in a number of different states. Not only Xhosa speakers may be found in both South Africa and Zimbabwe; other ethnic and linguistic groups such as Afrikaans speakers share a cross-border distribution. If there are language and ethnic groups found in different countries, it might be prudent to begin conceptualising language policies in terms of regions rather than restricting them to individual countries as is the general tendency currently: a notion which is widely shared by those who espouse an ecological perception of language planning and policy (Kaplan & Baldauf, 1999, 2003; Mühlhäusler, 1996, 2000).

The other names used to refer to dialects spoken by the Shona were *Korekore* and *Zezuru* both of which were originally terms for 'Highlanders' and 'Northerners', subsequently used as 'fixed' ethnic and linguistic labels. The Portuguese used the term Mocaranga to refer to ruling lineages in eastern Zimbabwe. In an 1867 map, the Portuguese used Macona as a variant of Shona to refer to the same people (MacGonagle, 2001).

The origins of the term *Ndau*, one of the dialects of Shona, is unclear. Renie, a historian, traces the term to a Portuguese document that refers to traders who crossed the river Save in 1739. However, Beach (1994) suggests that the term *Ndau* was first used to refer to Shona speakers living in the Eastern Highlands of Zimbabwe in the 18th century. The document described the people they encountered as *Mujao* similar to *Ndjao*. Both names are comparable in terms of the ways they are pronounced with the exception of the initial consonant. A British explorer in 1875 refers to the same people, subsequently called *Ndau*, as *Maandowa*. Linguistic analysis traces the term *Ndau* to the way in which the *Ndau* speakers greeted each other. According to Ndau customs people greet each other by saying: *Ndau-we, Ndau-we* which translates into: 'we salute you' (MacGonagle, 2002).

Shona speakers are found in Zimbabwe and Eastern Mozambique. Shona is classified as one of the languages falling within the south-central zone of the Bantu language group (Childs, 2003; Webb & Kembo-Sure, 1999). The development of a Shona identity is, however, a recent phenomenon. In the 19th century, the Shona identified themselves politically, but not culturally or linguistically, although hair styles and body marks were used to signal social class, gender and at times generational differences.

Despite many serious efforts to categorise the Shona into 'distinct' ethnic groups, no satisfactory classification has emerged because of the complex relationships between ethnic affiliation, dialects alleged to be spoken, and political units. Attempts to draw neat categorisation were also frustrated by the constant migration of families and ethnic groups. The term *Shona* socio-linguistically conjures an inaccurate image as it creates an image of simple ethnic groups, when "almost every modern Shona community is a complex ethnic amalgam" (Rubert & Rasmussen, 2001: 299). For example, the presence of the Dumbuseya, a group of refugees including Nguni elements, is defined as Shona in spite of their Nguni origins (Rubert & Rasmussen, 2001: 79).

Language is still not a necessary part of all Shona identity. Different Shona clans may identify themselves on the basis of their totems and unique praise poems. This phenomenon is also evident amongst the Ndebele who often identify themselves on the basis of their praise or clan names. However, unlike the Ndebele, not all persons who speak Shona necessarily identify themselves as Shona suggesting that language is not necessarily always tied to identity (May, 2002). For example, Mozambicans who speak Ndau, a dialect of Shona according to the 1930 Doke classification, do not identify themselves culturally as Shona. Historically, their ancestors would not have identified themselves either as Shona or Ndau in the 19th century. Ndau speakers were more likely to identify themselves as belonging to either Teve or Sanga political entities situated in the North and South of Eastern Zimbabwe/Mozambique respectively (Beach, 1994; McGonagle, 2002).

The emergence and evolution of these ethnic labels demonstrates that identities are not primordial. Identities are historically and situationally constructed. Even if identities are situationally constructed, this should not be construed to mean that speakers might select any identity they choose and arbitrarily assign meanings to any form of identity. Although identity is fluid it still is to some extent constrained by historical and situational factors (Joseph, 2004). Ethnic labels emerge in specific historical contexts, and ethnicity is one form in which the identities are expressed when they emerge. Nonetheless, ethnicity has been exploited by pre-colonial, colonial, and post-colonial rulers to heighten ethnic awareness, an argument well articulated in Vail's felicitous phrase, the 'Invention of Tradition'. Ethnicity was not only manipulated by rulers, but also by migrants who actively constructed their own identities as well.

Shona

In Zimbabwe, the Shona also shifted their identities so that they could take advantage of material benefits accruing from a new identity. During the colonial period, Europeans perceived the *Manyikas* as ideal domestic servants. In 1929 the Native Commissioner for Inyanga reported that the "*WaManyika* are in great demand as domestic servants . . . and they obtain good wages for this class of labor" (Ranger, 1989: 140). Ranger notes that the special treatment accorded to the *Manyika* led some Shona speakers who were not *Manyika* to assume an "extended *Manyika* identity" (Ranger, 1989: 13).

Migration strongly enhanced the migrants' sense of ethnic awareness. For example, in the 19th and 20th centuries migration to South African mines became a rite of passage for young Ndau men. When they arrived in South African mines, Ndau speakers assumed a new ethnic identity by adopting a Shangaan identity enabling them to receive better wages. Even when they returned from the mines, they did not invariably abandon the Shangaan identity. They amalgamated the newly acquired Shangaan identity to the Ndau identity. The dual identity was demonstrated by the way they retained Shangaan names while maintaining Ndau cultural habits. The Ndau are an example of transnational subjects, constantly moving between Mozambique, Zimbabwe and South Africa. The variety of African languages they speak because of their migration draws heavily from a number of different linguistic communities they have encountered in their migration.

The tendency to shift away from one ethnic identity and to embrace another identity is not peculiar only to Ndau labour migrants. According to Muzondidya (2001), some African immigrants from South Africa passed for 'coloureds' as the latter were paid relatively better than the former while some coloureds passed for whites, because they were the highest paid group. Read (1936) recounts an anecdote in which she met a group of men from what was then called Nyasaland (now Malawi) in the 1930s at the crown mines who told her "here we say we are *Ngoni*. We say we are *Ngoni* and people respect us" (Read, 1936: 456). Trans-border migrations raise important issues relating to: firstly, whether it is necessary to standardise these trans-border languages, secondly, if the languages are to be standardised, how could the standardisation be carried out so that it captures rather than suppresses the diverse range of styles, genres and registers characteristic of such languages. If early colonial standardisation of African languages suppressed variation, the model of standardisation being proposed here seeks to maximise variation, or at least to accommodate it. Trans-border migration is a reflection of the impact of globalisation on African languages. "Until recently the majority of linguistic studies which concerned themselves with global phenomena tended to depict the worst possible scenarios: linguistic imperialism, endangered languages, language death" (Jacquemet, 2005: 257). The argument being put forth in this monograph is against this dystrophic vision of linguistic catastrophe which conjures up images of contagion, disasters, panic, etc. by suggesting that globalisation, at least in southern Africa particularly amongst trans-border migrants, creates opportunities for them to recombine their identities while simultaneously maintaining presence in a number of different sites. Philosophically, trans-border migration challenges the idea of languages as reified structural systems tied to specific geographical regions, an idea which arose in the period of the French Enlightenment and German Romanticism.

The phenomenon of shifting identities due to migration is not restricted to Southern Africa; it has also been reported in other parts of Africa, particularly in West Africa. Wallerstein (2002) cites examples of how Northern Ghanaians adopted a Hausa and Islamic identity when they sought employment in Accra in Southern Ghana. The 'new' Hausa (unlike the Ndau of Zimbabwe) did not necessarily retain the Islamic religious practices when they returned to their original homelands in the North.

Ndebele
Having described the Shona trans-national subjects, attention is now turned to the Ndebele, the second largest African ethnolinguistic group in Zimbabwe. As stated at the beginning of this

paper, the second major ethno-linguistic group in Zimbabwe is the Ndebele. The Ndebele are found mainly in the south-western parts of the country, having originated from South Africa in an area referred to in contemporary South Africa as Kwa-Zulu Natal. Historically it is not clear when they were renamed Ndebele. It is possible that the name *Ndebele* has its origins from the Sotho word *kiMatebele* that was used to refer to all raiding Nguni groups and not specifically the Ndebele. *kiMatebele* meant "warriors with long shields" (Hadebe, 2002).

The Ndebele in their northward migration assimilated many Sotho speaking peoples. The Sotho modified their names linguistically so that they sounded Ndebele. For example, *Motlokwa* (Sotho) became *Mdlongwa* (Ndebele), *Tau* (Sotho) became *Dawu*, (Ndebele), *Mokgatla* (Sotho) became *Mnkandla* (Ndebele), *Nare* (Sotho) became *Nyathi* (Ndebele) (Khumalo, 2004).

When the Ndebele subsequently settled in south-western Zimbabwe, the other ethnic groups including the Nyubis, Kalangas, Nanzwas, Nambyas, and to some extent the Tonga and Shona (Khumalo, 2004) were assimilated. The Shona peoples who were previously known as *Mambo* subjects were referred to as *AbakaMambo* by the Ndebele (Hadebe, 2002). The assimilated groups subsequently outnumbered the Ndebele. However, in spite of these groups being in a majority they learnt the language of the dominant group, now called Ndebele. The language policy of the Ndebele state was therefore one in which the defeated peoples were expected to learn, and subsequently learnt, the language of the victorious Ndebele. Having described the language policies and practices in colonial Zimbabwe attention is now turned to an analysis of language and ethnicity in contemporary Zimbabwe.

Language and ethnicity in Zimbabwe
Until recently, African scholars have generally tended to be reluctant to write about ethnicity (Makoni & Meinhof, 2004).

Ethnicity has been portrayed as divisive, threatening the attempts at national integration. In South Africa there were more powerful factors discouraging scholars from researching ethnicity. Ethnicity was viewed as a reprehensible creation of the apartheid regime. The intellectual context seems to have changed. Issues of ethnicity have surfaced as research has shown that people can have multiple identities, but this is not to suggest that identities can be added ad infinitum.

This section is focused on issues concerning inter-ethnic relations for reasons that might not appear obvious. The land resettlement programme in Zimbabwe has brought to the fore complex inter-ethnic relations within Zimbabwe. The land issue raises interesting potential language policy issues. Zimbabweans who are categorised as aliens are not entitled to land claims. Different ethnic groups are not represented equally. The ethnic issue that has been created in Zimbabwe is that other ethnic groups that have lived in Zimbabwe for many generations have no claim to land as they are considered non-Zimbabwean. As a result, it is unlikely that a language policy in favour of ethnic minority languages could be developed.

This section of the paper is organised into two parts: firstly, a discussion of inter-ethnic relations in an urban setting (i.e. in Harare); secondly, a discussion of inter-ethnic relations in an agricultural setting. By focusing on inter-ethnic relations in an agricultural area rather than in an urban setting the purpose is to examine how ethnicity plays out in a rural setting. The way ethnicity is used to crystallise a diverse group of people, and the way differences in ethnicity can be traced to different agricultural practices are illustrated. The point is that language in the rural areas, unlike that in the urban settings, was not necessarily the key defining factor of ethnicity.

The emergence of urban vernaculars constitutes an attempt to create a common identity that is not ethnically based. Because of the constant migration of people from urban, rural and slum environments, these urban vernaculars are not confined to cities. It is these urban vernaculars, much more than English, that have begun to replace chiShona and isiNdebele as first languages. In terms of language policy, one that seeks to protect African languages from the socalled threat of English is misplaced because it is not English that is the source of the threat, but rather the urban vernaculars (see Makoni et al. 2007).

That is not to suggest that ethnicity is not an urban phenomenon. By analysing inter-ethnic relations among groups who ostensibly speak the same first language (i.e. chiShona), the way people may speak the same language but feel that they are affiliated to different ethnic groups is illustrated.

Last, ethnicity and identity formation within the coloured community are discussed. The general thrust in Zimbabwean scholarship has been to focus on the major ethnic and racial groups (i.e. Ndebele, Shona and white communities to the exclusion of coloured communities). The exclusion of Coloured speakers has led to a simplification of the sociolinguistic contexts within Zimbabwe, and unfortunately has downplayed the role of such other languages as Afrikaans and Portuguese. Notable exception to this research enterprise lies in the work by Logan and Makoni (2006), Mandaza (1997), Muzondidya (2005) and Sierlis (2004).

Language and ethnicity in urban Harare

This section explores the various ways in which inter-ethnic relations develop in urban Harare in contexts in which both Zimbabweans and Zimbabweans of Malawian origin share the same physical space as opposed to situations in which one had a dominant position.

First and second generation Malawian Zimbabweans whose parents are both of Malawian origin are typically bilingual in chiChewa and chiShona with chiChewa as a first language and chiShona as a second language. But the third and fourth generation Malawian Zimbabweans whose fathers are of Malawian descent but whose mothers are Shona ethnically tend to have chiShona as a first language and chiChewa as a second language. Most of these bilinguals are usually literate only in Shona irrespective of whether it's their first language or a second language. ChiShona functions within the Malawian Zimbabwean community as the language of inter-ethnic interaction, while chiChewa functions as the language of the home domain. Although there is a considerable amount of research into bilingualism in Africa, most of it has focused on bilingualism involving English or French and an African language but not bilingualism that involves two African languages, this despite the call by African scholars for an expanded use of African languages. The challenge with which Zimbabwean language policy is faced is how to foster bilingualism in African languages.

So far the nature of inter-ethnic relations has been explored. The following section examines social relations among groups, in which one group insists that it is indigenous, but that claim is not recognised by the other group. The ways in which agricultural practices are used to mark differences in ethnic loyalty and the implications thereof on language policy practices in pre-colonial Zimbabwe have been explored.

Language and ethnicity in rural Zimbabwe

This section examines the nature of inter-ethnic relations in a predominantly agricultural area, specifically, the area called Gokwe, situated in north-western Zimbabwe. In the 1950s a large influx of immigrants who had been evicted from 'Rhodesian crown land' (see Nyambara, 1999, 2002) settled in Gokwe. Divisions emerged between the immigrants and the 'indigenous' communities because the former willingly took to cotton farming, while the latter resisted. Cotton farming contributed towards a crystallisation of ethnic differences that focused not on language, since the groups shared the same language, but on the discourses used to describe the adoption of the agricultural practices and the adoption of new economic practices by the different groups. The immigrants coming into Gokwe portrayed the indigenous people in Gokwe as primitive, backward and resistant to change, and referred to themselves as modern in an idiom borrowed from colonial descriptions of Africans.

Modernity, however, meant different things to the colonial officers, to indigenous people and to the immigrants. To the colonial officers, modernity meant transforming the immigrants into cotton farmers. To the immigrant farmers, modernisation meant mimicking Western values. To the indigenous people of Gokwe, modernisation meant unnecessary interference into their lives. It is within this context that new terminology emerged both in chiShona and Ndebele.

The indigenous people referred to the immigrants as *Madheruka*, while the immigrants called the indigenous people *Shangwe*. Shangwe is not a name of an ethnic group but rather refers to a geographical location. Beach (1994) traces the word to *Shangwe*, a reference to a place which is susceptible to drought or, as Hannan (1959) defines it in his *Standard Shona Dictionary*, as famine or drought. The term was originally used by the Ndebele and not by the Shangwe peoples themselves. The term *Madheruka* referred to an amalgam of immigrants. The use of the term *Madheruka* marked the beginning of a process of ethnicisation of immigrants – a process that is similar to the formation of the Tsonga in Mozambique, and the Sotho in Lesotho (MacGonagle, 2002). Ethnic differences in the rural communities also corresponded with class differences. The Madheruka were more prosperous than the Shangwe.

The Ndebele, on the other hand, referred to immigrants as *omhambuma* (those who stopped during their long walk) whilst immigrants called the indigenous Ndebele as *omagcwala ibhavu* (those who filled the bath tub with their big bodies). The use of the term *omagcwala ibhavu* seems to have been influenced by the big physical appearance of Ndebele males.

Even though language was not a marker of ethnic difference, there were markings on the body that were used to capture social differences. For example, the Ndebele had *uphawu* (marks of identity) in the form of pierced ears and the Shona had *nyora* (cicatrix in which medicine has been added). *Nyora* tended to be specific to a local group, while marks on the abdomen were common among most Shona communities. Some Shona speakers in the north-east pierced their lips and added plugs. Hair styles were used to indicate to which ethnic group one belonged (Burke, 1996: 26). Hair was important as a symbolic marker not only of ethnic differences, but of generation and class as well.

Ethnicity played a crucial role during the colonial period resulting in what Manganga (2004) calls 'industrial ethnicity'. There was an interface of race, ethnicity and culture and in the division of labour. "Certain jobs came to be associated with particular groups. This division of labour tended to enhance ethnic awareness among blacks in Southern Rhodesia" (Kosmin, 1977, cited in Manganga, 2004: 2). For example, sanitary and municipal work such as rubbish collection and cleaning of public toilets was associated with men of Malawian and Zambian origin, domestic work with Shona men, whilst the Karanga dominated the police force.

This section argues for a conceptualisation of language policy from one which goes beyond simply identifying the number of languages and the role which they may play in government as medium of instruction to one which seriously takes into account the ethnicity and identities of Zimbabweans and the way these identities may shape and influence the way these people would react to language policies. For example, the emergence of urban vernaculars in urban areas may result in urban Africans adversely responding to language policies that are construed as undermining new pan-ethnic identities and reinforcing narrow ethnically based identities.

Language use in coloured communities
An analysis of the historical and contemporary experiences of the coloured communities is not only of interest in terms of

identity but because it has broader relevance to a much larger question about what constitutes being a Zimbabwean. The question has direct relevance when it comes to issues about language policy and language planning. If the individual is not allowed to be Zimbabwean irrespective of how long the individual has lived in the country or for how many generations the individual's ancestors have lived in the country, it is highly unlikely that the government will commit resources to promote and officially give recognition to the languages of such individuals. If this is the case, the Zimbabwean language policy will then seek to reduce rather than to enhance the degree of linguistic diversity within its borders.

We have used the term *coloured* without defining the concept within a Zimbabwean context. The term *coloured* defines a slippery category that quickly assumes the connotation *miscellaneous* (Sierlis, 2004: 406). Mamdani describes the analytical challenges where the miscellanies have become the object of analysis as part of a broader problem in colonial history's struggle to come to terms with the subject of race. An analysis of the census and statutes in Zimbabwe reflects the slippery nature of the category. Individuals were defined as coloured if they were racially mixed and living in an urban area. However, if they were racially mixed but living in the rural area those individuals would then be defined as natives.

What this shows is that the term *coloured*, and indeed the notion of race, was not consistently used because of the tendency to conflate race with geographical location, and with the urban/rural dichotomy. The slippery nature of the definition at times had negative consequences for some people as illustrated in the case of Mondam Adams who found himself denied the right to inherit his father's property because it was in a white man's land, and he could not purchase land in areas reserved for the natives because he was coloured (Muzondidya, 2002).

The term *coloured* was a product of European colonialism's preoccupation with race and racial mixing. The fixation with racial mixing produced a category that was intermediate between white and black. Although coloureds were discriminated against, they received better treatment than blacks (Muzondidya, 2002: 4). As a result, some Blacks and African immigrants during the colonial era assumed a coloured identity by changing their names and adopting a variety of coloured speech including using a variety of English associated with coloureds.

Coloured English is not homogeneous. If the coloured grew up with their African mothers, they are likely to have their English influenced by either Ndebele or Shona, one of which would be their first language. Some coloureds are likely to have Afrikaans as their first language, particularly if they live in the southern regions of Zimbabwe and their parents migrated to Zimbabwe from the Western Cape Province in South Africa. Another immigrant group classified as coloured was from the former Portuguese colony of Goa. This group is likely to have Portuguese as their first language.

As part of a process of identity construction, coloureds constructed a street language – an argot called *Kabid* – as a way of expressing resistance and a means of denying white colonial ideals. *Kabid* was also used as an in-group language to exclude outsiders. Historically, *Kabid* was initiated and popularised as a young coloured male's language in the 1960s. Unlike other argots, *Kabid* has withstood the test of time and spread across gender and generation boundaries. It is no longer predominantly a language of males and youth.

Linguistically, one of *Kabid*'s main features is inverted pronunciation – i.e. 'look out' becomes *kool tow* in *Kabid* (Sierlis, 2004: 420). *Kabid* can be described as a slang variety of new Englishes showing the extent to which English has permeated the coloured communities. Coloured communities previously spoke such other languages as Afrikaans, Ndebele, Portuguese and Shona in the period between 1890 and 1960. These languages have now been replaced by *Kabid*, reflecting the nature of intergenerational language shift towards a localised variety of English. The extensive use of *Kabid* as a variant of English means that English in Zimbabwe cannot be described as one entity – either as Zimbabwean English (i.e. as the English used by Zimbabwean second language speakers), or as white native-speaker English because of its different varieties. Zimbabwean coloureds may also attach different emotional significance to *Coloured English* than Zimbabwean second language speakers do to the English they speak as a second language. Zimbabwean language policy is therefore faced with the challenge of implementing a language policy even if it revolves around English that acknowledges and reinforces the diversities within English. English in Zimbabwe represents a cluster of varieties ranging form standardised native English, through non-standard English, to English as a second and at times as a foreign language. The crucial issue in such contexts is not the imposition of a single variety of English, but an awareness of the multiple roles these varieties play. Educationally, this entails encouraging teachers not only to teach a specific variety, but to teach students to develop strategies which enable them to negotiate cross, and to accommodate to, linguistic differences (Giles, 1984; Rampton, 1995).

DEVELOPMENT OF AFRICAN LANGUAGES IN ZIMBABWE

One of the major organisations which has played a key role in the political history of Zimbabwe is the British South African Company (hereafter BSACo). The following section examines the way the BSACo constructed its policies and implemented them, and the role of language in such policies.

Language policy and planning: The British South Africa Company

The BSACo regarded expertise by Europeans in the local languages as a valuable tool in the exercise of colonial power, particularly by the police and in criminal courts (Jeater, 2001: 451). Proficiency in local African languages was necessary both in order to enforce colonial orders and to collect hut taxes, as well as when enquiring into 'native law and custom'. Expertise in African languages also enhanced the BSACo's ability to control Africans. State control of local Africans was mediated by Africans who served as native police, interpreters, and messengers. In British colonial Africa, particularly in Southern Rhodesia, the colonial powers did not feel that it was necessary to impose their own languages on the local population. What was being imposed on the Africans was the Europeans' (partial) understanding or what can be roughly described as mishearing of African languages as apparent in the naming practices of the colonial period. For example, the names given to cities/towns such as *Selukwe* for *Shurugwi*, *Shabani* for *Zvishavani*, *Wankie* for *Hwange* and *Balabala* for *Mbalabala* reflect a tendency of Europeanising the African names of towns, a practice that differs from giving European names to African places. On the other hand, names like *Salisbury* for *Harare* and *Fort Victoria* for *Masvingo* are examples of the imposition of European names on African places. What was imperialistic here was not the imposition of English on Africans but the imposition of European variants of African languages on Africans either through the judicial system or through the educational system. This has not been adequately discussed even in current debates on linguistic imperialism (Brutt-Griffler, 2004; Skutnabb-Kangas, 1994).

Language expertise of the BSACo's personnel subdued the effectiveness of its own administrative policies, as the company could not directly intrude into African conversations. Traders and adventurers were the main sources of language expertise. The traders acquired their oral and cultural competencies in African languages through their daily encounters with Africans. BSACo's promotion of African languages was meant to gain control of the African population.

The notion of what constituted facility in a 'local' language was construed very broadly; at times it referred to expertise in 'Zulu', even in predominantly Shona speaking areas. For example, although the missionaries arrived in Eastern Zimbabwe in the 1890s, the first prepared Ndau reader was not available in print until 1914 in spite of the American Mission Board's commitment to using local languages. Zulu was widely used in the American Board Mission's everyday activities (Jeater, 2001; Makoni & Trudell, 2006).

The fact that the daily activities of the missionaries were carried out in Zulu instead of chiNdau does not mean that the missionaries were not aware of the importance of using chiNdau. In an attempt to rectify the problem created by the use of Zulu instead of chiNdau, the missionaries encouraged the training of chiNdau speakers in evangelism. Most of the evangelists were also salaried teachers, forging a link between education and Christianity. Those who were educated were Christians, and those who were Christians were also likely to be educated. Subsequently, a connection was forged between chiNdau, Christianity, and literacy. Schools that taught literacy also taught Christianity, so distinctions between literacy, Christianity and chiNdau became increasingly blurred. This argument was also captured in fiction by Zimbabwean novelist Tsitsi Dangarembwa in her novel *The Nervous Condition*. The point was not to reinterpret Christianity in light of local spiritual ideas, but to reinvent Africans as modern American Christians. Africans, however, were not amenable to being reinvented. Despite the intense attention to details in the translation, local evangelists had some discretion and autonomy in how they interpreted and understood Christian messages (Jeater, 2001).

Most of the whites were accompanied by Zulu speaking evangelists who used Zulu to speak to local Africans (Jeater, 2001). Even when the missionaries were proficient in chiNdau, proficiency was construed not as the ability to speak with local people, but as the ability to produce texts. A considerable investment was put into compiling lists of words rather than into writing grammars (Fabian, 1986), suggesting that language proficiency was construed as the knowledge of the meaning of words rather than as the ability to speak. Because of the scarcity of language expertise, knowledge of Zulu (i.e. knowledge of the meaning of a large number of words in Zulu) was construed as extremely important even in Shona. This is not to say that the BSACo did not distinguish among different African languages. For example, Jeater recites an anecdote in which a Native Commissioner allegedly physically assaulted a native when he was addressed in Shangaan rather than in Shona, the African's mother tongue (Jeater, 2001). Jeater speculates that the Native Commissioner felt the use of Shangaan instead of Shona was pretentious, as Shangaan was the language of the Nguni elites.

The BSACo felt that good interpretation played an important role in the delivery of justice to Africans, particularly in court trials. Yet archival records are replete with instances in which injustice is acknowledged to have been meted out by both Native Commissioners and court interpreters. For example, L.L. Robinson comments about a case in which he felt that there had been a miscarriage of justice because of the poor interpretation skills of the court interpreters:

> Had the judge in this case been assisted by experienced assessors, well versed in the mysteries of native evidence, is it too much to assume that they might have probed the matter to the bottom and discovered what was in the mind of the native. (Jeater, 2001: 458)

In an attempt to rectify the problem of poor interpretation, a two-tier salary scale for court interpreters was established. Junior interpreters were able to converse with Africans but, in order to be promoted to the status of senior interpreter, the candidate had to demonstrate social and cultural knowledge about the African's cultural habits and modes of thinking. The assessors themselves were inadequately skilled in African languages as their knowledge of these languages was limited to knowledge of meanings of words and not the structure of the language. What this means is that this linguistic inadequacy was perpetuated within the system, leading to miscarriages of justice in the administration of law.

Examinations were used to assess expertise in African languages. The first examination in African languages was the Civil Service Interpreter's Examination first administered in 1905. Although the enactment of this law was not necessarily a pre-requisite, it enhanced a candidate's chances for promotion. Army personnel, police officers and court interpreters were eligible to sit the examination.

Interestingly enough, although police officers were eligible to sit the examination, it was deemed too difficult for them and a relatively easier examination was subsequently set. When reflecting on the role of the white police and the significance attached to expertise in African languages, it becomes obvious that knowledge of the colonial language practices is limited by the nature of the archival data used to reconstruct the period. In order for the police to enforce the law, the police needed to mediate among different factions, to carry out their duties without relying on brute force, they had to accommodate the interests of the conflicting African groups. Insights into how the police were able to make these accommodations would have been useful, because they were 'stigmatised' (see Goffman, 1963 for an analysis of three types of stigmas) and treated as instruments of social oppression.

By and large, the BSACo had relied on interpreters who had acquired African languages through informal contacts with Africans, a majority of whom were Afrikaans speakers. Between 1925 and 1935, the company introduced a new language policy. Previously the company viewed competence in African languages as equivalent to knowledge of meanings of words. The new policy was one where competence meant an ability to analyse the language. As a result, between 1925 and 1935 there was a marked shift and language expertise was defined in terms of textual skills, which could not readily be acquired through interaction with Africans.

Additionally, the missionaries also regarded expertise in African languages as an indispensable tool for missionary work in Zimbabwe. For example, the American Mission Board (AMB) insisted that missionaries and their wives would be denied the rights to vote in elections until they had passed examinations in the vernaculars (see Jeater, 2001).

What is clear is that the missionaries and the BSACo were enforcing a bilingual language policy amongst Europeans working in Southern Africa in the early phases of colonial rule before the beginning of the 20th century. What was observed in colonial bilingualism is the learning of a second language by a dominant group. In Zimbabwe at times the acquisition of a local language by a dominant group is perceived negatively by the local community because they feel it threatens their sense of security because the dominant group will intrude into their social worlds without a corresponding access by local Africans into the world of Europeans. English/African bilingualism was not perceived as necessarily beneficial to Africans' interests.

This section tries to show that, although missionaries are credited with using and promoting local languages for religious and evangelical purposes, they tend to interpret what constituted local languages very broadly, and used Zulu more than chiNdau. The significance of Zulu in the history and contemporary language policy and practices has tended to be underestimated because of a tendency to associate Zulu more with South Africa than with such other countries as Zimbabwe and Swaziland. Arguably, Zulu was in some situations one of the dominant African languages even within Zimbabwe.

The impact of Christianity in language policy and planning
Although both the BSACo and the missionaries sought to foster development of expertise in African languages, they had different, if not conflicting, conceptualisations about the nature of

language, particularly during the early phases of colonial rule. The BSACo was interested in the ability of Europeans to know meanings of enough words to enable them to understand the natives. The missionaries, on the other hand, were more interested in the textual skills of Europeans, particularly the ability of Europeans to translate from English into an African language. The missionaries placed emphasis on written skills, particularly translation, because they were interested in finding words for such Christian concepts as *'God'*, *'sin'*, *'salvation'*, etc. which would not compromise the African's understanding of Christianity. The missionaries were much more interested in using vernacular words to describe new concepts than in creating new words to describe new concepts. Because the words they were using to describe religious ideas were based on African religious cosmology, the old words came to refer to new forms of religious cosmology that were neither European nor African. In that sense, Christianity not only affected African languages but African languages affected Christianity (Pennycook & Makoni, 2005).

The impact and effects of Christianity on language have been reported in other parts of Africa. For example, Masagara (1997) demonstrates the impact of Christianity on truth telling in Kirundi and Kinyarwanda, two closely related languages, by enumerating a number of words that changed their meaning under the influence of Christianity (Pennycook & Makoni, 2005).

The missionaries were interested ultimately in converting local Africans to adopt a Europeanised worldview, for both religious purposes and for more practical reasons such as farming. The general tendency among the Christians was to use existing words and to manipulate them so that they could have new meanings that were consistent with Christian beliefs. For example, in traditional Ndebele there is no preacher; in order to capture the notion of a preacher, the Christians used the word *tshumayela* and yet the word *tshumayela* meant 'to be talkative' in Ndebele. Another example of a word that shifted under the impact of Christianity in Ndebele is *khonz*, a word originally meaning to be loyal, but under the impact of Christianity it subsequently shifted to mean worshipful. In the Ndebele belief system, unlike in Christianity, the concept of prayer did not exist. The Ndebele belief system had a notion of pouring libation to appease one's ancestors (Khumalo, 2004) and yet the concept of prayer now exists in the language.

The construction of African languages was, therefore, of central importance if European phenomenology was to be clearly articulated to Africans. For the religious conversion to be successful, and for the conversion to have long-term effects, it was necessary for the missionaries to articulate their worldviews in a medium that would achieve maximum effect i.e. effect achieved through the use of indigenous languages (Pennycook & Makoni, 2005).

The focus on translation enabled missionaries "to appropriate African languages, and to reinvent them within the Christian tradition" (Jeater, 2001: 456). It is instructive to remember that missionaries were translating from their first language into a second language. The translation of the Bible and religious texts into chiShona changed the way that the Africans viewed their languages. It led them to view their languages as texts in which there was a stable relationship between language and meaning, a notion that was subsequently reinforced in the production of dictionaries. The impression that African languages were fixed texts also affected the contexts in which they were used. In that sense, translation affected the natives' conceptualisations of their own languages.

Prior to colonialism and the introduction of translation for the natives, African languages only had an existence in so far as they were spoken and could not be separated from other social practices. Seeing African languages in translation shifted the Africans' conceptualisations of their own languages. This was further reinforced by the religious literature that each mission station produced. The literary versions of Shona led to the production of a special type of Shona that the Africans called *Chibaba* (the missionaries' language). *Chibaba* was produced by missionaries in collaboration with interpreters who generally spoke Zulu more fluently than Shona. Because of the restricted linguistic sophistication of the interpreters, the missionaries produced literary dialects that varied in terms of spelling conventions, word division, and sounds used to mark phonological contrasts. Some missionaries used a different type of spelling in which the morphemes were kept distinct from each other while the others fused them into single words. In a 1929 occasional paper on the problem of word-division in Shona, Doke gave an example of lack of uniformity in word-division by quoting a section of the New Testament (Mark 10: 46) as it existed in four different versions current at the time, in Karanga, Zezuru, Manyika and Ndau. Only the Karanga and Ndau versions are repeated here as an illustration:

>Karanga: Va ka sike Yeriho; ipopo a chi buda Yeriho na vadzidzgwa vake na vazhinjizhinji, Bartimeo, mgana wa Timeo, rombe ri ri bofu, wa ka nga a gere pa zhira.
>Ndau: Va ka sika ku Jeriko: e I bva apo mu Keriko na vadzidzi vake nembungano huru, Bartimiosi, mukororo wa Timiosi, bofu murombo, inga a ka gara pamphiri penjira.
>
>*Standard orthography*: Vakasvika Jeriko; zvino akati achibuda Jeriko vadzidzi vake navazhinji-zhinji, Bhatimeo mwanakomana waTimeo, raiva bofu riri rombe, wakanga agree panzira. (Bible Society of Zimbabwe, 1996: 48)
>
>*English translation*: They came to Jericho and as he went out of Jericho with his disciples and a great number

of people, blind Bartimaeus, the son of Timaeus, sat by the highway side begging.

Missionary work subsequently had a huge effect on the socio-genesis of languages, as they had had in other parts of the world. This is not to say that, prior to colonialism and Christianity, there were no African languages, but rather to suggest that some of our contemporary ways of thinking and imagining African languages do have their origins in Christianity and literacy. In that sense one can say that, prior to the introduction of Christianity and colonialism, Africa was a language-free zone.

In his explanation to Recommendation 1 on the unification of Shona dialects, Doke says, "By the main Shona-speaking area I mean the area covered by the Zezuru, Karanga, Korekore, Manyika, and Ndau groups..." (Doke, 1931: 76). Thus, according to Doke Shona has five dialects – (1) Zezuru, (2) Karanga, (3) Korekore, (4) Manyika, and (5) Ndau – which tended to correspond to different religious denominations, reflecting the impact of Christianity on ways of thinking about African languages. The dialects subsumed under the label Shona can be constructed as discrete entities.

When the dialects of Shona were being identified by Doke, Kalanga was excluded from the unification proposed for Shona although there were missionaries to the Shona working in the Kalanga dialect area, even though it was mutually intelligible with the other dialects of Shona. The exclusion caused Kalanga to develop some linguistic features distinct from Shona and to borrow considerably from Ndebele since Ndebele is the official national language in the districts where Kalanga is spoken as the first language. Because of the official dominance of Ndebele, Kalanga is rapidly being absorbed into Ndebele (*Ethnologue* 10th Edition, Maseko, 2004). Contrary to what *Ethonologue* and Maseko suggest, there seems to be a heightened awareness of Kalanga identity emerging as separate from an expanded Ndebele identity. For example, after Zimbabwe's independence in 1980, speakers of Kalanga formed an association to promote and advocate the development of Kalanga.

The unification of Shona and the proposed use of African vernaculars were a source of acute controversy within the Native Conference, an association of African evangelists. The controversies are reported in *The Bantu Mirror* – an African owned newspaper. The fact that the controversies were reported in *The Bantu Mirror* is significant because *The Bantu Mirror* carefully controlled its contents and avoided addressing controversial topics.

The Bantu Mirror printed in full the reaction by Reverend Rusike in a paper he had delivered at the Native Conference in May, 1934. He objected that:

> No African was given a seat in the unification committee, and one of the results is that the newly formed language is all a mixture of Xhosa, Zulu, Ndebele, Kitchen Kaffir, Swahili, Nyanja and English. To my mind, it is not Shona language that the white people are trying to force; it is a white man's native language. (*Bantu Mirror*, 1934: 8)

In this quotation, Rusike raises two objections: firstly, that there was no African representation on the committee that finally determined the nature of Shona; secondly, that the newly formed language was an amalgam of different languages/dialects. His first argument, noting a lack of representation, is a valid one. However, his second argument, noting that Shona is an amalgam, is only partially true. To some extent whilst Shona is an amalgam of different languages/dialects, it is also an exaggeration to claim that the amalgam included Nyanja, Swahili, Kaffir English, Xhosa, and Zulu. The key issue is that the amalgamation of different 'dialects' and languages into Shona made it look inauthentic to Shona speakers, hence Rusike's argument that it is a "white man's native language" even if it is classified as an indigenous language.

There was a strong argument for the learning of English that was described as the 'language of the marketplace' (Rusike, 14 March 1936). Four decades later, during the period of the conflict between African guerrillas and the white state in Rhodesia, English was to be described as the "language of the revolution" (Ranger, 2003: xvii). This might appear strange, but it has to be noted that guerrillas came from different linguistic groups and English was the only language that they could use amongst themselves and with those from the organisations that were funding the liberation movement. What is interesting, however, is that the role of English has always been debated. This debate is also still found in present day language discourses in most African countries.

If there was a general agreement in Africans' responses that the vernaculars were 'alien' and had been appropriated by Europeans, there was a sharper division among Africans on the status and role of Ndebele, and the role it could play in schools in Matabeleland. The Ndebele language issue divided Africans along religious and political lines. Commenting on this division, Ranger (1995: 21) writes:

> The Methodists, who had always used Zulu texts, favoured that language; the London Missionary Society, who had worked to systematise Sindebele, argued strongly for the vernacular. (Ranger, 1995: 21) [What is referred to here as Sindebele is what we are referring through out the monograph as Ndebele, the second largest spoken African language in Zimbabwe.]

If Shona was construed as a mixture of Nyanja, Kitchen Kaffir, Ndebele, etc, then Ndebele was presented as a mixture of Zulu and Kalanga. For example, the Reverend T.D. Samkange, in a commentary that appeared in *The Bantu Mirror* 18 April 1936, states that:

> There appeared two articles in your issue of March 28th and April 4th on 'SINDEBELE OR ZULU AS A STANDARD LANGUAGE' [sic.] written by supposed thinking Bantu advocating the use of Sindebele books in all our schools in Matebeleland in place of Zulu books at present used by many denominations working in this country save one or two books in this so called Sindebele language – a mixture of Zulu words and Kalanga. (p. 23)

The quotation is important because it captures the controversies which revolved around whether Ndebele or Zulu should be used as the medium of instruction in Zimbabwe.

Cultural nationalists like the Reverend Samkange objected to the use of Sindebele by appealing to a combination of linguistic and political arguments for ethnic unity, as well as to the validity of taking advantage of the English model, and Christianity. It is important to stress that the debate at this historical juncture was not between using either English or an African language, but whether Sindebele could be constructed as authentically an African language, and if so whether it could be used instead of Zulu. Similarly, Sindebele was pejoratively seen as inauthentic. Sindebele was construed by the cultural nationalists as inauthentic because it was a mixture or a combination of Zulu words and Kalanga. The ideology that Sindebele was a mixture was based on the belief that the pure form of Sindebele was Zulu. Sindebele was therefore, according to cultural nationalists, a 'Colonial language'. In these discussions it was not English that was being defined as the colonial Language but Sindebele. Cultural nationalists also objected to the use of Sindebele because it was construed as ethnically divisive as it would "manufacture more tribal distinctions demarcated by red ink" (*Bantu Mirror*, 1936: 8).

The use of Sindebele instead of Zulu was also regarded as unchristian and highly divisive. In addition, the argument for Sindebele instead of Zulu was regarded as alienating the Ndebele from their main language, Zulu. The cultural nationalists, in their arguments in support of the continued use of Zulu, appealed to English as a model to support their arguments. According to Samkange, the British were divided into separate 'tribes' until they saw the wisdom of being united under the 'King's English' (Samkange, 1936). The historical argument which is being articulated is not tenable linguistically.

The debates are illuminating because they capture the controversies in the roles of languages and in the ways in which African languages were construed. The key issue is that 'colonial' from the viewpoint of cultural nationalists referred to European variants of African languages and not to English. If that is the case, language policies which sought to promote standardised African languages would be received negatively by educated Africans as promoting European values under the guise of so-called indigenous languages. Such perceptions may partially account for the negative responses to African languages as mediums of instruction by educated Africans.

RESPONSES TO COLONIAL EDUCATION BETWEEN 1890 AND 1940

The previous section analysed how some Africanists, e.g. Samkange and Rusike, reacted to the unification of Shona and announcements of the intent to use vernaculars as media of instruction. This section will analyse the general responses of Africans to efforts to set up African schools by missionaries and by the white-settler Southern Rhodesian government. Missionaries, white governments, and Africans each had different political interests. The negative response of Africans was predicated on the assumption that education provided an opportunity for social engineering that might successfully challenge white dominance. But Africans pursued education because education ostensibly provided access to civilised society and to social and political opportunities (Summers, 2002: 2).

The establishment of the schools was the result of acquiescence by, or even of demands from, Africans. At times, Africans demanded not only a school, but a specific type of school. Chief Mdala reports that the people demanded not only a school, but a college. Africans were motivated by a host of factors to demand the establishment of schools. One of the prominent reasons was the belief that, when a school was established, the land on which it was built automatically became mission land and therefore could not be annexed by white settlers (Summers, 2002).

Africans not only demanded the establishment of schools but a voice in the content of the curriculum. In 1929, students marched 19 miles from Domboshawa to what was then called Salisbury (i.e. Harare) to demand that instruction include not only religion but also reading in English. At Umchingwe School the communities not only demanded English, but also that the teaching of English should come before they study industrial subjects (Stoneman, 2002: 67). At other times the students might strike if the reader they preferred was not employed. The African communities were "strikingly sophisticated consumers of education" (Stoneman, 2002: 12).

The notion of a teacher as distinct from a preacher is a relatively new phenomenon emerging after the massive expansion of teacher education for Africans. Between 1890 and 1945 teachers occupied a dual position, functioning as both teachers and preachers. The same space that was used for teaching was also used for Sunday worship. The same activities that characterised school activities were also the defining features of Sunday school worship – attendance register taking, singing, catechism and Bible reading.

This section shows that demands for English went hand in hand with demands for education. Consequently, a connection was being forged between formal education and English. The demands which the Africans were making reflect the extent to which they played a key role in shaping the nature of the language-in-education policies which affected their children. The demands for English during the colonial era are not substantially different from those being made in the 21st century by African parents.

LANGUAGE POLICIES DURING THE NATIONALIST STRUGGLES 1965 TO 1980

A considerable amount of research that examined language policies and practices in Africa has been state-based; that is, the tendency has been to concentrate on either the role of the colonial or the post-colonial state in shaping language policies and practices. The usefulness of a notion of the state as a basis for analysing language policies and practices has gradually come under scrutiny in the light of trans-border migration (see Makoni & Meinhof, 2004). Exclusive focus on the role of the state in formulating and shaping language policies and practices has led to the exclusion of the analysis of language policies and practices of some of the national liberation organisations whose defacto language policies during the liberation struggle might have strongly influenced language policies in post-independent Africa. This monograph analyses the language policies and practices of the three major political parties in Zimbabwe: the Zimbabwe African National Union (ZANU), the Zimbabwe African People's Union (ZAPU) and the United African National Council (UANC). The liberation army for ZANU was called the Zimbabwean African National Liberation Army (ZANLA); the liberation army for ZAPU was called the Zimbabwean African People's Resistance Army (ZIPRA). ZANU and ZAPU were banned in 1964.

The analysis of the language policies and practices of the ZANU will illustrate the way in which policies evolved within the liberation movement, but will also fill an important gap in Zimbabwean war studies by providing a linguistic lens to an important phase in the history of Zimbabwe – a perspective which has frequently been missing in the war-studies literature.

The linguistic lens shows not only the *de facto* language policies but also how languages changed under the impact of war. For example, Bhebhe and Ranger (1995) sum up the main criticisms of Zimbabwean war research that had been dominated by the authorised version of Zimbabwean history by Martin and Johns which had functioned as the official account of events in Zimbabwean history. Martin and Johns' account ignores the role of the common soldier in the Zimbabwean war (see e.g. Bhebhe & Ranger, 1995: 6).

Conceivably, ZAPU party structures survived through proxy organisations such as women's organisations and youth leagues even after ZAPU was officially banned. The young men who assisted the guerrillas were called *mujibas*, a term which originally referred to Zimbabwean migrant workers in Johannesburg, South Africa. The workers were perceived to be brave and brilliant. The young girls who assisted the guerrillas were called *chimbwidos*. Linguistically, it is interesting that the terms used to refer to either the young male or the female assistants were morphologically marked using English plurals in addition to the Shona plural prefix. The guerrillas themselves were referred to by the populace as *vakomana*, or *obhudi* (brothers) in Ndebele, and yet the term *vakomana*, prior to the war, simply referred to boys. During the war the meaning of the term was then narrowed to refer to young men who were fighting in the liberation army; it seems this was a corrupted translation of the English term 'soldier boy'.

The interesting thing about the evolution of the combatant term is that, although there were female combatants, the term seems to have been confined to male combatants. This is also evident from the use of such terms as *vakomana/obhudi* which refer to males, despite the fact that there were female combatants in the liberation struggle. In a parallel manner, the term 'ex-combatant', when used to describe war-veterans after the 2000 elections, refers exclusively to males. Over a period of two decades the term has been 'masculinised' (Nhongo-Simbanegavi, 2000). One possible explanation may lie in the voluntary and involuntary relegation of women combatants to the political margins. Given the fact that nationalism was strongly male-oriented, it is unlikely that post-independent Zimbabwe would generate a gender-neutral policy.

One of the terms that entered Zimbabwean popular usage from the war is *Povo* in Shona (or *ipovo* in Ndebele) originating from Portuguese and having the meaning *civilian population*. Some Zimbabwean guerrillas received their military training in Angola and Mozambique, both former Portuguese colonies. They brought back with them Portuguese words which subsequently entered Shona and Ndebele. A term such as *Chef* [English/French], *Chefe* [Portuguese] (boss) was adopted during the Zimbabwean war to refer to someone holding a senior position of authority. The guerrillas adopted it from their ally, the Mozambican Liberation Movement, since Mozambicans spoke Portuguese as their first language (Lopez, 1998). However, in contemporary usage the term now refers to anyone holding a senior position irrespective of whether they held senior positions during the liberation war.

The history of African politics has been marked by frequent military and political conflicts. The war of liberation invoked here is one such conflict. The impacts/effects of such military conflicts on language use and language practices have not been systematically investigated. In the Zimbabwean situation, it is unclear whether the reluctance of the Zimbabwean government to recognise the role and position of Portuguese, inspite of its wide spread impact on Shona, is the result of the association that has been created between Portuguese and armed conflicts in the history of Zimbabwe.

Unlike ZIPRA, ZANLA held all night political rallies aimed at educating the peasants politically in the areas in which it operated. The all-night political vigils were referred to as *pungwes*, a term which was also used interchangeably with *mapungwe*, a term which follows Shona morphological marking for plural, marked by the prefix *ma-* (Bhebhe & Ranger, 1995: 43).

Another party that was heavily involved in the struggle for Zimbabwean liberation was the United African National Congress (UANC) headed by Bishop Abel Muzorewa.

The language policies of the liberation movements led to the introduction of new words, or a reinterpretation of existing words. The various liberation movements differed in the degree to which they used either English or Shona and Ndebele. In its official announcements and propaganda ZANU was more likely to use a considerable amount of English, while the UANC relied on a combination of Shona and English. ZIPRA tended to use English and Ndebele for its propaganda and official announcements.

Language and gender
There is a considerable amount of ongoing research that has examined issues about language and gender in African contexts; however, in Africa, the research has rarely focused on language and gender within popular movements. This section examines language and gender from two historical points: during the struggle, and after liberation. The previous section showed that, during the liberation war, terminology existed to refer to male combatants, but no equivalent terms existed for female combatants, suggesting an imbalance in terminology across the gender divide. This imbalance was not highly likely to lead to a gender sensitive post-independent language policy. This section briefly examines the treatment of women during the liberation war, focusing on the role of nationalism.

Nationalism provides an important opportunity to examine the nature of the relationships between elites and non-elites, elders and the young and men and women. Since the notion of *nation* is typically a male construct, examining the nature of the relations between men and women in situations of political conflict is interesting; it sheds light on how political rhetoric in conflict situations may mask or accentuate gender differences (Nhongo-Simbanegavi, 2000: 79). This section explores the nature of the relationship between language and gender in the Zimbabwean nationalist movement in a specific historical period (1975 and 1980), the period during which Zimbabwe attained its independence.

Nhongo-Simbanegavi (2000) points out that women *guerrillas* were informally divided into three categories: wives, mistresses, and casual sex providers. Any women who tried to challenge these categories were regarded as unpatriotic. Sexual activity, particularly when women were servicing men, was considered patriotic. In other words, women were defined as servicing men who were taking part in nationalistic struggles, and therefore they were not treated as equal contributors to the political struggle. Nhongo-Simbanegavi (2000) suggests that, during nationalistic struggles, the discourse of gender equality is replaced by that of nationalism. The discourse of rights and nationalism was dominated by men. The irony is that the nationalist struggle was fought to challenge political inequalities between the colonised and the colonisers, but not inequalities in gender relations between males and females, thus suggesting that issues of rights were being interpreted in a very restricted sense. In terms of either language policies or language rights, nationalism was not consequently perceived as an instrument to rectify gender inequalities. The issue of equal rights socially, politically and linguistically was therefore not one of the strengths of the nationalist struggle. It is, therefore, not surprising that it was viewed as secondary even in post-independence Zimbabwean state discourses. Thus, it may be argued that comprehensive discourse dealing with rights cutting across different ethnic and gender groups has yet to emerge in Zimbabwe.

Language and gender: Cross-border women
In the post-independence period, despite the declining economic situation in Zimbabwe, a new group of enterprising and independently minded women actively involved in cross-border trade of material goods has emerged since the early 1990s. The women are collectively referred to as *vakadzi vekuSouth Africa*, a term not referring to women who are from, or resident in, South Africa, but rather to women who travel to and from South Africa for purposes of business (Tevera & Zinyama, 2002). These women are shrewd, assertive, ambitious, confident, goal oriented and determined to succeed. Because of their success, they are increasingly described in masculine terms; i.e. *varume pachavo* (they are real men). The women have developed extensive social networks that they use to access clients and other commercial resources. At times their networks include whites who migrated to South Africa. Such networks are based upon a shared past historical identity felicitously referred to as *Rhodie* which means former Rhodesian. Even though the networks are described in a kinship idiom, women were treated neither equally nor fairly.

The women are subject to abusive language and described as *Makwerekwere* (foreigners) and have to endure name-calling rituals directed against Robert Mugabe.

Although the notion of a firm border separating South Africa from Zimbabwe seems to be encoded in the minds of South Africans, the separation of South Africa from Zimbabwe only took effect in 1929 when the Rhodesian whites voted against continuing to be a South African province. An analysis of the cross-border women is important, not only because of what it may reveal about emerging gender identities, but because of its impact on conceptualisations of language. Because of their extensive cross-border travels that at times include travels as far as Mauritius, the women are building up a linguistic repertoire that includes linguistic fragments drawn from many different geographical regions and from various languages spoken in Southern Africa. A new language repertoire reflecting the social travel experiences of these women is therefore emerging. The emergence of new language repertoires is significant because it suggests that language policies which are predicated upon conventional views of standardised African languages are likely to fail to capture the complex language use characteristics of the speech of such individuals as cross-border women. A radical reconceptualisation of African language which takes into account these new cross-border languages is necessary if language policies in Zimbabwe are to address comprehensively the diverse contemporary experiences of Zimbabweans, so that research is freed in part from views of languages and indeed people being contained within national political boundaries.

Language-in-education policy
Prior to 1980, class distinctions tended to correlate with race-based distinctions. That is not to say there were no class distinctions either within the black or the white communities, but rather that as a rule whites belonged to a higher social class than blacks. In 1980, when Zimbabwe became independent, the new elites who took over the management of the country were anxious to provide their children with educational opportunities that were previously the privilege of whites. The new elites did so by enacting legislation that allowed their children to attend schools that had previously been reserved for white children.

Given the fact that government schools in suburbs, previously restricted for whites only, still had white children in attendance, children of black elites living in those suburbs had the opportunity to be taught by white first-language speakers of English, unlike their counterparts from less affluent families who were taught by African second-language speakers of English. Students who attend formerly white-only schools are stigmatised by other African students who refer to their pronunciation as belonging to the 'nose brigade' referring to their Europeanised English accent. Because politicians and the economic elites were generally satisfied with the status quo, there was no concerted effort to change the status of English in Zimbabwe. The training and recruitment policies for employment in both public and private institutions require(d) a pass in English even if there was very little English required to perform successfully. English proficiency served, and still serves, a gate-keeping function.

Some nominal changes in policy were officially made in 1987 when a new Education Act was introduced. The Education Act had a language section under the title 'Languages to be taught'. That section identifies Shona, Ndebele and English as the three main languages of Zimbabwe that were to be taught as follows in all primary schools starting from the first grade:

(a) Shona and English in all areas where the first language of the majority of the residents is Shona; or

(b) Ndebele and English in all areas where the first language of the majority of residents is Ndebele.
(Nziramasanga Commission Report, 1999: 628)

The Act uses 'mother tongue' to mean the first language that a child acquires and uses at home before attending school. The Act is silent on situations in which a language is spoken by the majority of the residents but it is not their 'mother tongue'. However, in practice, such situations obtain, for example, where Ndebele is used as the language of instruction because it is spoken by the majority of people whose 'mother tongue' is a minority language.

Prior to the fourth grade, either of the languages referred to in paragraphs (a) or (b) may be used as the medium of instruction, depending upon which language is commonly spoken and better understood by the pupils. From the fourth grade onwards, English is the medium of instruction, provided that Shona or Ndebele are taught as subjects on an equal allocation basis with the English language. In areas where minority languages exist, the Minister may authorise the teaching of these languages in primary school. Interestingly enough there are some areas where neither Ndebele nor Shona is the first language of the majority of residents, and yet minority languages are not used as the medium of instruction. In Hwange, for instance, Ndebele was used as the medium of instruction from the first grade when the first language of the majority of the residents was Nambya (Dube, 2001). In this case, the language that may be regarded as imperialist is not English, but an African language, i.e. Ndebele.

According to the 1987 Education Act, Shona and Ndebele were to be used as medium of instruction in lower primary schools before shifting to English. The policy was motivated by pragmatic considerations rather than by psycholinguistic factors. Even if the Zimbabwean government had legislated that English should be used as the medium of instruction from the first grade, this would not have been feasible because most of the teachers whom one encounters in early primary schools are not competent enough to teach in English. There is a greater likelihood that one would encounter teachers with adequate proficiency to teach in English in grade four and above when the switch to English is expected to occur. The metaphor of a switch to English is, however, misleading because there is a protracted period after grade four when the teachers characteristically use a mixed variant of Shona/Ndebele and English for instructional purposes. The continued importance attached to English even in post-independent Zimbabwe reflects a disconcerting continuity with pre-colonial language policies in which, in part as a result of the demands of African parents, English continued to play a significant role.

Teaching and assessment of Shona and Ndebele
There are two groups of Shona speakers in Zimbabwe: those who have Shona as a first language, and those who have Shona as a second language. Students who have Shona as a first lan-

guage typically also have English as a second language, while those who have Shona as a second language have competencies in a variety of languages as these students may have been born outside the borders of Zimbabwe. There is also an important social class difference between the two groups. Shona first-language speakers are usually drawn from the lower working class, while those who have Shona as a second language and speak English (or any other language spoken outside the borders of Zimbabwe) as a first language are typically part of the Zimbabwean elite. However, within the group that speaks Shona as a second language are Ndebele first language speakers who may not be viewed as elites because they do not have English as part of their repertoire of languages. In this regard, there has been an intergenerational language shift in some households. Children who have Shona as a first language usually have parents who speak Shona as a first language but English as a second language. The shift which has taken place within these families is from having Shona as a first language to having Shona as a second language and English (and any other language) as a first language.

Shona was first offered as a subject for examination by Cambridge University's Local Examinations Syndicate for African Students in 1957 and for white students in 1964. Initially, Shona was taught in both English and Shona; currently, teachers are encouraged to teach Shona through the medium of Shona. The teaching of Shona through another language seems to undermine the status of Shona in the minds of the students, instead of reinforcing the idea that Shona can be seriously used as a medium of instruction. Chiwome and Thondhlana (1992: 257) state:

> Jocular digressions are generally carried out in Shona, whereas serious content is delivered in English. One lecturer observed that whenever English is used during a

lecture, students take notes and whenever Shona is used students stop taking notes.

Although there is a distinction between Shona as a first and Shona as a second language, both groups of speakers sit for the same language examination. The examination seems to disadvantage both groups but for radically different reasons. It is too difficult for first-language chiShona speakers because the variety of Shona they encounter in the examinations is different from the everyday language they use. The *Sunday Gazette* observes: "The Shona they set is not spoken any more. Nobody speaks using those proverbs, idioms and complex grammar written by Fortune, Hodza and the early missionaries" (*Sunday Gazette Magazine*, 24 April 1994).

The Shona in the examination is also too difficult for learners who have Shona as a second language. There is neither a chiShona as a second language examination nor a form of grading that accommodates chiShona for second-language speakers because "the children who learn Shona as a second language are a minority" (Mr Hartmann, quoted in the *Sunday Gazette Magazine*, 24 April 1994).

The examiners feel that the Shona used in the examinations (according to the Permanent Secretary) is "standard, its pure idiomatic Shona and not the polluted Shona". There clearly are major differences of opinion about the variety of Shona that should be assessed in the examinations. The government's thinking about Shona, as reflected in the comments of the Permanent Secretary, seems to be strongly influenced by an ideology of language 'purity'. The failure rate, according to the Zimbabwean government, is therefore a consequence of the unwillingness of the students to take Shona seriously.

The status of English relative to Shona is also reinforced by the nature of the examinations themselves. For example, in the Shona examination, it is possible to answer some of the questions in English, while the converse does not apply; it is not possible to answer any English questions in Shona or any other indigenous languages. English also has a higher status than the 'indigenous' language; if a candidate passes all subjects but fails English, the candidate will not be awarded a certificate. This practice illustrates that English is still used for screening purposes, because candidates are said to have failed even if they have passed all the subjects except English. The discourse on language purity in the current discussion echoes the earlier discourses by Samkange and Rusike (Bantu Mirror, 1934) in the 1930s.

African language scholarship
In order to understand some of the problems that are emerging about the nature of language policy and planning in Zimbabwe, it is necessary to situate the discussion within a framework that examines the nature of academic enquiry into African languages. Scholarly studies of African languages have a relatively long history; Errington (2001) traces that history back to the late 19th century. In spite of this relatively long tradition, scholarly studies have hardly made a sizeable impact on linguistic theory, unlike the theoretical contributions of such other areas of enquiry as anthropology or creative literature.

One of the strongest traditions in academic studies of African languages is what Blommaert (1999) refers to as a descriptive tradition. In this descriptive tradition, the main focus is on linguistic structure rather than on linguistic praxis (Blommaert, 1999: 178). Collections of grammar, structure and vocabulary that subsequently developed into lexicography were the key preoccupations of scholarly descriptions of African languages, hence the notion "bringing grammar and structure to the languages" (Fabian, 1986). The label 'descriptive tradition' is potentially misleading because what was being described in the early phases of studies of African languages were the varieties of African languages which the missionaries themselves spoke, rather than what was spoken by Africans.

However, the missionaries were not only describing, but were also creating and socially legitimising specific varieties of African languages. Missionaries, therefore, ended up describing what they expected to hear as well as language that could be used to serve commercial purposes and that were demanded by labour.

Lexicography is one of the most well-established areas in the study of African languages, not only in Zimbabwe but also across the continent (Makoni & Meinhof, 2004). It is intriguing that, while the focus of most sociolinguistics is moving from a concentration on monolingual models to bilingual and multilingual models, Zimbabwean lexicography is embracing both models but with emphasis on monolingual dictionary making. This section seeks to explain why Zimbabwean lexicography is going in this direction.

Multilingual dictionaries have not been common in Zimbabwe lexicography. The closest attempt was by a member of the London Missionary Society, Elliot, who published a *Dictionary of the Tebele and Shuna languages* (1897), in which he listed English terms with 'Tebele' (Ndebele) and 'Shuna' (Shona) equivalences.

Bilingual dictionaries are of two types: dictionaries made up of a number of different languages, and those seeking to establish equivalence between languages – typically Shona-English dictionaries. Monolingual dictionaries are typically produced by Shona native-speakers while bilingual or multilingual dictionaries are typically compiled by people who have Shona as an additional language. The first Shona dictionary, compiled by Bleek in 1856, was entitled *The Languages of Mosambique*. The most recent dictionary is Chimhundu's (2001) *Duramazwi Guru reChiShona*.

The bilingual phase of Zimbabwean lexicography in general and Shona, in particular, is intimately linked with the colonisation of Africa, dated between 1850 and 1930. The compilation of dictionaries was part of a broader project to comprehend the native. Dictionaries during this period were aimed at Europeans, not at Africans. Chimhundu, one of the authors of the Zimbabwean indigenous lexicographic tradition, is quoted in a review of the first monolingual Shona dictionary by Shona speakers, *Duramazwi ReChiShona* (1996) in the weekly paper *The Zimbabwe Independent* saying, "Those people who had resources were missionaries and because of their background they were writing for their own people" (*Zimbabwe Independent*, 1996: 6). The missionaries constituted a broad range of professionals working in close relationship with such colonialists as tax collectors, court interpreters and police officers. Missionaries typically worked in isolation from each other; they relied heavily on Bible translations for headwords and lexical items in their dictionary-compiling activities. Since the work of missionaries was intended to bring the message of religion to the natives, their lexical compilations drew most heavily upon those registers and ignored other, normally more common, registers. Furthermore, because most of the compilers spoke Shona as an additional language, some of their interlanguage forms found their way into the dictionaries. For example, Fortune (1979: 42) noted that 'Father Hartman found difficulty in distinguishing between voiced and voice-less sounds so the results, though quite intelligible, look strange today'.

The only Ndebele bilingual dictionary that is known, but appearing in the form of a glossary of terms, is Weale's (late D. Troop B.S.A. Cos. Police) (1903) *Matabele and Makalaka Vocabulary Intended for the use of Prospectors and Farmers in Mashonaland. Makalaka* in the title refers to the Karanga dialect and, as Weale claims in the introduction, the entries are drawn from 'mostly spoken' sub-dialect although a native speaker's perusal of the entries reveals glaring errors and misrepresentations resulting from the compiler's limited proficiency in the language.

The second phase of Shona lexicography can be said to begin in the early 1930s after the formal declaration by Clement

Doke that Shona was indeed a language. The function of lexicography during this period was to promote the harmonisation of the principal dialects of Shona. Previously, each missionary had compiled a dictionary for the geographical region in which she/he was working. After 1930 the objective was to create a dictionary for all the dialects.

Two notable dictionaries were produced during the second phase of the history of Shona lexicography – one by Hannan and one by Dale. Hannan tried to be comprehensive in his compilation. He tried to include words from as many Shona dialects as possible. The words from chiNdau that he included were, however, arbitrarily removed by the Shona language committee before the dictionary was published. The crucial effect of Hannan's work was an increasing awareness that his limited knowledge of Shona had a detrimental effect on his lexicographic projects. In terms of space and content in Hannan's bilingual dictionary, English occupies larger space than Shona. Dale's dictionary had as its primary targets Europeans learning Shona at beginner's stage.

The third period – the post-independence period – was characterised by a major shift in Zimbabwean lexicography. The focus shifted from bilingual dictionaries to primarily monolingual Shona and Ndebele dictionaries produced by linguists who were Shona and Ndebele native speakers. The dictionary compilation work was also generously funded by the Norwegian government. Dictionary production ceased to be a hobby and became a professional pursuit. Lexicographical projects in Zimbabwe are housed in the African Languages Research Institute in the Department of African languages and Literature at the University of Zimbabwe. The major product of the new monolingual dictionary focus is Chimhundu's (1996) *Duramazwi Re-ChiShona* and Hadebe's (2001) *Isichazamazwi SesiNdebele*. The publication of the monolingual dictionaries in Shona and Ndebele attracted a lot of attention from various sectors of the Zimbabwean community. The dictionaries were positively viewed, with some reviews being highly sentimental, as reflected in such titles as 'The real Shona dictionary' (Zenenga, 1994: 14). The dictionaries were viewed as vehicles for language raising, rationalisation and standardisation. Plans for dictionaries for other minority languages in Zimbabwe are at an advanced stage of development.

It is also important to mention that the bilingual agenda has not been abandoned outright. In fact, 'the master plan of the ALLEX Project include a Ndebele-Shona/ Shona-Ndebele dictionary in its proposed dictionary projects' (Hadebe, 2005: 265). While earlier bilingual dictionaries were commonly the language pairs English-Ndebele/Shona and vice versa, the proposed type in which African languages, Ndebele and Shona form a language pair. The proposal to compile Ndebele-Shona/Shona-Ndebele dictionaries reflects a shift in the language planning needs from those of the missionary-linguists. Hadebe (2005) discusses the challenges associated with the compilation of such bilingual dictionaries, the purposes for and efficacy of such dictionaries. With regards to language planning, Hadebe concludes that, "the successful completion of the proposed dictionary would be a landmark in Zimbabwean lexicography and a crucial contribution of lexicography towards language policy and planning" (274).

This section has revealed that an analysis of the scholarship on African languages is important, showing that there is limited systematic research into the nature of actual language practices that can inform language policy decisions because of a strong preoccupation with the production of dictionaries. A shift in linguistic research would be most welcome.

References
Baker, C. (2001) *Foundations of Bilingual Education and Bilingualism* (3rd edn). Clevedon: Multilingual Matters.
Beach, D. (1994) *A Zimbabwean Past*. Gweru, Zimbabwe: Mambo.

Beach, D. (1984) *Zimbabwe Before 1900*. Gweru: Mambo.
Bhebhe, D. and Ranger, T. (eds) (1995) *Soldiers in Zimbabwe's Liberation War*. Harare and London. Currey, Heinemann and University of Zimbabwe.
Bhebhe, N. and Ranger, T. (2001) *Soldiers in Zimbabwe's Liberation War*. London: Currey.
Bible Society of Zimbabwe (1996) *Bhaibheri: Magwaro Matsvene aMwari* [Bible: Letters about God] Harare: Bible Society of Zimbabwe.
Bleek, W.H. (1856) *The Languages of Mosambique*. London: Harrison.
Blommaert, J. (1999) "Reconstructing the sociolinguistic image of Africa: Grassroots writing in Shaba (Congo)" *Text* 18 (2), 175–200.
Brutt-Griffler, J. (2004) *World English: A Study of its Development*. Clevedon: Multilingual Matters.
Burke, T. (1996) *Lifebuoy Men, Lux Women: Commodification, Consumption and Cleanliness in Northern Zimbabwe*. Durham, NC: Duke University Press
Canagarajah, S. (2006) "After disinvention: Possibilities for communication, community and competence" In S. Makoni and A. Pennycook (eds) *Disinventing and Reconstituting Languages*. Clevedon: Multilingual Matters.
Caftanzoglou, R. (2001) "The shadow of the Sacred Rock: Contrasting discourses of place under the Acropolis" In B. Bender and M. Winer (eds) *Contested Landscapes: Movement, Exile and Place*. Oxford: Berg.
Childs, T. (2003) *An Introduction to African languages*. Amsterdam/ Philadelphia: John Benjamins.
Chimhundu, H. (1992) "Early missionaries and the ethno-linguistic factor during the invention of tribalism in Zimbabwe" *Journal of African History* 33, 87–109.
Chimhundu, H. (ed.) (1996) *Duramazwi ReChiShona*. Harare: College Press.

Chimhundu, H. (ed.) (2001) *Duramazwi Guru reChiShona*. Harare: College Press.

Chiwome, E.M. and Thondhlana, J. (1992) "Sociolinguistics and education: A survey concerning attitudes on the teaching of Shona through the media of Shona and English" In R. Herbert (ed.) *Language and Society in Africa: The Theory and Practice of Sociolinguistics* (pp. 247–263). Johannesburg: Witwatersrand University Press.

Cobbing, J.R.D. (1976) *The Ndebele under the Kumalos, 1820–96*. PhD Thesis, University of Lancaster.

Dale, D. (1975) *A Basic Shona Dictionary*. Salisbury: Rhodesia Literature Bureau. Daily Gazette (1994) 14 February.

Doke, C. (1931) *Report on the Unification of the Shona Dialects*. Hertford: Austin.

Dube, S. (2001) *An Investigation Into the Effects of Multilingualism in Hwange Urban Area*. BA Dissertation, Open University, Bulawayo, Zimbabwe. E-mail sdube@crlcommission.org.za.

Dwyer, D. (2002) "The Language/Dialect Problem" On WWW at http://www.msu.edu/: course/426.

Elliot, W.A. (1897) *Dictionary of the Tebele and Shuna Languages*. London: David Nutt.

Epstein, A.L. (1992) *Scenes from African Urban Life*. Edinburgh: Edinburgh University Press.

Errington, J. (2001) "Colonial linguistics" *Annual Review of Anthropology* 30, 19–39.

Fabian, J. (1986) *Language and Colonial Power: The Appropriation of Swahili in the Former Congo 1880–1938*. Cambridge: Cambridge University Press

Fortune, G. (1979) "Shona lexicography" *Zambezia* 7(1), 21–47.

Garlake, P.S. (1973) *Great Zimbabwe*. London: Thames and Hudson.

Giles, H. (ed.) (1984) "The dynamics of speech accommodation" *International Journal of the Sociology of Language* 46. (Special topic issue.)

Goffman, E. (1963) *Stigma: Notes on the Management of Spoiled Identity.* New Jersey: Prentice Hall.
Hadebe, S. (2005) "Reflections on the proposed Ndebele–Shona / Shona–Ndebele dictionary" *Lexicos* 15, 265–275.
Hadebe, S. (2002) *The Standardization of the Ndebele Language Through Dictionary Making.* PhD Thesis, University of Zimbabwe. E-mail: Samukeleh@yahoo.com.
Hadebe, S. et al (eds) (2001) *Isichazamazwi SesiNdebele.* Harare: College Press.
Hannan, M. (1959) *Shona Standard Dictionary.* London: Macmillan.
Harris, R. (2006) *Integrationist Notes & Papers: 2003–2005.* Crediton: Tree Tango.
Hill, J. (2002) "Expert rhetorics in advocacy for endangered languages: Who is listening and what do they hear?" *Journal of Linguistic Anthropology* 12 (2), 119–133.
Hyatt, P. (1969) *The Old Transport Road.* London: Andrew Melrose Ltd.
Jacquemet, M. (2005) "Transidiomatic practices: Language and power in the age of globalization" *Language and Communication* 25 (3), 257–277.
Jeater, D. (2001) "Speaking like a native" *Journal of African History* 43, 449–468.
Jeater, D and C. Hove (undated) "And the God was made word: Exploring the implications of translation and power in the 1920's" E-mail: Diana.Jeater@uwe.ac.uk
Joseph, J. (2004) *Language and Identity.* Basingstoke: Palgrave Macmillan.
Kaplan, R.B. and Baldauf Jr., R.B. (eds) (1999) *Language Planning in Malawi, Mozambique and the Philippines.* Clevedon: Multilingual Matters.
Kaplan, R. and Baldauf Jr., R.B. (eds) (2003) *Language and Language-in-education Planning in the Pacific Basin.* Dordrecht: Kluwer Academic.
Khumalo, L. (2004) "Language contact and lexical change: A

lexicographical terminographical interface in Zimbabwean Ndebele" *Lexikos* 14, 105–17.
Kumbirai, J.C. (1979) "Shona Bible translation: The works of the Revd Michael Hannan" *Zambezia* 7 (1), 61–74.
Logan, I. and Makoni, S. (2006) "Coloured identities in Zimbabwe in the 1930's ethnicities" (unpublished manuscript). E-mail: sbm12@psu.edu.
Lopez, A.J. (1998) "Language planning situation in Mozambique" *Journal of Multilingual and Multicultural Development* 19 (5), 440–487.
MacGonagle, E. (2001) *A Mixed pot: History and Identity in the Ndau Region of Mozambique*. PhD Thesis, Michigan State University
Makoni, S. (2003) "From misinvention to disinvention of language: Multilingualism and the South African Constitution" In S. Makoni, G. Smitherman, A. Ball and A. Spears (eds) *Black Linguistics, Language, Society, and Politics in Africa and the Americas* (pp. 132–153). London and New York: Routledge.
Makoni, S. and Meinhof, U. (2004) "Western perspectives on applied linguistics in Africa" *AILA Review* 17, 77–104.
Makoni, S., Brutt-Griffler, J. and Mashiri, P. (2007) "The use of urban and indigenous languages in Zimbabwe" *Journal of Language in Society*, 36, 1-36.
Makoni, S. and Trudell, B. (2006) "Complementary and conflicting discourses of diversity and implications for language planning" *Per Linguam* 22 (2), 14−28.
Mandaza, I. (1997) *Race and Colour and Class in Southern Africa*. Harare: Sapes.
Manganga, K. (2004) "Industrial ethnicity in African Salisbury: 1890–1950. Some preliminary investigations" Unpublished paper, University of Zimbabwe. E-mail: history@ arts.uz.ac.zw.
Masagara, N. (1997) "Negotiating the truth through oath forms"

Journal of Multilingual and Multicultural Development 18 (5), 385–400.

Maseko, B. (2004) *Patterns of Language use by L1 Kalanga Speakers in an Urban Bilingual Setting: The Case of Bulawayo*. BA Honours dissertation, Department of Linguistics, University of Zimbabwe. E-mail: linguistics@arts.uz.ac.zw.

May, S. (2001) *Language and Minority Rights*. Harlow: Longman.

Mazarire, G. (2004) "The rise and fall of the Dutch Reformed church in the Victoria circle with particular reference to the Chibi circuit 1880–1950" Unpublished paper, University of Zimbabwe. E-mail: gmazarire@yahoo.com.

Mazarire, G. (2003) "Who are the Ndebele and the Kalanga in Zimbabwe?" Unpublished paper, University of Zimbabwe. E-mail: gmazarire@yahoo.com.

Mühlhäusler, P. (1996) *Linguistic Ecology: Language Change and Linguistic Imperialism in the Pacific Region*. London: Routledge.

Mühlhäusler, P. (2000) "Language planning and language ecology" *Current Issues in Language Planning* 1 (3), 306–337.

Muzondidya, J. (2001) *Sitting On The Fence Or Walking A Tight Rope: A Political History Of Coloured Communities 1845–1980*. Unpublished PhD, University of Cape Town.

Muzondidya, J. (2002) "Towards a historical understanding of the making of the Colored community in Zimbabwe, 1890–1920" *Journal of Identity, Culture and Politics* 3 (2), 73–99.

Nhongo-Simbanegavi, J. (2000) *For Better or Worse: Women and ZANLA in Zimbabwe's Liberation Struggle*. Harare, Zimbabwe: Weaver.

Nyambara, P. (1999) "Colonial policy and peasant cotton

agriculture in Southern Rhodesia" *International Journal of African Historical Studies* 33 (1), 81–111.

Nyambara, P. (2002) "Madheruka and the Shangwe: Ethnic identities and the culture of modernity in Gokwe, Northern Zimbabwe, 1963–79" *Journal of African History* 143, 287–306.

Nziramasanga Commission (1999) *Report on the Presidential Commission Inquiry into Education and Training.* Harare.

Pennycook, A. and Makoni, S. (2005) "The modern mission: The language effects of Christianity" *Journal of Language, Identity, and Education* 4 (2), 137–157.

Pikirayi, I. (1998) "The threatened landscape. Historical period sites from the Northern Zimbabwe AD 1500–Present" In E.M. Chiwome and Z. Gambahaya (eds) *Culture and Development: Perspectives from the South* (pp. 89–92). Harare: Mond.

Rampton, B. (1995) *Crossing: Language and Ethnicity Among Adolescents.* London: Longman.

Ranger, T. (1985) *Peasant Consciousness and Guerilla War in Zimbabwe. A Comparative Study.* Oxford: Oxford University Press.

Ranger, T. (1989) "Missionaries, migrants and the Manyika: The invention of ethnicity in Zimbabwe" In L. Vail (ed.) *The Creation of Tribalism in Southern Africa* (pp. 118–51). Berkeley, CA: University of California Press.

Ranger, T. (1995) *Are We also not Men? The Samkange Family and African Politics in Zimbabwe, 1920–64.* Portsmouth: Heinemann.

Ranger, T. (ed.) (2003) *The Historical Dimensions of Democracy and Human Rights in Zimbabwe.* Harare: University of Zimbabwe Publications.

Read (1936) On WWW at http://www.thuto.org/ubh/bw/colad/coloff.htm. Accessed January 29th, 2007.

Rubert, S. and Rasmussen, R.K. (2001) *Historical Dictionary of Zimbabwe*. Lanhaman, MD and London: Scarecrow.

Samkange (1936) Samkange to Carter, 2 December 1938 file ms 239/5/15/1.

Seirlis, J.K. (2004) "Islands and autochthons, Coloureds, space and belonging in Rhodesia and Zimbabwe" *Journal of Social Archaeology* 4 (3), 405–427.

Sinamayi, D. (1998) "Heritage in politics: Great Zimbabwe in the struggle for self-determination" In E.M. Chiwome and Z. Gambahawa (eds) *Culture and Development Perspectives from the South* (pp. 93–98). Harare: Mond.

Skuttnab-Kangas, T. (1994) *Multilingualism for All.* Amsterdam: Swets + Zetlinger.

Stoneman, C. (2002) (ed.) *Zimbabwe's Inheritance.* New York: St. Martin's.

Summers, C. (2002) *Colonial Lessons: Africans' Education in Southern Rhodesia, 1918–1940*. Portsmouth: Currey.

Tevera, D. and Zinyama, L. (2002) *Zimbabweans Who Move: Perspectives on International Migration in Zimbabwe*. Cape Town: Southern African Migration Project, Dachs Miller.

Vail, L. and White, L. (eds) (1989) *The Creation of Tribalism in Southern Africa*. London: James Currey.

Wallerstein, I. (2002) *The Essential Wallerstein*. New York: New Press.

Webb, V. and Kembo-Sure (1999) *African Voices: An Introduction to the Languages and Linguistics of Africa*. Cape Town, South Africa: Oxford University Press.

Wolf, H.E. (2000) *Pre-school Child Multilingualism and Educational Implications in the African Context*. PRAESA. Occasional Papers 4. http://www.praesa.org.za/wp-content/uploads/2017/01/Paper4.pdf

Wolf, H.G. (2003) "The contextualization of common core terms in West Africa: Evidence from computer corpora" In P. Lucko, L. Peter, and H.G. Wolf (eds) *Studies of*

African Voices of English (pp. 3–21). Frankfurt: Peter Lang.

Yngve, V. (1996) *From Grammar to Science: New Foundations for General Linguistics.* Amsterdam & Philadelphia: John Benjamins.

Yngve, V. (2004) "Issues in hard-science linguistics" In V. Yngve and Z. Wasik (eds) *Hard-Science Linguistics* (pp. 1–47). New York. Continuum.

Zenenga, P. (1994) "The real Shona dictionary" *Sunday Gazette Magazine.* 30 January 1994.

Zimbabwe Independent (1996) "Controversy over first Shona language dictionary" *Zimbabwe Independent* 27 September 1996.